The Self-managing School

Education Policy Perspectives

General Editor: Professor Ivor Goodson, Faculty of Education,
University of Western Ontario, London,
Canada N6G 1G7

Education policy analysis has long been a neglected area in the United Kingdom and, to an extent, in the USA and Australia. The result has been a profound gap between the study of education and the formulation of education policy. For practitioners such a lack of analysis of the new policy initiatives has worrying implications particularly at such a time of policy flux and change. Education policy has, in recent years, been a matter for intense political debate — the political and public interest in the working of the system has come at the same time as the consensus on education policy has been broken by the advent of the 'New Right'. As never before the political parties and pressure groups differ in their articulated policies and prescriptions for the education sector. Critical thinking about these developments is clearly necessary.

All those working within the system also need information on policy-making, policy implementation and effective day-to-day operation. Pressure on schools from government, education authorities and parents has generated an enormous need for knowledge amongst those on the receiving end of educational policies.

This series aims to fill the academic gap, to reflect the politicalization of education, and to provide the practitioners with the analysis for informed implementation of policies that they will need. It will offer studies in broad areas of policy studies. Beside the general section it will offer a particular focus in the following areas: School organization and improvement (David Reynolds, University College, Cardiff, UK); Social analysis (Professor Philip Wexler, University of Rochester, USA); Policy studies and evaluation (Professor Ernest House, University of Colorado-Boulder, USA); and Education and training (Dr Peter Cuttance, University of Edinburgh, UK).

School Organization and Improvement Series

Editor: David Reynolds, University College, Cardiff, UK

The Comprehensive Experiment
David Reynolds and Michael Sullivan with Stephen Murgatroyd

The Self-managing School
Brian J. Caldwell and Jim M. Spinks

Education Policy Perspectives

The Self-managing School

Brian J. Caldwell
and
Jim M. Spinks

RoutledgeFalmer
Taylor & Francis Group

LONDON AND NEW YORK

First published 1988.
By Routledge Falmer
11 New Fetter Lane, London EC4P 4EE
Reprinted 1988, 1989, 1990, 1991 and 1993

Transferred to Digital Printing 2004

Library of Congress Cataloging in Publication Data

Caldwell, Brian.
   The self-managing school/Brian J. Caldwell and Jim M. Spinks.
   (Education policy perspectives)

   Bibliography: p.
   Includes index.
   1. School management and organization. 2. Public schools—
Business management. 3. School management and organization—
Decision-making. I. Spinks, Jim M. II. Title. III. Series.
LB2805.C15 1988 371.2—dc 19 87-33077
ISBN 1-85000-330-0
ISBN 1-85000-331-9 (pbk.)

Jacket design by Caroline Archer

Typeset in 10½/12 Caledonia by
Imago Publishing Ltd, Thame, Oxon

Contents

Foreword

This book concerns one of today's key educational issues: how schools can be encouraged to develop their own management skills. The present British government has introduced legislation for schools to manage their own budgets and to enable schools to opt out of LEA control and become independently run and financed by central government. In other countries such as Australia, Canada, the Scandinavian countries and also in some parts of the United States, the devolution of budgeting and management power to schools and the decentralisation of educational administration are being pursued with vigour.

Experience of past top-down change programmes or improvement schemes was one of dismal failure and it is therefore easy to see why the self-managing school is currently such a popular concept. The school effectiveness literature also shows that the more effective schools in all countries have staff groups who 'own' their school because they as staff are responsible for its management and general well-being. It is also clear from the various school improvement programmes that commitment to personal and institutional change is greatest where the individual school is in charge of its own schemes.

Brian Caldwell and Jim Spinks' book is therefore an important one for policy-makers and practitioners alike. It outlines how schools can 'self-manage' themselves and the detailed experience of one school in Australia that attempted a long-term programme of Collaborative School Management. It will be useful for practitioners in that it is above all a *practical* guide to the process of school management that gives a large quantity of work sheets, check lists and documents that can be used by any staff group in their own school. It will also be a useful book for policy-makers since it surveys the current decentralisation attempts of the educational systems in Britain, the United States and Australia.

The book is lucidly written, sensibly structured and full of perceptive ideas and policies on the ways schools can be managed. In a world moving rapidly towards self-managed schools it is a timely and important practical contribution to our knowledge of school organisation and our chances of effective school improvement.

David Reynolds
University College, Cardiff

Preface

The title of this book may be greeted with incredulity or scepticism by the reader who has been associated with publicly funded schools which have been directed and supported for decades in a complex arrangement of roles and responsibilities involving authorities at the national, state and local levels. While believing that such schools must continue to work within a framework of policies and priorities which will ensure that a system of education will meet public as well as private purposes, it is our belief that schools can now be otherwise largely self-managing. We believe that the values of effectiveness, efficiency, equity, liberty, choice and, indeed, excellence, are not mutually exclusive, and that the time is now at hand in many countries to bring about a shift in the centralisation-decentralisation continuum as far as the management of education is concerned. This shift is already underway in a number of places including Britain, Australia, Canada and the United States.

We have defined a self-managing school as one for which there has been significant and consistent delegation to the school level of authority to make decisions related to the allocation of resources (knowledge, technology, power, materiel, people, time and finance). This decentralisation is administrative rather than political, with decisions at the school level being made within a framework of local, state or national policies and guidelines. The school remains accountable to a central authority for the manner in which resources are allocated. Our purpose in this book is to describe an approach which was identified in a study of highly effective schools and which has now been successfully implemented in hundreds of schools in a once highly centralised system. We offer a model we describe as the Collaborative School Management Cycle because it provides for the appropriate involvement of teachers, parents and students in an ongoing management process of goal-setting, need identification, policy-making, planning, budgeting, implementing and evaluating. The focus is on programmes for students and the effective and efficient allocation of resources to support learning and teaching.

Our work began in 1983 with a limited focus in one state in Australia. What was an attempt to describe a promising way of allocating resources in a strictly financial sense has evolved into a framework for the key functions in school administration, including the management of curriculum change, which can be adapted to suit a variety of settings. We began in Tasmania with an interest in identifying and disseminating information which would help head teachers manage their finances in more efficient and effective ways. Such a capability was important in this state since, at the time, a greater proportion of the Recurrent Grants of the Commonwealth Schools Commission was decentralised to schools than in any other state. Receipt of a Commonwealth Schools Commission grant for a Project of National Significance led to a joint Education Department of Tasmania-University of Tasmania effort to accomplish the same ends on a national scale through the Effective Resource Allocation in Schools Project.

Following a trial seminar based on model practices at Rosebery District High School in Tasmania, we were invited to serve as consultants to the Department of Management and Budget in Victoria to assist the Education Department in that state in the introduction of programme budgeting in all schools at a time when the government was introducing the most far-reaching powers at the school level in any of the countries we mentioned above. By the end of 1986, we had conducted more than 100 seminars for representatives of about 1,100 schools — head teachers, teachers, parents and students — with many hundreds of these schools already making good progress in the adoption of the approach. In 1986, the Education Department of Tasmania published an earlier version of this book under the title *Policy-making and Planning for School Effectiveness: A Guide to Collaborative School Management*. This edition sold within months, with interest beyond the borders of Tasmania and Victoria. It was apparent that the book was relevant to changes in other parts of Australia, especially in Western Australia, where shifts in the centralisation-decentralisation continuum were also underway.

In 1987, it became evident that the approach we describe is of value in other countries, especially in Britain, where the government, following its re-election in June 1987, announced its intention to provide governing bodies and head teachers of all secondary schools and many primary schools with powers to control their own budgets. In the United States, the powerful National Governors' Association announced in August 1986, its support of school-site management, an approach we have described more generally as self-management for schools. With revisions to suit the wider international scene, this Falmer Press edition is offered as a contribution to achieve the intents of these changes and recommendations.

The book is intended to serve the needs of everyone who is involved in the management of schools which now have, or intend to have, greater autonomy within a system of education than is now the case. While the book will be of value to those who support the work of schools, including people in central offices of school systems and those who conduct professional development programmes, the needs of practitioners at the school level have been foremost in our minds. The book assumes that a framework exists for an equitable allocation of resources to all schools: this is a necessary starting point for self-management. We do not deal with the means of establishing this framework although we note in chapter 1 that it has been successfully accomplished in many school systems, notably in Edmonton, Canada. Several years are required to establish such a framework and it is fortunate that governments or authorities in the several countries we have mentioned have allowed time for this to be accomplished. Our experience has also shown that several years are also required for people in schools to acquire the knowledge and skills of self-management. Hopefully, these efforts to ensure equity across a school system and the development of school-level capability can proceed together.

We wish to acknowledge the invaluable assistance of many organisations and individuals. The Commonwealth Schools Commission in Australia provided financial support for the initial study of highly effective government and non-government schools in the Effective Resource Allocation in Schools Project (ERASP). This project was guided by a Steering Committee of nominees of the Commonwealth Schools Commission, Education Department of Tasmania, Catholic Education Office in Tasmania, Institute of Educational Administration, and the Australian Council for Educational Administration. Studies of highly effective schools were carried out in Tasmania and South Australia with the assistance of the Directors-General of Education in each state as well as officers of the Commonwealth Schools Commission and systems of non-government schools. The Director-General of Education and senior officers in the Education Department of Victoria provided strong support to our consultation in that state. We are indebted to hundreds of head teachers, teachers, parents and students who gave their time in the initial studies and who worked with us in our consultancies related to the self-management of schools. The approach at Rosebery District High School was developed with the commitment and skill of staff and council over a number of years. The illustrations of policies, plans, budgets and evaluation reports throughout this book are testimony to their efforts.

On a personal note, we would like to acknowledge the support of Mr. Ken Axton, Director-General of Education in Tasmania, for support of the entire venture, especially the initial study, the publication of the first edition of the book, and the release of Jim Spinks for consultancy work in many parts of Australia; Professors Phillip Hughes and Kevin Collis of the Centre for Education at the University of Tasmania for the encouragement and support of Brian Caldwell; Dr. Josie Misko, who served as Project Officer for ERASP and conducted most of the studies of highly effective schools; Kingsley Curtis, who facilitated studies in South Australia; Dr.

Preface

Colin Moyle, Director of the Institute of Educational Administration, for his personal contributions and invitations to serve as consultants on the approach in residential programmes at the Institute; and Dr. Jeffrey Dunstan, Executive Director of Schools, and Dr. Philip Creed, Director of Policy and Planning who supported our efforts in Victoria.

More recently, the opportunity for Brian Caldwell to observe current developments in other countries at first hand in 1986 and 1987 was aided greatly by the Dean and faculty of Fordham University at Lincoln Centre in New York, especially Dr. Robert J. Starratt who has broadened immensely our view of leadership in education, Dr. Michael Usdan, who also serves as Director of the Institute of Educational Leadership and who provided a base and a host of contacts in Washington, DC; and Dr. Bruce Cooper, then on leave at the University of London Institute of Education, who facilitated much of our work in England. Michael Strembitsky, Superintendent, and Robert Smilanich, Associate Superintendent, helped ensure that our knowledge of 'lighthouse' practice in Edmonton, Canada was up-to-date. A base at the University of London Institute of Education was provided by Professor Denis Lawton, Director, and Professor Gareth Williams, Department of Economic, Administrative and Policy Studies in Education. Information about pioneering efforts in self-management in Britain was obtained with the assistance of Colin Humphrey, former Director of Education, Solihull, and Geoffrey Morris, Chief Education Officer, Cambridgeshire.

We were indebted throughout to Julie Goninon, Rosebery District High School, and Christine Monks, All-Electric Typing, Sandy Bay, for their outstanding typing services.

It is our hope that this book will make a contribution to self-management for school effectiveness, with the prime beneficiaries being the students in our schools.

Brian J. Caldwell
Jim M. Spinks

London, June 1987

Part A

A Framework for Self-management

1   *Toward the Self-managing School*

There have been initiatives in a number of countries to increase the autonomy of schools within publicly-funded systems of education. In Britain, for example, the Conservative government of Margaret Thatcher proposes[1] to give control of their own budgets to governing bodies and head teachers of all secondary schools and many primary schools, with provision for schools to opt out of control by the local education authority and receive grants directly from the Department of Education and Science. In Australia, where control of education has traditionally been highly centralised at the state government level, several states have enacted or are contemplating legislation which provides a high degree of decentralisation in school management. In the state of Victoria, for example, more than two thousand state schools now have school councils of parents, teachers and, for secondary schools, students, which have the power to set the educational policy and budget of the school within guidelines established by the Minister of Education. In the United States, the influential National Governors' Association has called[2] for the support of school-site management to bring about school improvement, thus extending a practice which has been adopted in a small number of districts in recent years.

This book is intended to serve the needs of everyone who is involved in the management of schools which now have, or plan to have, greater autonomy within a system of education than has traditionally been the case. In brief, it is a guide to 'the self-managing school'. Its purpose is to describe an approach which was identified in a recently conducted study of highly effective schools and which has now been successfully implemented in hundreds of schools in a once highly centralised system. The approach, described as Collaborative School Management, has the following characteristics:

- It integrates goal-setting, policy-making, planning, budgeting, implementing and evaluating in a manner which contrasts with the often unsystematic, fragmented processes which have caused so much frustration and ineffectiveness in the past.

- It secures appropriate involvement of staff, students and the community, with clearly defined roles for governing bodies where such groups exist and have responsibility for policy-making.
- It focuses on the central functions of schools — learning and teaching — and, accordingly, organises the management of the school around 'programmes' which correspond to the preferred patterns of work in the school.

The book goes beyond a description of the approach. Detailed guidelines and illustrations are provided for every phase of the management process, with account taken of the diverse population involved in that process. While practice varies from country to country, among state or local authorities within each country, and among schools within each system, these guidelines concern the work of the head teacher, other teachers with formal positions of responsibility, teachers in general, support staff, students, members of the school community at large, and members of the school community in groups such as governing boards or councils or parents and friends' organisations. The description of the approach and guidelines for its implementation are also intended to serve the needs of those who direct, support or study the management of schools, including people employed by local, state, national or other central authorities as well as lecturers and students in tertiary programmes in educational administration. The needs of the practitioner have, however, been foremost in the minds of the authors in the preparation of the book.

The Self-managing School Defined

Efforts to increase the autonomy of schools have differed in scope and nomenclature. In Britain, where the focus so far has been on decentralisation of decisions related to the allocation of financial resources, the initiative has been described by pioneering authorities as Local Financial Management (Cambridgeshire) and the School Financial Autonomy Scheme (Solihull). In Canada, the initial focus in a 'lighthouse' scheme in Edmonton, Alberta was also on the school budget, with the practice described as school-based budgeting. With the introduction of teacher effectiveness programmes and school-by-school approaches to programme evaluation, school-site decision-making became the preferred descriptor. In Victoria, Australia, the general term 'devolution' has been used to described the quite sweeping change to the pattern of school governance which began with the enactment of legislation giving policy powers to school councils. The term 'self-governing school' was used in a proposal to give a very high measure of autonomy to state schools meeting certain requirements. In the small number of districts in the United States where changes along these lines have been made, a financial focus was known as school-site or school-based budgeting, with a more comprehensive approach, especially where teacher and community involvement was sought, being described as school-site or school-based management.

The common thread in all of these developments has been the shift of power to make certain kinds of decisions from a central authority to a school. In each instance, the school has continued to work within a framework of legislation, policies and priorities determined by the central authority. These decisions have been concerned with the allocation of resources, in the narrow financial sense in all instances, but often in the broader sense in the areas of curriculum, personnel and facilities. In general, the intent has been to foster a measure of self-management in the school. It is for this reason that we have coined the term 'self-managing school' to describe the kind of school which results from these efforts, although we acknowledge that the extent of autonomy has varied among the settings we have reviewed.

We define a self-managing school as one for which there has been significant and consistent decentralisation to the school level of authority to make decisions related to the allocation of resources. This decentralisation is administrative rather than political, with decisions at the school level being made within a framework of local, state or national policies and guidelines. The school remains accountable to a central authority for the manner in which resources are allocated.

Resources are defined broadly to include knowledge (decentralisation of decisions related to curriculum, including decisions related to the goals or ends of schooling); technology (decentralisation of decisions related to the means of teaching and learning); power (decentralisation of authority to make decisions); materiel (decentralisation of decisions related to the use of facilities, supplies and equipment); people (decentralisation of decisions related to the allocation of people in matters related to teaching and learning, and the support of teaching and learning); time (decentralisation of decisions related to the allocation of time); and finance (decentralisation of decisions related to the allocation of money).

The Case for Self-management

It is useful to briefly review some of the arguments which have been offered in support of self-management. The case can be presented from several perspectives drawn from fields of inquiry such as economics, politics or organisation theory. Advocates have traditionally argued on these grounds but, more recently, appeal has been made to findings from research on school effectiveness and to the need for increased professionalism among teachers. What follows is just a sample of what may be found in the literature. Public and private values pervade each perspective, with current interest explained in large measure by the ascendancy of certain of these values.

Political-economy

The case for self-management which draws on concepts from economics or politics seems at first sight paradoxical since it challenges the belief that equity or equality are achieved through relatively uniform, centralised allocations of resources to all schools. This challenge was mounted in strong terms by Garms, Guthrie and Pierce[3] who based their case on the view that education is a prime instrument for the promotion of three strongly held values: equality, efficiency and liberty. A fourth value, choice, may be promoted through efficiency and equality, with efficiency ensuring that resources are conserved for other activities, thus expanding choice, and equality of opportunity ensuring that choice can be exercised. These writers contend that centralised budgeting, with relatively uniform allocations to schools and minimal opportunity for re-allocation, impairs the achievement of equality and efficiency and, by implication, of choice. Equality of opportunity is impaired because a centralised budget makes it difficult for schools to match services to student needs. Efficiency is impaired for the same reason but also for other reasons: centralised budgeting seldom provides incentives for efficiency, frequently fails to foster diversity through which more efficient and effective approaches to teaching and learning may be identified, and invariably excludes key actors such as governing bodies, heads, teachers, parents and students who have perhaps the most powerful motivation to see that resources are used to best advantage. The solution, according to these writers, is school-site management, with lump-sum budget allocations to schools, a high degree of community involvement in school decision-making, and the fostering of diversity within and among schools to ensure choice.

Organisation theory

A self-managing school operates within a framework of local, state or national legislation, policies and priorities. Some decisions remain centralised. Support for an appropriate balance of centralisation and decentralisation may be drawn from the field of organisation theory. Perrow,[4] for example, suggested that the pattern of centralisation and decentralisation in an organisation can be determined through analysis of the techniques or technology required to get the work done as well as the nature of the people with whom the organisation must deal. For example, for techniques or technology, where few exceptional cases must be dealt with and problems are relatively simple, allowing for the development of routines, a relatively centralised structure is appropriate. Where many exceptional cases are encountered, and problems are more complex so that non-routine processes are required, a relatively decentralised structure is more appropriate. For organisations where people are central to the work, when people with whom the organisation deals are relatively uniform in nature and the processes for dealing with those people are well understood, a relatively centralised structure is appropriate. Where people are diverse in nature and the processes for dealing with them are not well understood, a relatively decentralised structure is more appropriate.

Applying Perrow's analysis to education results in patterns of centralisation and decentralisation of the kind found in places where self-management of schools has been encouraged. Many matters related to support services, such as pupil transportation or the distribution of instructional supplies, allow for the development of routines applicable to all schools, suggesting a relatively centralised structure for the delivery of such services. On the other hand, if pupils are seen as having diverse needs, with each school expected to provide programmes to meet these needs, and if the nature of teaching and learning for each child cannot be well understood from a central perspective, then a more decentralised structure is appropriate. It is evident that establishing an appropriate balance of centralisation and decentralisation requires careful analysis if this perspective is adopted. It is also evident that such analysis will be embedded in values related to the purpose of schooling and the nature of the child. For example, if education is seen as being concerned with a relatively narrow range of cognitive skills with the expectation that all children should have the same learning experiences in pursuit of similar outcomes and, further, if children are seen as similar in nature with little account of individual differences necessary, then a relatively high degree of centralisation may be appropriate. These values may have prevailed in former times or may be evident in other cultures, thus accounting for and making acceptable a different pattern of centralisation and decentralisation than is assumed in this book.

An echo of this perspective from organisation theory may be found in the work of people such as Peters and Waterman,[5] whose studies of excellent companies led them to the identification of 'simultaneous loose-tight properties'. They found that excellent companies are both centralised and decentralised, pushing autonomy down to the shop floor or production team for some functions but being 'fanatical centralists about the core values they hold dear'.[6] The parallel in education is the centralised determination of broad goals and purposes of education accompanied by decentralised decision-making about the means by which these goals and purposes will be achieved, with those people who are decentralised being accountable to those centralised for the achievement of outcomes.

School effectiveness

Increasingly, however, the case for self-management is being argued on the basis of findings from studies of school effectiveness. Some writers, after reviewing the characteristics of effective schools, have concluded that a form of self-management provides the best framework wherein these characteristics may be fostered in all schools. Foremost are Purkey and Smith[7] who, while expressing some reservations about the effective schools movement, concluded that 'existing research is sufficiently consistent to guide school improvements based on its conclusions'.[8]

Purkey and Smith offered a model 'for creating an effective school' which drew from literature in four areas: classroom research on teacher effectiveness, research on the implementation of educational innovations and school organisation which identify the role of school culture in school improvement, research in workplaces other than education, and consistency between effective schools research and the experience of practitioners. Their model contains thirteen characteristics, nine of which can be implemented relatively quickly, while four defining the school's culture will take time because they require the development of an appropriate climate. In the first group of nine they include school-site management and democratic decision-making wherein 'the staff of each school is given a considerable amount of responsibility and authority in determining the exact means by which they address the problem of increasing academic performance. This includes giving staffs more authority over curricular and instructional decisions and allocation of building resources'.[9]

Four policy recommendations were offered by Purkey and Smith, each of which has implications for self-management. They included recommendations that 'the school [should be] the focus of change; its culture, the ultimate policy target';[10] 'resources, especially time and technical assistance, must be provided that will encourage and nurture the process of collaboration and participation necessary to change both people and structures in schools';[11] and 'an inverted pyramid approach to changing schools [must] be adopted that maximises local responsibility for school improvement while it recognises the legal responsibility of the higher government levels'.[12]

Finn[13] addressed another implication of the effective schools research when he called for 'strategic independence' for schools. He noted that 'the central problem faced by policy makers who attempt to transform the findings of "effective schools" research into improved educational practice at state or local level is the tension between school-level autonomy and systemwide uniformity'.[14] His nine commandments for strategic independence included recognition of the school as 'the key organisational unit in the public school system';[15] the setting of 'rigorous educational standards for entire states and communities but [emphasising] broad goals and essential outcomes, not specific procedures, curricula, or timetables';[16]

encouraging 'schools to be different, except for the core of cognitive skills and knowledge that all students in a system or state should acquire';[17] and devolving 'more budgetary authority ... to the school level'.[18] Finn's recommendations, along with the model of Purkey and Smith, are consistent with the contingency view of organisations offered by Perrow as far as centralisation and decentralisation are concerned: a point must be found in the continuum which provides for centralisation of authority for some functions but decentralisation for others.

Professionalism

Increased autonomy for teachers and fewer bureaucratic controls have invariably been included as elements in the case for the enhancement of teaching as a profession. In the United States, for example, reports by the Carnegie Forum on Education and the Economy[19] and the Holmes Group[20] advocated this course, with the latter setting a goal of making schools better places for teachers to work, and to learn: 'This will require less bureaucracy, more professional autonomy, and more leadership for teachers'.[21]

Initiatives in Self-management

Efforts to increase the autonomy of schools have been made in a number of countries for a variety of reasons. What follows is a summary of developments in Britain, Australia, Canada and the United States. The purpose is to provide an account of what has been accomplished and what is emerging as well as the major issues and concerns. This account sets the stage for the remaining chapters of the book which are concerned with an approach to ensuring effective adoption of the self-management concept.

Britain

What is proposed in Britain is potentially the most far-reaching development in any of the countries considered in this review. The Conservative Manifesto for the 1987 national election contained proposals for four major reforms,[22] each of which has implications for the management of schools and a shift in the centralisation-decentralisation continuum toward self-management:

- A national core curriculum.
- Control over school budgets to be given to governing bodies and head teachers of all secondary schools and many primary schools within five years.

- Increasing parental choice by fostering diversity and increasing access.
- Allowing state schools to opt out of LEA (local education authority) control, with grants from the national government being made directly to the school.

These proposals reflect each of the four values described by Garms, Guthrie and Pierce in their advocacy of school-site management. The values of equity, efficiency, liberty and choice are addressed in the intents to decentralise control of budgets, increase access, foster diversity and allow state schools to be independent of LEA control. While details of implementation on a national scale have not yet been addressed, a picture has been painted of a broad framework of national policy in the area of curriculum, with an equitable allocation of resources to schools. Schools will then be encouraged to allocate resources in a manner which best meets needs at the local level, with independence from the LEA an option which might be considered on a school-by-school basis.

These proposals are contentious, with representatives of local authorities expressing concern about impact on the quality of education should schools be allowed to opt out of the LEA.[23] Some heads do not wish to assume responsibility for the budget, fearing that this will detract from their preferred role of educational leader.[24] However, these proposals have been made against a background of successful experience by six local authorities in the area of school finance, with that in Cambridgeshire and Solihull considered briefly here.

Chief Education Officer of Cambridgeshire, Geoffrey Morris, has provided an account of the introduction of Local Financial Management (LFM).[25] The initiative was consistent with the tradition in the county for close links between community and education. With the encouragement of management consultants to 'delegate to the lowest level compatible with effective management', the county commenced a pilot in April 1982, with six secondary and one primary school volunteering for the scheme. Schools were provided with a lump-sum allocation based on historical patterns of expenditure, with freedom of virement (transfer) across all categories of expenditure, including staff. No special training was provided and no additional staffing resources were supplied. While the scheme continues to evolve with a number of problems yet to be resolved, Morris believes that it is worth pursuing. Another pilot in other schools in the county involves the trial of a system of accountability based on careful specification of performance measures. Morris also believes that establishing an appropriate pattern of accountability is necessary in the current environment in Britain. He concludes that a link between accountability and local financial management is essential 'if the way forward is to be towards the self-managing instituion . . .'.[26]

Practice in the metropolitan borough of Solihull has steadily evolved since the commencement of the 1981–82 financial year, involving three schools initially and now ten, with further expansion to remaining schools now that commitments have been made to the permanence of the approach. Decisions related to about 90 per cent of costs, including staff, have been decentralised to the school level in this initiative which is known locally as the School Financial Autonomy Scheme. Implementation was the subject of regular internal and external appraisal, with several published accounts by the Director of Education in Solihull, Colin Humphrey, and the external consultant, Hywel Thomas, Department of Social and Administrative Studies in Education, University of Birmingham.[27]

It was the chairman of the borough's education committee who took the initiative in Solihull: 'he held the view that if you applied the same sort of procedures to running a school as he used in running a small business, there could be some improvement in performance, and that if you are spending your own money you exercise more care than if you are spending somebody else's'.[28] Implementation proceeded in a matter of weeks, with three schools selected for trial (sixth form college, secondary school, primary school) based on the interest of the heads and the desirability of having a range of schools. The principal aim was 'to make more efficient use of scarce resources'. A review of reports in the early years of the trial reveals similar problems and issues as encountered elsewhere, with difficulty in determining the amount of the total allocation to each school; concern at the lack of understandable, reliable, and up-to-date information related to school accounts; debate about categories of income and expenditure which should be the subject of school decision, especially those related to maintenance of buildings and debt servicing; and the time-consuming nature of clerical tasks.

After five years' experience with school-based budgeting, Humphrey and Thomas described[29] the following outcomes: a willingness on the part of schools to use their power of virement; a more responsive approach to school maintenance, with schools now able to set their own priorities; greater awareness among teachers of the financial parameters; and steady improvement in the quality of financial information made available to schools. Plans have been made to improve the financial information system, and for in-service training of teachers and officers of the authority as autonomy is extended to other schools.

A reading of published accounts suggests that the handling of finance was almost exclusively the focus of these early initiatives in Britain. These accounts do not describe linkages with planning for curriculum and instruction or with systematic approaches to programme evaluation. Furthermore, in none of these initiatives has the basic relationship between school and LEA been at issue. Even with a preference for self-management, Geoffrey Morris, Chief Executive Officer, sees a balance of centralisation and decentralisation which is consistent with the theoretical analysis of Perrow, the 'simultaneous loose-tight' organisation of Peters and

Waterman, and the concept of 'strategic independence' proposed by Finn. Writing at a time of increasing tension between national and local authorities, Morris contends that

> Central and local governments have vital roles of course but these should be concerned with establishing frameworks, distributing resources, monitoring standards and not with prescribing content or process or pace. That, paradoxically, seems to me to be the most effective way of ensuring that education remains local; at the very time when all the pressures are towards centralisation, we should resist and delegate. But it is a risk-taking formula and letting go can test the nerves.[30]

Australia

Developments in Australia in terms of distribution of responsibilities among different levels of governance often come as a surprise to those from other nations who recall its traditional pattern in a highly centralised system of education. These developments have been uneven among states and, for the most part, would not be the reason for any special comment in this chapter. However, the change in one state, Victoria, has been so far-reaching that in many respects it provides the outstanding example of *existing* approaches to self-management among the countries being reviewed here.

It was not until 1987 that plans were made in Victoria for significant decentralisation of responsibility in budgeting. However, this development was preceded by sweeping reform which saw the decentralisation of perhaps the major resource — power — to the extent that every state school now has a school-site council of parents, teachers and for secondary schools, students. These councils have the power, within a framework of state policies and priorities, to set educational policy for the school, approve the budget, and evaluate the educational programme. Principals (head teachers) are now appointed through a local selection process. A comprehensive in-service programme in the last three years has endeavoured to develop the knowledge, skills and attitudes of participants in the process, thus setting the scene for what many see as the final stage of a decade of decentralisation, namely, the decentralisation of financial responsibility. A major part of this in-service programme was based on the model for Collaborative School Management described in this book.

Education is a state responsibility in Australia and, for more than one hundred years until the early 1970s, public education at primary and secondary levels was administered in each state through highly centralised state government departments of education. Curriculum was for the most part determined centrally, with tight control exercised through an inspectorial system and state-wide external examinations at the end of secondary schooling. Most funds for education came from state sources, with centralised allocation of resources which provided little money for discretionary use by schools other than that raised by voluntary contributions from parents and the local community. The federal government provided very limited support until the 1960s when aid for libraries and science facilities in both government (state or public) and non-government (private or independent) schools was introduced.

There have been dramatic changes to this pattern of governance since the early 1970s. The federal government became involved in a very significant way through the Australian Schools Commission (now called the Commonwealth Schools Commission) established in 1973. A comprehensive grants scheme administered by the commission for both government and non-government schools was designed to achieve greater equity among schools and equality of opportunity for students. The task of administration in state departments of education became immediately more complex, with several states, notably Tasmania, decentralising to the school level decisions related to a substantial portion of recurrent grants received from the commission. The early 1970s were also marked by administrative decentralisation of education departments through the formation of regional units in several states. South Australia and the Australian Capital Territory led the way in providing greater freedom and autonomy for schools, with provision in both instances for school-site councils or boards having advisory and limited decision-making powers. The factors underlying these trends fall neatly into frameworks drawn from the fields of economics, politics and organisational theory outlined earlier in the chapter. The concern for equity was evident in the grant structure of the Australian Schools Commission. A movement toward decentralisation was associated in large part with increasing complexity in the administration of education. Political values in the form of a desire to participate in decisions were also evident in the positions taken by some parent and teacher organisations.

The trend to a decentralised system of school governance continued most markedly in Victoria,[31] with proposals currently under consideration for similar changes in Western Australia.[32] In Victoria, administrative decentralisation to regional units proceeded throughout the 1970s and 1980s. In 1975, the state government required all government schools to establish school-site councils of teachers, parents and other members of the school community. A variety of models were offered as a guide, with most providing powers of advice only to the principal and staff. These initiatives in regionalisation and decentralisation to the school level were taken by a relatively conservative Liberal government. In 1983, however, the election to government of the Australian Labour Party saw a dramatic change, with substantial commitment to decentralisation.

The immediate environment for public education was turbulent when government changed in 1983. A succession of extended strikes by teachers throughout the previous decade and a perceived reluctance or incapacity on the part of government and education department to respond to community and professional concerns led to some loss of confidence in the government system and an increase in enrolments in non-government schools where almost one-third of the state's students were soon receiving their education. It seems that decentralisation was not so much a response to demands from the school level, though some parent and professional bodies were strong advocates of this course, but an effort to restore confidence in the state system.

Shaping recent developments in Victoria was a series of Ministerial Papers, the first of which enunciated five guiding principles: genuine devolution of authority and responsibility to the school community; collaborative decision-making processes; a responsive bureaucracy, the main function of which is to serve and assist schools; effectiveness of educational outcomes; and the active redress of disadvantage and discrimination.[33] The Ministerial Papers in Victoria signalled government intent to ensure that school councils would in future have the major responsibility for deciding the educational policies of their schools. Planning and budgeting responsibilities were also envisaged for school councils.

Two further priorities of government then laid the foundation for the far-reaching approach to school-based management which has now emerged. One was a comprehensive School Improvement Plan with purposes which included 'to encourage and support collaborative practices between parents, students and teachers in schools' and 'to encourage and support a cylical process of school evaluation, planning, implementation and re-evaluation'.[34] The other priority was the decision to introduce programme budgeting in all departments and agencies of government, including schools. The Education Department, soon re-formed as a Ministry of Education, was faced with the challenge of introducing programme budgeting to schools in a manner which was consistent with its other policies related to devolution, with their emphasis on collaborative structures and processes.

A five-year strategy commencing in 1984 was adopted for the introduction of programme budgeting in approximately 2,200 public schools in Victoria. A pilot project in 1984 involved three to five schools in each of the twelve administrative regions of the state. The emphasis in the first three years was on the development of the necessary knowledge, skills and attitudes, and an extended series of seminars was conducted for principals (head teachers), teachers, parents and students. By the end of 1986, more than 1,100 schools had participated in these seminars with the majority making good progress in the adoption of collaborative approaches to policy-making and planning. As noted earlier, the approach described in this book was the centre-piece of these seminars.

The government in Victoria gave consideration in late 1986 to recommendations of its Ministry Structures Project Team which would allow government schools meeting certain criteria to become 'self-governing schools'. If adopted, this would have established the most comprehensive form of school-based management to be found in the countries under consideration here. The recommendation is similar in some respects to that of the provision in the Conservative Manifesto in Britain in 1987 for schools to 'opt out' of an LEA. Such schools would be fully-funded by the state but, apart from operating a programme consistent with the general policies and priorities of the government, would be governed independently by their councils. These recommendations were generally opposed by organisations having an interest in education, with concerns about equity being expressed and opposition to what was seen as an effort by the Labour government to 'privatise' public education. While rejecting the concept of 'self-governing schools', the government accepted in principle that schools should be given greater control over the allocation and management of resources, the need to shift resources from the centre to schools, the need for improved support of school councils, the need to develop new forms of block (lump-sum) funding for schools, and the principle of decentralisation of management and operational functions in the areas of curriculum, special programmes, finance and administration, and facilities.[35] It is likely, however, that the intents of recommendations for 'self-governing schools' will be largely met if the government proceeds along these lines.

United States

Public education is a state responsibility in the United States. However, a substantial level of community control has been achieved with the creation and empowerment under state law of locally-elected school boards having responsibility for schools in a district, subject to state laws and regulations. Concern for efficiency and equity led to substantial consolidation, with the number of districts reduced from about 128,000 in 1932 to about 15,000 at present. There has traditionally been heavy reliance on local property tax as the chief source of funds but a succession of legal challenges and general concern for equity have shifted the balance so that most finance now comes from the state. The federal government has played a small, significant but now diminishing role through a series of categorical grants generally designed to promote equality of opportunity. Private schools must generally raise their own funds although some support comes in the form of categorical grants from and access to services provided by federal and state governments on condition that such support is delivered in non-sectarian fashion.

Guthrie and Reed reported[36] that the term 'school-site management' was originally used by a New York State reform commission and was intended to cover a comprehensive approach to decentralisation, with resources defined broadly to include matters related to curriculum and personnel in addition to finance, and with a greater measure of lay control at the school level. After a brief review of developments around the country, these writers concluded that, although there was widespread adoption of parent advisory councils as required for several federal aid programs, there were few efforts to comprehensively decentralise, inspiring the view that the reform 'was only superficial'.[37]

Most of the more comprehensive attempts at school-site management were in California and Florida but, even in these states, the numbers are small. Lindelow reported[38] five of sixty-seven county districts in Florida and sixty-one of about 1,100 districts in California. A few districts in other states have also been identified. The practice was adopted in most instances in the seventies, a decade which also saw administrative decentralisation to regional or sub-district units and political decentralisation to community boards in some large urban school districts. Lindelow saw these developments in the context of the continuing, historical 'tug-of-war between the concepts of autonomy and control'.[39]

The intents of school-site management were mainly addressed through the mechanism of the budget. The usual approach was to provide the school with a lump-sum allocation determined on the basis of a per pupil allocation, with weighting factors which varied according to level of schooling and category of educational need. The principal (head teacher) was then responsible for preparing a budget for the school, subject to the constraints of state and district requirements. The budget for teaching and non-teaching staff used system-wide average salaries as the basis for costing. Allocations for maintenance and utilities were often included in school-site budgets. The general intent was to match resources to the needs of students. The principal was accountable to the superintendent of the district for the use of funds and for ensuring that district-wide instructional goals and priorities were addressed in the school. The most extensive preparation for the introduction of the approach seems to have been in Florida, where a five-year phased introduction allowed time for development of team management and decision-making skills.

Until recently, it seems that the mid- to late-seventies marked the peak of interest in school-site management in the United States. Lindelow reported that two pioneers of the approach, Alachua County in Florida and Newport-Mesa in California, had re-centralised in some respects at the start of the eighties. Despite the fact that implementation occurred in a number of districts in the intervening years, it is fair to say that relatively low levels of interest have been generated around the nation. One explanation might be found in the rather narrow focus of initial attempts at school-site management, where the budget was the chief mechanism for encouraging schools to more closely match their resources to the needs of pupils, and where resources tended to be narrowly conceived in terms of money and basic consideration of time and personnel. While extended training of the kind provided in Florida fostered team management and decision-making skills, additional knowledge and skill in the technical core of education are clearly demanded if the outcome is to be a contribution to school effectiveness. This technical core is largely concerned with curriculum and instruction.

There has, however, been a renewal of interest in school-site management in the United States. Recent interest has been generated by reports such as that of the National Governors' Association. The governors called for 'incentives and technical assistance to districts to promote school site management and improvement', reflecting a belief that 'providing discretionary resources to schools gives them a major incentive to improve. Where this has been tried, it has unleashed creative energies and helped schools develop a diversity of approaches and strategies to meet particular goals'.[40] The National Education Association and the National Association of Secondary School Principals issued a joint report stating that 'The NASSP and NEA remain committed to the principle that substantial decision-making authority at the school site is the essential pre-requisite for quality education'.[41] These proposals and beliefs are consistent with recommendations of scholars such as Theodore Sizer and John Goodlad following their respective studies of schooling in the United States. Sizer believes that one 'imperative for better schools' is to give teachers and students room to take full advantage of the variety among them, a situation which 'implies that there must be substantial authority in each school. For most public and diocesan Catholic school systems, this means the decentralisation of power from headquarters to individual schools'.[42] Goodlad proposed 'genuine decentralisation of authority and responsibility to the local school within a framework designed to assure school-to-school equity and a measure of accountability'.[43] He noted that 'the guiding principle being put forward here is that the school must become largely self-directing'.[44]

What is occurring in the United States may be seen as part of the so-called second wave of educational reform, with the first wave being the welter of state commissions and regulations and the diminution of federal involvement which, at least in the public mind, followed the report in 1983 of the National Commission on Excellence in Education.[45] There now seems to be general acceptance that the intents of the first wave of reform will only be achieved if changes occur in the classroom. In the second wave of reform, the focus is the school and the support of schools. Resources are now being mobilized to achieve this end, with the National Governors' Association, for example, securing the financial support of the Carnegie Foundation as it plans the implementation of its report.

Canada

The most interesting development in Canada is in the Edmonton Public School District in Alberta, where the approach is generally described as school-site decision-making and where a number of factors make its experience over ten years of special interest. It has become a 'lighthouse' for both Canada and the United States, with conferences organised by the district in 1983 and 1986 drawing large numbers of participants from both countries. Decisions related to the allocation of resources have been decentralised to schools for teaching and non-teaching staff, equipment, supplies and services. A pilot project of school-based budgeting for consulting services is currently underway. System-wide and school-based opinion surveys involving principals, teachers, parents and students have been conducted since the inception of the programme, with major attention now being given to school-by-school appraisal of student performance on centrally-administered achievement tests. With more than sixty thousand students, this is probably the largest system in North America to have adopted such a comprehensive approach to school-site management.

Of special interest in Edmonton is the decision in 1986 to pilot an extension of the approach to include centralised consulting services. Fourteen schools reflecting the diversity in the district were selected from eighty-four which volunteered for the project, whose purposes are to ensure the effective and efficient deployment of consulting services, to improve capability at the school level to determine the nature and level of consulting services required to meet the needs of students, and to improve the way in which consulting services are accessed and delivered. Schools in the project had their lump-sum allocations supplemented by amounts which reflected the historical use of consulting services according to type of school and level of student need. Allocations were then included in school-based budgets. Standard costs for various types of service were then determined, on a per hour or per incident basis, with costs charged to the school as service is requested. Schools may choose services outside those provided by the district.

The district also established a teacher effectiveness programme in the early eighties. Commencing in 1981 as a small centrally-funded project, by 1986–7 most schools were represented in the one-half day per week professional development programme, with funding from school-based budgets. It is estimated that about half of all teachers in the district have been involved as expertise is shared within schools.

The continuing evolution of the approach in Edmonton Public through the eighties contrasts with an apparent levelling of interest in the United States after the initiatives of the mid-seventies. It was suggested in connection with the United States that undue emphasis may have been given to the budget as the mechanism for educational reform in some districts and that the approach may not have been strongly linked to curriculum and instructional processes. In contrast, Edmonton Public established a teacher effectiveness programme in the early eighties and maintained a high profile for evaluation from the outset, although an instructional focus for the latter has emerged only recently. The commitment to central responsiveness to school needs continues with the current pilot project in school-site decision-making on the use of consulting services.

Issues and Concerns in Self-management

A number of issues and concerns have emerged from a decade of experience in Britain, Australia, United States and Canada. Some concern the system as a whole. For example, can equity be maintained with lump-sum allocations to schools on a per pupil basis? The answer lies in the affirmative if successful experience in Edmonton, Alberta is taken as a guide. In this system, lump-sum allocations to schools involve eleven levels of per pupil allocation to meet forty-seven categories of student need. What is the role of local, state or national authorities as schools become self-managing? Can schools really 'opt out'? Experience to date suggests that other authorities have an important role to play, not only in providing a framework of goals, policies and priorities but also in determining levels of funding and setting appropriate standards of accountability. Consultant and other specialist support for schools can also be efficiently and effectively provided by a local authority, although the pilot project in Edmonton, Alberta includes provision for schools to seek such support from other sources.

This book is intended to address issues and concerns at the school level. Four are identified, reflecting the importance of a focus on teaching and learning; a framework of accountability; appropriate involvement of staff, parents and students; and professional development programmes for the acquisition of knowledge, skills and attitudes among participants in the management process.

Focus on teaching and learning

The limitations of a narrow focus on finance have been noted throughout this account of experience to date. The intents of increasing the autonomy of schools can only be achieved if financial plans reflect educational plans, ensuring that resources are allocated to meet priorities among the special needs which have been identified for the school. Furthermore, the manner in which resources are allocated must be reflected in what actually transpires in the classroom as far as learning and teaching are concerned. What is needed, then, is a comprehensive approach to school management which links goal-setting, need identification, policy-making, planning, budgeting, learning and teaching, and evaluating.

The concerns of head teachers and others that greater autonomy as far as the school budget is concerned will turn them into accountants and purchasing agents are justified unless the focus is clearly on learning and teaching. If this focus is maintained, the role of the head teacher as an educational leader is likely to be enhanced rather than diminished as a school moves toward self-management. The approach described in this book is intended to foster educational leadership in the school.

A framework for accountability

The school must be managed within a framework of national, state and local guidelines. These guidelines may be in the form of legislation, policies, priorities, and conditions in collective agreements and funding arrangements. The school must be able to demonstrate that these guidelines have been honoured.

Three patterns of accountability are suggested in the self-management of schools: accountability to a central authority, accountability to the local community, and accountability of each school programme to the governing body or appropriate policy group within the school. Included then among procedures which ensure accountability will be an approach to the dissemination of information which is easy to prepare and easy to read as well as timely and accurate. Guidelines for these patterns and procedures are contained in this book.

Appropriate involvement of staff, parents and students

A school which is responsive to the needs of its parents and students will ensure their appropriate involvement in the management process. Since these needs must be addressed through the various programmes for teaching and learning, there must similarly be a process for securing appropriate involvement of teachers. Indeed, this kind of involvement is seen by advocates of self-management as a means of enhancing the professional status of teachers.

Involvement must be appropriate to the extent that it reflects the interests and expertise of participants. It should not be excessive and burdensome otherwise the expected gains in professional satisfaction may be lost. The approach to self-management described in this book is intended to provide for this appropriate involvement.

Programmes for professional development

The self-managing school will require a range of knowledge, skills and attitudes not demanded in schools which have worked within a framework of centrally-determined policies, plans and budgets and with few requirements as far as accountability is concerned. Knowledge and skill of a technical, human and educational nature will be required as needs are identified, goals are set, policies are formulated, priorities are determined, resources are allocated, and teaching and learning proceeds, with systematic approaches to programme evaluation. This book describes this knowledge and skill and provides guidelines for their utilisation. Some attention is also given to higher-order attributes of leadership, namely, the capacity to articulate and win commitment to a vision for the school and ensure that vision is institutionalised in the structures, processes and procedures which shape everyday activities. Also addressed is the management of change as a school moves toward self-management.

The Approach

Origin in studies of highly effective schools

The approach to school management described in this book addresses the four issues set out above. It was identified in a study carried out in 1983 of approaches to resource allocation in highly effective government and non-government schools in two states in Australia (Tasmania and South Australia). This study was the Effective Resource Allocation in Schools Project (ERASP), a joint endeavour of the Education Department of Tasmania and the Centre for Education at the University of Tasmania, funded by the Commonwealth Schools Commission as a Project of National Significance. The purpose of ERASP was to prepare a professional development programme to assist people in all kinds of schools acquire knowledge and skills necessary for effective allocation of resources. This programme was trialled, refined and then used as the centre-piece of an extended consultancy from 1984 to 1986 in another state in Australia, Victoria, where the government was proceeding with plans for self-management of schools as described earlier in the chapter. The authors conducted seminars for principals, parents, teachers and students representing an estimated 1,100 schools during this time, with the majority making good progress in adopting the recommended approach at the conclusion of the consultancy. Adoption proceeds in Victoria as the government provides even greater autonomy to the more than 2,000 schools in the state. A review of developments in other Australian states as well as in Britain, United States and Canada suggests wide applicability of the approach.

Collaborative School Management Cycle

The approach is best described as a Collaborative School Management Cycle as illustrated in Figure 1.1. The management cycle has six phases:

Figure 1.1 The Collaborative School Management Cycle

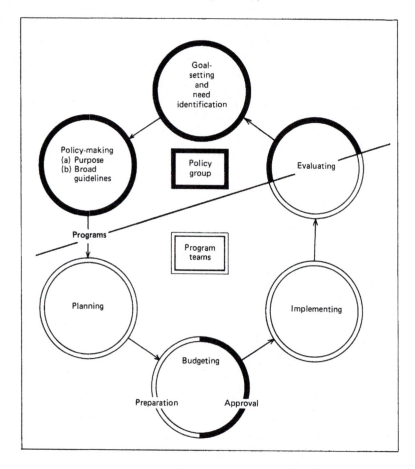

- Goal-setting and need identification
- Policy-making, with policies consisting of purposes and broad guidelines
- Planning of programmes
- Preparation and approval of programme budgets
- Implementing
- Evaluating

The cycle is similar to others which may be found in general texts on management and administration. The special contribution which it may make is based on three characteristics: (1) the clear and unambiguous specification of those phases which are the concern of the group responsible for policy-making in the school ('policy group') and of other phases which are the concern of groups responsible for implementing policy ('programme teams'), (2) a definition of policy which goes beyond a statement of general aims or purposes but is not so detailed as to specify action — it provides a brief statement of purpose and a set of broad guidelines, and (3) it organises planning activities around programmes which correspond to the normal patterns of work in the school.

The distinction between 'policy group' and 'programme teams' provides the framework for a workable approach to Collaborative School Management. The people who constitute the policy group vary according to the setting. For state schools in Britain, the policy group will be a board of governors. In government schools in Victoria, Australia, it will be a school council. Where the wider community is not involved in school governance, the policy group may be the head teacher (principal)* alone, the head teacher and senior teachers, or the head teacher and senior teachers with advice from other teachers and members of the school community. There may, in some instances, be different policy groups in the school, each addressing different sets of issues.

The activities of the school associated with learning and teaching and which support learning and teaching are divided into programmes. The policies and priorities set by the policy group shape the planning of these programmes by members of the programme teams who will be teachers in most instances. Programme teams are responsible for preparing a plan for the implementation of policies related to their programmes and for identifying the resources required to support that plan. A programme plan and the proposed pattern for resource allocation together constitute a programme budget.

While programme budgets are prepared by programme teams, they must be approved by the policy group; they must reflect the policies and priorities established earlier by that group. Following implementation by programme teams, the evaluating phase is again a shared responsibility, with programme teams gathering information for programme evaluation and the policy group gathering further information as appropriate to make judgements on the effectiveness of policies and programmes.

In general, then, referring again to Figure 1.1, the policy group has responsibility for those phases which are emphasised in black — largely those above the diagonal line — while programme teams work within a framework of policy to take responsibility for the remaining phases — largely those below the diagonal line. It is important to note that while a clear distinction is made between the responsibilities of the policy group and programme teams, there will, in fact, be a high degree of overlap as far as personnel are concerned and a continuing, high level of formal and informal communication. The head teacher and some teachers will, for example, be members of the policy group and programme teams where the

---

*The term 'head teacher' is used in remaining chapters to describe the position designated in some countries as 'principal'.

A Framework for Self-management

Figure 1.2 The organisation of the book

PART A: A FRAMEWORK FOR SELF-MANAGEMENT

Chapter 1 Toward the Self-managing School

Chapter 2 In Search of Effectiveness

Chapter 3 Effectiveness through Collaborative School Management

Chapter 4 Alternatives in Collaborative School Management

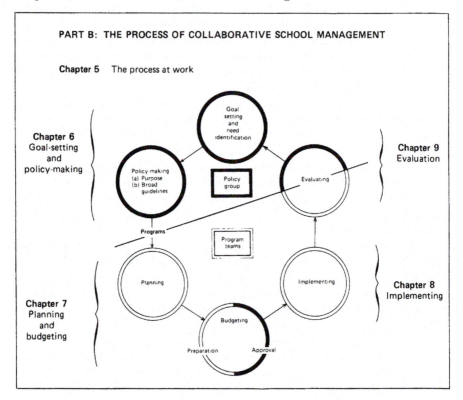

PART B: THE PROCESS OF COLLABORATIVE SCHOOL MANAGEMENT

Chapter 5   The process at work

Chapter 6
Goal-setting
and
policy-making

Goal
setting
and
need
identification

Chapter 9
Evaluation

Policy making
(a) Purpose
(b) Broad
guidelines

Policy
group

Evaluating

Programs

Program
teams

Planning

Implementing

Chapter 8
Implementing

Chapter 7
Planning
and
budgeting

Budgeting

Preparation   Approval

PART C: MAKING IT WORK

Chapter 10 Getting Started

Chapter 11 Leadership and Management of Change

Chapter 12 Management of Conflict

Chapter 13 Management of the Staff Resource

Chapter 14 Questions That People Often Ask

policy group is a school council or board of governors which includes representatives of teachers. The policy group may frequently depend on the head teacher and programme team for the development of policy options.

Organisation of the Book

The organisation of this book is illustrated in Figure 1.2. The remaining chapters of Part A provide further information about the general approach, with chapter 2 describing the search for highly effective schools which led to the formulation of the Collaborative School Management Cycle and identification of the school which provided the working example for illustration throughout the book. This school is Rosebery District High School, a primary-high school (Kindergarten to Grade 10) in Tasmania. Chapters 3 and 4 describe the Collaborative School Management Cycle in some detail, with alternatives for settings which vary according to the composition of the policy group.

Part B provides guidelines for the process of Collaborative School Management, with explanations and illustrations which will enable readers to implement the approach in their own settings. Chapter 5 describes the process at work at Rosebery District High School. Chapters 6 to 9 address each phase in the Collaborative School Management Cycle: chapter 6 is concerned with policy-making, including goal-setting and need identification; chapter 7 is concerned with programme planning and the preparation and approval of programme budgets; chapter 8 is concerned with the implementation of programme plans and budgets; and chapter 9 is concerned with evaluating.

Part C provides guidelines for 'making it work'. Chapter 10 describes alternative strategies for implementing the approach in schools. Chapter 11 demonstrates how the approach may be used as a framework for the exercise of educational leadership and the management of change. Chapter 12 provides guidelines for the management of conflict in schools, demonstrating how the Collaborative School Management Cycle is itself a valuable framework for dealing with conflict. Chapter 13 is concerned with the allocation of the staff resource in schools. Chapter 14 provides answers to questions which are commonly asked about the approach, with the authors drawing on their experiences in the school setting and in seminars and consultations associated with the introduction of the approach.

2   *In Search of Effectiveness*

The Effective Resource Allocation in Schools Project (ERASP) commenced in December 1982 as a partnership of the Education Department of Tasmania and the Centre for Education at the University of Tasmania. Supported by the Commonwealth Schools Commission as a Project of National Significance, its purposes were to identify the processes and skills which are required for the effective allocation of resources in government and non-government schools and to establish a programme for the assessment and development of the requisite skills among those in or preparing for positions of responsibility. The identification of processes and skills required first, the nomination of schools considered to be highly effective in both a general sense and in the manner in which resources were allocated, and second, the careful study of practices related to resource allocation in these schools.

The purpose of this chapter is to provide a brief outline of ERASP, giving particular attention to the criteria used in the search for highly effective schools. The listing may afford readers a basis for assessing in a general sense the settings in which they have an interest. The reader is then introduced to the exemplary approach of one school which provides a working example of the Collaborative School Management Cycle.

Effective Resource Allocation in Schools Project

Rationale

The value of the project was suggested by developments in Tasmania where schools have had for a number of years a relatively high degree of responsibility for allocating resources compared to their mainland counterparts. For example, more than 70 per cent of Recurrent Grants paid by the Commonwealth Schools Commission to the Education Department are channelled directly to schools. The White Paper on Tasmanian Schools and

Colleges in the 1980s recommended an extension of this responsibility toward the end of the decade.[1] The introduction by the Government of Tasmania in early 1982 of a form of programme budgeting had implications for the way resources were allocated among and within schools. In anticipation of further change, the Education Department of Tasmania and the Centre for Education at the University of Tasmania sought the support of the Commonwealth Schools Commission in a project for the professional development of school administrators. Awareness of similar developments in other places, notably South Australia, suggested the value of support as a Project of National Significance.

Nature and purpose

The purposes outlined in the introduction to this chapter were achieved in three stages: (1) a nationwide survey to determine the manner in which resources were allocated to schools, (2) case studies in two states — Tasmania and South Australia — of schools where resources were seen to be allocated effectively, and (3) the design, writing and testing of an integrated, comprehensive programme for the assessment and development of skills in school-based resource allocation. South Australia was selected as the second state for detailed study because a national survey revealed that, after Tasmanian schools, government and non-government schools in South Australia had the highest degree of responsibility for allocating resources as indicated by the per capita total of grants to schools.

The project was supported by a grant of $35,000 from the Commonwealth Schools Commission. It commenced on 1 December 1982, and concluded on 31 December 1985, with reports of all stages published in 1986. A Steering Committee of five people was established, these being nominees of the Director-General of Education in Tasmania, the Director of Catholic Education in Tasmania, the Commonwealth Schools Commission, the Australian Council for Educational Administration, and the Institute of Educational Administration. Project Director was Dr Brian J. Caldwell, Senior Lecturer in Educational Administration in the Centre for Education at the University of Tasmania. Working with Dr Caldwell were Dr Josie Misko, Research Fellow in Educational Administration in the Centre for Education, who served as Project Officer, and Mr Chris Smith, Assistant to the Headmaster of the Hutchins School, who served as Research Officer for Non-Government Schools.

Outcomes

The findings of the project are described in a report in five parts.[2] Part 1 is a summary of the project written by Brian Caldwell. Parts 2 and 3 were written by Josie Misko and are concerned with highly effective approaches to resource allocation in government schools in Tasmania and South Australia. The former provides a detailed account of the method which was used in the search for highly effective schools and a summary of case studies in sixteen such schools, and the latter contains a detailed account of the sixteen case studies. Part 4 was written by Mr Kingsley Curtis, Senior Project Officer, School Management Systems Team, Education Department of South Australia, and is concerned with approaches to resource management in government schools in South Australia which are characterised by payment to school councils of a single lump-sum grant. Such a grant is in contrast to the fragmented approach to the payment of grants which prevails in most states. Workshop materials are included in the book. Part 5 is a report of case studies in non-government schools, written by Chris Smith.

This book is based on the successful use of a number of ERASP materials in two settings: (1) in a seminar in Hobart in January 1984, attended by thirty-five administrators from central offices and schools in Tasmania, Victoria, South Australia and the ACT; and (2) in the adoption of school-level programme budgeting in Victoria from 1984 to 1986, in which the authors conducted over one hundred seminars and workshops for head teachers, teachers and parent members of school councils from more than 1,100 schools. Other materials developed independently by Brian Caldwell and used in all states and the NT from 1981 to 1986 have also been incorporated.

The Search

In similar fashion to Peters and Waterman's *In Search of Excellence: Lessons from America's Best-Run Companies*,[3] a decision was made from the outset to base books and other materials in ERASP on practice in highly effective schools. The strategy was to identify schools which were highly effective in a general sense and in the manner in which resources were allocated, with schools identified in both categories being chosen for detailed study. Two issues had to be resolved in implementing this strategy: first, which criteria would be used to identify schools, and second, what the process of identification would be.

A comprehensive review of literature associated with the effective schools movement was undertaken to provide a list of the characteristics of highly effective schools. The limitations of this literature were acknowledged. Literature related to the allocation of resources was examined to identify characteristics of a high degree of effectiveness in this area. It is beyond the scope of this book to summarise the literature; a detailed account may be found in the ERASP report prepared by Misko.[4]

Both sets of characteristics were validated in the Tasmanian setting on the basis of a critical review, first, by a group of practising teachers and administrators in government and non-government schools, and second, by a Criteria for Effectiveness Advisory Committee consisting of Professor Phillip Hughes, then Dean of the Centre for Education at the University of Tasmania and a former Deputy Director-General of Education in Tasmania; Mr Bryce Ward, Deputy Director-General of Education in Tasmania; and Professor Emeritus Richard Selby Smith, former Dean of the Faculty of Education at the University of Tasmania and one-time Principal of Scotch College, Melbourne. Refinement based on this critical review resulted in two lists of characteristics. No further changes were made by people who reviewed the lists prior to their use in government schools in South Australia and in non-government schools in Tasmania and South Australia.

The second issue to be resolved was the process of identifying highly effective schools. Time and resources did no permit an empirical study based on the characteristics which had been selected. A decision was made to use a modification of the so-called 'reputational approach', with the people best suited to judge the reputations of schools considered to be regional superintendents, regional directors, directors of primary and secondary education for government schools; senior officers for systemic schools and Schools Commission personnel for non-government schools. In addition, it was decided to employ two different sets of judges: one set to nominate schools on the basis of their general effectiveness and the other to nominate schools on the basis of their effectiveness in resource allocation. Those schools selected by both sets were included in the case studies.

The process of identification is illustrated here for government schools in Tasmania. Schools from two of the three regions of the state were considered, with a total of fourteen people providing nominations of schools which were highly effective in a general sense. Regionally-based people considered only those schools in their own regions and centrally-based people considered schools in both regions. Two people provided nominations, on a statewide basis, of schools which were considered to allocate their resources in a highly effective manner. Those providing nominations in each instance were asked to read the relevant set of characteristics and then nominate schools on the basis of their knowledge. They were also asked to consider schools which had shown marked improvement in areas in which they had been deficient and to take account of the location and socio-economic environment of schools. Each person provided up to three nominations in categories which reflected differences in terms of level of schooling (primary, high and district high), size (large, medium, small), socio-economic status (high, low) and location (country, city). After each school was nominated, judges referred again to the characteristics and checked those which applied to the school concerned. Schools which were nominated by both sets of judges were then considered further, and those receiving the highest number of nominations were selected for detailed case study. Senior officers with responsibility for special schools and secondary colleges provided single nominations in each category after reading the two sets of characteristics.

Characteristics of Highly Effective Schools

The forty-three characteristics used in the search for schools which were highly effective in a general sense are listed in Figure 2.1. These lie in six areas: climate (20), leadership (11), curriculum (4), decision-making (3), outcomes (3) and resources (2). Taken together, these characteristics describe an 'ideal type' of school. It is acknowledged that not all will be found in any one highly effective school and that some schools which are considered highly effective may have some characteristics which are in fact the opposite of those listed.

Each of the characteristics in Figure 2.1 was selected at least once by the fourteen people who provided nominations. The characteristic selected most frequently (n = 50) was CU1 'the school has clearly-stated educational goals'. Others mentioned frequently were related to the leadership of the head teacher: L3 'is responsive to and supportive of the needs of teachers' (n = 46), L1 'enables the sharing of duties and resources to occur in an efficient manner' (n = 46), L6 'has a high level of awareness of what is happening in the school' (n = 45), L5 'encourages staff involvement in professional development programmes and makes use of the skills teachers acquire in these programmes' (n = 42) and L11 'ensures that a continual review of the school programme occurs and that progress towards goals is evaluated' (n = 40). Two characteristics related to climate were also selected in at least forty instances: CL2 'the head teacher, teachers and students demonstrate commitment and loyalty to school goals and values' (n = 45) and CL10 'students have respect for others and the property of others' (n = 40).

Chosen least often were CL16 'a low delinquency rate among students' (n = 4), O2 'scores on tests reflect high levels of achievement' (n = 5), CL14 'there is a low absentee rate among students' (n = 6), O1 'a low student drop-out rate' (n = 6) and CL13 'few occasions where senior administrators in the school need to be directly involved in the discipline of students' (n = 6). It is possible that many did not select these criteria when describing the schools they nominated because they did not have information on hand to make a judgement.

The twelve characteristics used in the search for schools which allocated resources in a highly effective manner are listed in Figure 2.2. Nine are concerned with the process of resource allocation while three are concerned with the outcomes of resource allocation.

Figure 2.1 Effective Resource Allocation in Schools Project — characteristics of highly effective schools

CURRICULUM

CU1   The school has clearly stated educational goals.

CU2   The school has a well-planned, balanced and organised programme which meets the needs of students.

CU3   The school has a programme which provides students with required skills.

CU4   There are high levels of parental involvement in the children's educational activities.

DECISION-MAKING

D1   There is a high degree of staff involvement in the development of school goals.

D2   Teachers are highly involved in decision-making at the school.

D3   There are high levels of community involvement in decision-making at the school.

RESOURCES

R1   There are adequate resources in the school to enable staff to teach effectively.

R2   The school has motivated and capable teachers.

OUTCOMES

O1   There is a low student drop-out rate.

O2   Scores on tests reflect high levels of achievement.

O3   There is a high degree of success in the placement of students in colleges, universities or jobs.

LEADERSHIP

A head teacher who:

L1   Enables the sharing of duties and resources to occur in an efficient manner.

L2   Ensures that resources are allocated in a manner consistent with educational needs.

L3   Is responsive to and supportive of the needs of teachers.

L4   Is concerned with his or her own professional development.

L5   Encourages staff involvement in professional development programmes and makes use of the skills teachers acquire in these programmes.

L6   Has a high level of awareness of what is happening in the school.

L7   Establishes effective relationships with the Education Department, the community, teachers and students.

L8   Has a flexible administrative style.

L9   Is willing to take risks.

L10   Provides a high level of feedback to teachers.

L11   Ensures that a continual review of the school programme occurs and that progress towards goals is evaluated.

Figure 2.1 cont.

CLIMATE

CL1   The school has a set of values which are considered important.

CL2   The head teacher, teachers and students demonstrate commitment and loyalty to school goals and values.

CL3   The school offers a pleasant, exciting and challenging environment for students and teachers.

CL4   There is a climate of respect and mutual trust among teachers and students.

CL5   There is a climate of trust and open communication in the school.

CL6   There are expectations at the school that all students will do well.

CL7   There is a strong commitment to learning in the school.

CL8   The head teacher, teachers and students have high expectations for achievement.

CL9   There is high morale among students in the school.

CL10 Students have respect for others and the property of others.

CL11 There is provision for students to take on responsibility in the school.

CL12 There is good discipline in the school.

CL13 There are few occasions when senior administrators in the school need to be directly involved in the discipline of students.

CL14 There is a low absentee rate among students.

CL15 There is a low student suspension rate.

CL16 There is a low delinquency rate among students.

CL17 There is high morale among teachers in the school.

CL18 There are high levels of cohesiveness and team spirit among teachers.

CL19 There is a low absentee rate among teachers.

CL20 There are few applications from teachers for transfer.

Effectiveness and the Collaborative School Management Cycle

Twenty-two of the fifty-five characteristics describe features of the Collaborative School Management Cycle introduced in chapter 1. These may be grouped according to their collaborative nature (described further in chapters 3 and 4), and according to the major phases of the cycle as outlined in chapters 6 to 9.

The collaborative nature of school management (chapters 3 and 4)

D1   There is high degree of involvement of staff in the development of school goals.

D2   There are high levels of teacher involvement in decision-making at the school.

Figure 2.2 Effective Resource Allocation in Schools Project — characteristics of schools which allocate resources in a highly effective manner

---

PROCESS

There is a systematic and identifiable process in which:

P1	Educational needs are determined and placed in an order of priority.
P2	The order of priority takes full account of local as well as system needs.
P3	Financial resources are allocated according to priorities among educational needs.
P4	There is opportunity for appropriate involvement of staff, students and the community.
P5	Participants are satisfied with their involvement in the process.
P6	Consideration is given to evaluating the impact of resource allocation.
P7	A budget document is produced for staff and others which outlines the financial plan in an understandable fashion.
P8	Appropriate accounting procedures are established to monitor and control expenditure.
P9	Money can be transferred from one category of the budget to another as needs change or emerge during the period covered by the budget.

OUTCOMES

O1	High-priority educational goals are consistently satisfied through the planned allocation of resources of all kinds.
O2	Actual expenditure matches intended expenditure, allowing for flexibility to meet emerging and/or changing needs.
O3	There is general understanding and broad acceptance of the outcomes of budgeting.

D3	There are high levels of community involvement in decision-making at the school.
CL18	There are high levels of cohesiveness and team spirit among teachers.
P4	There is opportunity for appropriate involvement of staff, students and the community (in the process of resource allocation).

Goal-setting and policy-making (chapter 6)

CU1	The school has clearly-stated educational goals.
CU2	The school has a well-planned, balanced and organised programme which meets the needs of students.
CU3	The school has a programme which provides students with required skills.
CL1	The school has a set of values which are considered important.
CL6	There are expectations at the school that all students will do well.

CL8   The head teacher, teachers and students have high expectations for achievement.

P1   Educational needs are identified and placed in an order of priority.

P2   The order of priority takes full account of local as well as system needs.

Planning and budgeting (chapter 7)

R1   There are adequate resources in the school to enable staff to teach effectively.

L1   The head teacher enables the sharing of duties and resources to occur in an efficient manner.

L2   The head teacher ensures that resources are allocated in a manner consistent with educational needs.

P3   Financial resources are allocated according to priorities among educational needs.

P7   A budget document is produced for staff and others which outlines the financial plan in an understandable fashion.

Implementing (chapter 8)

P8   Appropriate accounting procedures are established to monitor and control expenditure.

P9   Money can be transferred from one category of the budget to another as needs change or emerge during the period covered by the budget.

Evaluating (chapter 9)

L11   The head teacher ensures that a continual review of the school programme occurs and that progress towards goals is evaluated.

P6   Consideration is given to evaluating the impact of resource allocation.

The Exemplary Approach at Rosebery District High School

Rosebery District High School received more nominations as a highly effective school than any other in the Effective Resource Allocation in Schools Project. These nominations were in both categories, as a highly effective school in a general sense, having in large measure the characteristics listed in Figure 2.1, and in the manner in which resources were allocated, having in similar large measure the characteristics listed in Figure 2.2. The Collaborative School Management Cycle is based on the approach which has been adopted at Rosebery.

Rosebery District High School is located in a relatively remote setting on the west coast of Tasmania. Total school enrolment is 600 with approximately half at the primary (K–6) level and half at the secondary (7–10) level. Rosebery is a one-industry town associated with the mining operation of the Electrolytic Zinc Company which operates two mines, both producing silver, lead and zinc. The area is very mountainous, densely forested and has a cold wet climate. Annual rainfall is 2250 mm and snowfalls are relatively frequent in winter, especially on the high slopes of the surrounding mountains. The nearest major centre is Burnie, 125 kilometres distant on the north-west coast.

The Collaborative School Management Cycle has evolved at Rosebery over a number of years, commencing in 1977. One feature of the school is its council, which, despite the voluntary nature of such bodies in Tasmania, has policy-making powers almost identical to those for school councils in Victoria. Another feature is a well-established form of programme budgeting, making it the first school in Australia to have implemented such an approach.

Details of the Collaborative School Cycle are given in chapters 3 and 4, with chapter 5 containing a detailed account of the process at Rosebery.

3   Effectiveness through Collaborative School Management

This chapter contains an explanation and illustration of each phase of the Collaborative School Management Cycle. If the purpose of chapter 1 was to develop awareness of the approach, then chapter 3 is intended to provide the reader with an opportunity to move further, from awareness to a broad understanding. Further development, taking readers to the application level of knowledge with guidelines which can be applied in the work setting, comes in chapters 5 to 9.

The first part of the chapter provides an explanation and illustration of the process and product of each phase. This sets the stage for a listing of the benefits to those who participate in the process or who are affected by the outcomes.

Phases of Collaborative School Management

The Collaborative School Management Cycle is illustrated again in Figure 3.1. In summary, its general characteristics are as follows:

- The cycle integrates goal-setting, need identification, policy-making, planning, budgeting, implementing and evaluating.
- The approach secures appropriate involvement of staff, students and the community.
- The focus is on the central functions of schools — learning and teaching — and, accordingly, organises the management of the school around 'programmes' which correspond to the preferred patterns of work in the school.
- The 'policy group', the composition of which varies according to the setting, has responsibility for those phases emphasised in black, mainly those above the diagonal line: goal-setting and need identification, policy-making, approving the budget, and evaluating the extent to which goals and policies are being achieved and needs are being satisfied.

Figure 3.1 The Collaborative School Management Cycle

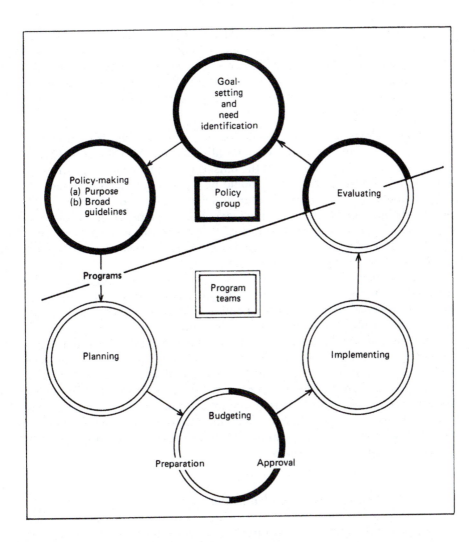

- The 'programme teams', which usually consist of teachers, work within a framework of policies and priorities set by the 'policy group' to prepare plans for the implementation of policy and to identify the resources required to support those plans.
- A programme plan and the proposed pattern for resource allocation to implement that plan together constitute a programme budget.

- Implementing and evaluating are largely the concern of programme teams whose tasks, taken together, are those shown below
the diagonal line.
- While responsibilities are clearly designated, there is overlap in
activity to the extent that some people may be members of the
policy group as well as of one or more programme teams, and that
members of programme teams frequently provide information for
the policy group, for example, in preparing policy options and a
programme budget.

What follows is a more detailed explanation and illustration of the
product of each phase of the Collaborative School Management Cycle.
Three reassurances are offered at the outset. First, that each phase calls for
a minimum of writing. Each goal should be written in a single sentence. A
policy should occupy no more than a page. A programme plan, with
proposed allocation of resources, is a maximum of two pages. An evaluation
report should never exceed two pages. In each instance, what is written
should be free of technical language so that it can be read and understood
by all members of the school community.

The second reassurance concerns the order of the phases. As illustrated in Figure 3.1, there is the suggestion that planning, for example,
must be preceded by policy-making and goal-setting, with the implication
that a school cannot commence the process until goals are set and policies
are formulated. While these are desirable starting points, this order is not
necessary for the success of the approach. A school may 'enter' the
Collaborative School Management Cycle at any phase knowing that, over
time, others will be completed in a manner suited to each setting. The third
reassurance concerns the time required to fully implement the approach. It
is the authors' experience that a minimum of three to five years is required
for most schools. This allows ample time to integrate the approach with
existing management processes.

Goal-setting and need identification

A *goal* is a statement of broad direction, general purpose or intent; it is
general and timeless and is not concerned with a particular outcome at a
particular moment in time.[1]

The goals of the school are usually expressed as desired outcomes for
students and most will usually be of this type. It is recommended, however,
that schools give consideration to four types of goals:

1 Goals related to outcomes for students.
2 Goals related to learning experiences for students.
3 Goals related to the provision of resources.
4 Goals related to the management of the school.

Figure 3.2 contains samples of each type of goal statement.

It is evident that a school with goals such as those sampled in Figure 3.2 has a more fundamental set of beliefs which have shaped those goals. Consider, for example, the goal related to the management of the school. Providing a variety of opportunities for parental involvement in the activities of the school suggests that a value is placed on community involvement. This more fundamental belief or value constitutes part of the philosophy of the school which may be set out in a brief statement which precedes the school goals. Considering another, the goal related to parental involvement may be derived from a statement in the school philosophy which reads 'In planning our school programme we believe it is important to take account of the nature, interests, values, expectations and ambitions of our community.'

Similarly, a number of goals in Figure 3.2 reflect a high degree of sensitivity to individual differences and needs associated with a statement in the school philosophy which may read 'We recognise and take account of the difference between individual children in planning our school programme and in our dealings with them.' In all instances, it is recommended that each goal and each statement of philosophy be limited to a single sentence, written as simply as possible to ensure understanding by all members of the school community.

The second aspect of the first phase of the Collaborative School Management Cycle is *identification of needs*. A need is usually considered to exist if *what is* falls short of *what should be*.[2] Referring again to the statements in Figure 3.2, a goal related to the provision of resources was 'to provide resources for each programme at a level commensurate with standards for the school system.' A recommended standard for support in the curriculum resource centre of a school having more than 500 students might be a half-time aide. A need would exist if the school currently has the services of an aide on a 0.3 Full-Time Equivalent (FTE) basis for three half-days per week.

The above is, however, a rather simplistic view of specifying needs. A number of additional considerations should be made when needs are specified. A gap between *what is* and *what should be* may not necessarily result in action. Even if action is suggested, the policy group will usually establish some priorities for action in the knowledge that resources may not enable all needs to be satisfied. One consideration is the extent to which the gap has resulted in some identifiable harm. For the curriculum resource centre discussed above, it may be considered that no harm is being done because the library support of 0.3 FTE falls short of a state standard of 0.5 FTE.

In general, the policy group must ask a number of questions before a need can be specified in a particular programme. A goal is just the starting point. The group must determine in practical terms *what should be*. It must

Figure 3.2 Samples of each type of goal statement

GOALS RELATED TO OUTCOMES FOR STUDENTS
1   To develop an understanding of those factors which have contributed to our way of life.
2   To develop knowledge, attitudes and skills necessary to participate in the political process.
3   To develop a love of learning and a realisation that learning is a life-long activity.
4   To develop to the full each student's creative talents in the various artistic fields.

GOALS RELATED TO LEARNING EXPERIENCES FOR STUDENTS
1   To ensure that all students experience the use, meaning and development of language through stories, poetry, drama and related activities.
2   To ensure that students' learning is through direct experience wherever possible.
3   To provide opportunities for all children to pursue and develop their capabilities.
4   To provide experiences for special students designed to overcome their disabilities.

GOALS RELATED TO THE PROVISION OF RESOURCES
1   To provide resources for each programme at a level commensurate with standards for the school system.
2   To promote the appropriate use of the community as a school resource.
3   To provide programmes for the professional development of teachers.
4   To provide transport for excursions, sport and general school activities, at relatively low cost to students.

GOALS RELATED TO THE MANAGEMENT OF THE SCHOOL
1   To provide a variety of opportunities for parents to be involved in the activities of the school.
2   To develop a reward system appropriate to the age of students which recognises and applauds excellence in achievement.
3   To administer the school in a manner which reflects the continuity of the curriculum.
4   To provide ways for regularly informing parents about school matters and about the progress of their children.

---

gather information about *what is*. A judgement must then be made as to whether a gap is large enough for action to be taken. Will some harm be done if the gap is not closed? How important is this need compared with others? In answering these questions the policy group will usually seek information from programme teams.

Policy-making

Policy-making is in many ways the key to successful implementation of the Collaborative School Management Cycle. This is especially the case in situations where the policy group is a board of governors or school council, that is, the group which has responsibility for approving a policy is a group which is broadly representative of the school community, usually including parents, the head teacher and teachers. Some head teachers and teachers do not believe that parents can or should be involved at the point of decision when a policy is approved. This difficulty can be resolved if an appropriate meaning is attached to the term 'policy'.

A *policy* consists of a statement of purpose and one or more broad guidelines as to how that purpose is to be achieved, which, taken together, provide a framework for the operation of the school or programme.[3] A policy may allow discretion in its implementation, with the basis for that discretion often stated as part of the policy. A sample, simplified policy on homework at the secondary level is contained in Figure 3.3. This is a sample of a policy which applies to all areas of instruction in the school. Other policies may apply to only one area or programme, for example, a high school may have a policy related to the mathematics programme.

Some differences between this view of policy and those which often prevail should be noted. An examination of policy handbooks sometimes reveals that what are referred to as policies are really statements of philosophy or are goals. Other policy handbooks are often simply collections of rules or procedures, that is, detailed specifications of what can or cannot be done, or of how something is to be done. The view of policy offered here is a balance between the two, with a statement of purpose which is usually derived from the philosophy of the school or from a statement of goals, and guidelines which are clear enough to make the intent and pattern for action clear, but broad enough to allow those concerned with implementation the opportunity to use their professional judgement from situation to situation.

Two other features of the recommended view of policy are the length and the language. It is recommended that no policy be more than one page in length: any longer and it will rarely be read and rarely changed. One page is sufficient to state the purpose and broad guidelines for any programme or area of operations in a school. Such a statement can be quickly read and, being just a page in length, can be easily replaced or amended. Equally important is the language of the policy. It should be free of technical language of a kind teachers use in the course of their professional work. Words like 'conceptualize', 'streaming', 'core curriculum', and 'individualisation' should be replaced by simple words or phrases of a kind which can be understood by all members of the school community.

The process of policy-making is considered in detail in chapter 6. It is briefly noted here, however, that building a base of policies for a school is not as complex a task as is often suggested. Most policies can be quickly written by documenting the current approach in the format recommended for a policy. Only for programmes or areas of activity which are contentious should a more formal approach to policy-making be adopted. The formation

Figure 3.3 A sample statement of policy on homework at the secondary level

---

SCHOOL HOMEWORK

Purpose

Regular homework is a valuable aspect of the learning process and contributes to the development of sound study habits. Consistent with this belief, homework shall be implemented according to the following guidelines:

Broad guidelines

1 Each child will be assigned homework in each subject on a regular basis.
2 While the amount of homework will vary according to age and learning needs, every child will be assigned some homework on each day of the school week, with at least two days per week assigned for each of language, mathematics and social studies.
3 Teachers will be responsible for reviewing the homework assignment of each child.

Framework for planning, implementing and evaluating

---

of small working parties to prepare options for consideration by the policy group is recommended. In the collaborative approach, the policy group will usually be assisted by teachers and others who document existing practice or prepare policy options.

Programmes

Goal-setting and need identification, together with policy-making, are two phases of the Collaborative School Management Cycle which are the responsibility of the policy group. Once completed, other phases become the responsibility of programme teams, the first being planning the implementation of policy. Consideration must be given first, however, to programmes and to programme structure for the school.

A programme is an area of learning and teaching, or an area which supports learning and teaching, corresponding to the normal pattern of work in a school. For example, mathematics is invariably taught at the secondary level so it is appropriate in a secondary school to refer to 'the Mathematics Programme'. A number of people in the school will be involved in administration — a collection of activities which support learning and teaching — so it is also appropriate to refer to 'the Administration Programme'. The programmes found in a school will or should reflect the philosophy and goals in that school, many of which will, in turn, reflect the philosophy and goals for all schools in the state in a government system.

Rarely, however, will two schools have the same set of programmes if there is an intention for each school to reflect local as well as national needs. Figure 3.4 contains a sample list of two sets of programmes, one of which may be found in a primary school (eleven programmes) the other in a secondary school (twenty-four programmes). The list of programmes constitutes the programme structure of the school.

Programmes should be carried out within a framework of policy, with some policies relating to individual programmes and others relating to the school as a whole. For example, the Mathematics Programme will be shaped by school policy on mathematics as well as by key policies on issues such as homework, testing, reporting on pupils' progress and the grouping of students for instruction.

In the collaborative approach, a programme team is responsible for certain matters related to a programme. It may provide the policy group with information concerned with programme needs and with options for a policy related to the programme. It will be responsible for preparing a programme plan and a programme budget in a manner consistent with the policies and priorities set by the policy group for the school. Once the budget is approved by the policy group, the programme team is responsible for implementation and, subsequently, for gathering information as part of programme evaluation.

A programme team is usually composed of everyone involved in the delivery of the programme. In a secondary school, the programme team for mathematics will normally consist of all who teach mathematics. It is important that the work of teachers in programme planning is manageable so it is recommended that no teacher be a member of more than four programme teams. Each programme team should have a designated team leader who will usually be a person with formal authority related to the programme, such as a subject co-ordinator or a head of department.

Planning

Planning is simply determining in advance what will be done, when it will be done, how it will be done and who will do it.[4] There are different levels of planning related to a particular programme, described here as programme planning, curriculum planning and instructional planning. Programme planning is determining in general terms how a programme is to be implemented, specifying such things as the manner in which students will be grouped vertically (among grade or year levels) and horizontally (within a grade or year level); the number and nature of the teachers and support staff associated with the programme; the supplies, equipment and services required and initiatives (additions or deletions) which are noteworthy. Curriculum planning provides a relatively detailed specification of what will be taught, how it will be taught and when it will be taught. Instructional

Figure 3.4 Sample programme structures

A PRIMARY SCHOOL

* K–2 General studies
* 3–6 General studies
  Art
  Music
  Physical education

Early intervention
Special education
Computer studies
Administration
Learning resources
Cleaning and grounds

Note

* Programmes which integrate language,
  maths, science and social studies.

A SECONDARY SCHOOL

English
Mathematics
Social studies
* Science
* Commerce
* Second languages
  History
  Physical education
  Music
  Art
  Speech and drama
  Home economics

Technical subjects
Computer studies
Special education
Transition education
Extra-curricular activities
Administration
Learning resources
Cleaning
Grounds
Canteen
Book sales
Transportation

Note

* Programmes such as Science, Commerce
  and Second Language include discrete
  subjects of study. Science, for example,
  includes general science, physics,
  chemistry and biology.

---

planning is considered here to be the planning undertaken by individual teachers when implementing a curriculum plan in their own classrooms. This book is concerned primarily with programme planning.

Figure 3.5 contains a plan for the Learning Resource Programme in a school. The 'Plan for implementation' is preceded by statements of purpose and broad guidelines which are summaries of the school policy related to learning resources, illustrating that aspect of the Collaborative School Management Cycle which links policy-making and planning. The plan for implementation is consistent with policy in that it describes services and resources which are made available through a learning resource centre staffed by a teacher and an aide. It is also consistent with priorities established by the policy group in that it refers to a major evaluation in the last year which drew attention to shortcomings. It is recommended that a

Figure 3.5 A sample plan for a Learning Resource Programme

A summary of school policy on learning resources which was adopted by the policy group

Purpose

The purpose of the Learning Resource Programme is to provide learning resources for staff and students. More specifically, the purpose is to ensure that:

1. the full range of learning resource services is made available to staff and students in an efficient and effective manner;
2. new and replacement materials are provided to meet ongoing learning needs.

Broad guidelines

1. The Learning Resource Programme is implemented through a Learning Resource Centre.
2. The Learning Resource Centre provides print and non-print materials together with facilities and staff for their housing, maintenance, organisation and use.
3. The staff of the Learning Resource Centre includes a trained teacher who will provide instruction in other aspects of the school programme as well as to all students in the use of learning resources.
4. The trained teacher who is responsible for the programme is assisted by an aide in the maintenance and organisation of the centre.

The plan for Learning Resources which is consistent with the policy as summarised above and with priorities established by the policy group

Plan for implementation

A major evaluation of the Learning Resource Programme last year made use of a specially devised Learning Resource Services Survey to obtain staff and student views on the services and resources offered by the Learning Resource Centre. It revealed a backlog of work associated with the preparation of materials, delays in providing services for a number of teachers and lack of print materials to provide central support to the mathematics and science programmes. The policy group has assigned a high priority to overcoming these shortcomings during the next year. The following is the plan for implementation with elements of that plan placed in an order of priority:

1. to maintain the service provided by the teacher-librarian at the current level of 0.4 FTE (16 units of time per week);*
2. to acquire and maintain resources at the current level with the exceptions noted below;
3. to reduce backlogs and delays by increasing the library aide's time from 0.5 FTE (20 units) to 0.8 FTE (32 units);
4. to acquire new texts to provide central support to the mathematics and science programmes;
5. to acquire new periodicals in science;
6. to acquire new shelving space for the materials listed in elements 4 and 5;
7. to provide a reserve to meet contingencies throughout the year.

*The school has 40 units or periods scheduled each week, hence a 0.4 Full-Time Equivalent (FTE) teacher is committed to 16 units of time.

plan for implementation which proposes an addition to a programme be accompanied by a brief statement of need and a reference, where appropriate, to the priority placed on the programme.

The plan for implementation in Figure 3.5 contains seven parts described as planning elements which are placed in an order of priority by the programme team. An order of priority is an acknowledgement that resources are limited and that all elements of the plan may not necessarily be implemented in the year ahead. An order of priority is thus valuable in the programme budgeting phase of the Collaborative School Management Cycle.

Preparation and approval of the budget

In simple terms, a *budget* is a financial plan which contains estimates of expenditure and forecasts of revenue.[5] A school budget may be viewed as a financial translation of an educational plan for the school. Budgeting is thus one aspect of planning, but for purposes of illustration, it is considered here to be a separate phase in the Collaborative School Management Cycle.

Taking the view of budgeting set out above, a programme budget is simply a financial translation of a programme plan. A programme budget contains a listing of the resources required to support the plan, with each listing accompanied by an estimate of expenditure and a forecast of revenue. The illustration and explanation which follow contain estimates of expenditure only.

Figure 3.6 contains an illustration of the resources required to implement the plan for the Learning Resource Programme set out in Figure 3.5. Each of the elements in the plan for implementation has a counterpart in the estimates of resources required. For example, the estimated cost of Element 1 in the plan (service of teacher–librarian) is the first item in the list of resources required ($9,600). Resources are classified as teaching staff, support staff, supplies, equipment and furniture, services and reserve. An allocation is made for salaries even though the school may not be responsible for the payment of salaries or the hiring of staff. It is simply a financial translation of a time allocation which is made in every school.

In the illustration, a teacher devotes four-tenths of working time in the learning resource centre, representing sixteen periods of the forty-period week at the school. The average salary of a teacher at this school for one period or unit of time per week over the full academic year is $600, hence the cost of the four-tenths teacher–librarian is entered as 16 x $600; that is, $9,600. The allocation for the library aide is costed in similar fashion for 32 units at $250 per unit; that is, $8,000.

The benefits of costing staff resources in this fashion are set out in chapter 13 along with a description of the techniques for making the estimates. It is noted at this point, however, that the inclusion of such

Figure 3.6 Resources required to support a plan for implementing a Learning Resources Programme

Plan for implementation which is consistent with policies and priorities (see Figure 3.5.)

Plan for implementation

1. To maintain the service provided by the teacher-librarian at the current level of 0.4 FTE (16 units of time per week).
2. To acquire and maintain resources at the current level with the exceptions noted below.
3. To reduce backlogs and delays by increasing the aount of time of the library aide from 0.5 FTE (20 units) to 0.8 FTE (32 units).
4. To acquire new texts to provide central support to the mathematics and sciences programmes.
5. To acquire new periodicals in science.
6. To acquire new shelving space for the materials listed in elements 4 and 5 above.
7. To provide a reserve to meet contingencies throughout the year.

A financial translation of the plan for implementation

Resources required

Planning element (see Plan for implementation)	Teaching staff	Support staff	Supplies	Equipment and furniture	Reserve	Total
1 Teacher-librarian 16 units at $600 per unit	9 600					9 600
2 Acquisition of print and non-print material at current levels			1 045			1 045
3 Library aide 32 units at $250 per unit		8 000				8 000
4 Textbooks for maths and science			500			500
5 Periodicals in science			120			120
6 Shelving space for new materials				500		500
7 Reserve					150	150
TOTAL	9 600	8 000	1 665	500	150	19 915

estimates is an acknowledgement that the major resource in a school is the staff and that the most important task in resource allocation each year is making the school timetable.

The plan for implementation and statement of resources required of the kind illustrated in Figure 3.6 are consolidated with plans and statements for all programmes in the school. A process of 'reconciliation' must then occur, with estimates of expenditure adjusted in the light of estimates of revenue. This reconciliation is carried out by a group such as the senior staff of the school or by a committee appointed by the policy group for the purpose. The consolidation of plans and budgets, with estimates of revenue and expenditure reconciled, is then forwarded to the policy group with a recommendation for adoption. The policy group is involved again at this point to ensure that plans and budgets are consistent with policies and priorities established earlier in the Collaborative School Management Cycle.

The group which carries out the reconciliation and the policy group which has responsibility for adoption must examine plans and budgets in the light of policies and priorities. This can be an unwieldy process if policies, priorities, plans and budgets are contained in separate documents. To assist these groups, it is recommended that a single document be produced which is essentially a combination of information of the kind illustrated in Figures 3.5 and 3.6. Such a document should not exceed two pages for each programme, and should contain a statement of the purpose of the programme and broad guidelines as to how the purpose is to be achieved (the purpose and broad guidelines being a summary of the policy or policies which provide the framework for the programme), a plan for implementation, a statement of resources required, and a plan for evaluation. Figure 3.7 illustrates such a document for the Learning Resource Programme outlined in Figures 3.5 and 3.6.

The document illustrated in Figure 3.7 is usually described as a programme budget. The term is to some extent unfortunate since most people associate a budget with a simple listing of estimates of revenue and expenditure whereas Figure 3.7 contains very little financial information. 'Programme plan' is perhaps a better descriptor, but, with the increasing rate of adoption of the practice, the term 'programme budget' is retained but defined broadly to include the characteristics illustrated in Figure 3.7. A *programme budget* at the school level is a comprehensive plan for an area of learning and teaching or an area supporting learning and teaching which contains a statement of purpose, a listing of the broad guidelines as to how the purpose is to be achieved, a plan for implementation with elements listed in order of priority, an estimate of resources required to support the plan and a plan for evaluation. Detailed illustrations and guidelines for the preparation of a programme budget are contained in chapter 7.

Implementing

With the adoption of a programme budget by the policy group, programme teams have the authorisation to proceed with implementation of plans in the forthcoming year. There is no need for further reference to the policy group unless there is a major change to these plans. This applies, in particular, to resources: there is no need for approval to acquire each of the resources in the budget and there is no need for approval of accounts for payment. Revenue and expenditure are monitored by programme teams and the policy group in regular financial statements. Illustrations and guidelines are contained in chapter 8. Members of programme teams proceed with the curriculum and instructional aspects of the programme plan through the regular teaching programme of the school. It is beyond the scope of this book to consider these aspects of implementation.

Evaluating

The sixth phase of the Collaborative School Management Cycle is concerned with evaluation. *Evaluation* is the gathering of information for the purpose of making a judgement and then making that judgement.[6] Two kinds of evaluation should occur during or following the implementation of programme plans. One is evaluation of learning, where information is gathered to form judgements about the progress or achievement of students. Another is evaluation of programmes, when information is gathered to form judgements about the extent to which progress toward goals has been made, needs have been satisfied and policies have been implemented. Information gathered in an evaluation of learning may be used in an evaluation of programmes. This book is mainly concerned with programme evaluation.

The illustration of the Collaborative School Management Cycle contained in Figure 3.1 shows that programme evaluation is a shared responsibility, with part carried out by programme teams and part carried out by the policy group. The policy group has a major responsibility in programme evaluation since it must be concerned with the extent to which goals, needs and policies have been addressed. Planning teams have a similar interest and gather much of the information in programme evaluation, for their own use and for the policy group. The cyclic nature of Collaborative School Management takes effect when judgements in programme evaluation result in the setting of new goals, the identification of new needs, the formulation of new policies or the introduction of new programmes.

Illustrations and guidelines for programme evaluation are set out in chapter 9 where a distinction is made between minor evaluation carried out annually, and major evaluation carried out less frequently on a three- or five-year basis. A plan for a minor evaluation is illustrated in the programme budget in Figure 3.7. The emphasis is on a manageable and usable approach to programme evaluation, in contrast to the frequently exhausting approach to school review and evaluation which has been encountered in many schools in recent years. It is recommended, for example, that a report of a minor evaluation for a programme be a maximum of one page and that a report of a major evaluation be a maximum of two pages.

Benefits of Collaborative School Management

A well-implemented system of Collaborative School Management offers many benefits, twenty-five of which are listed on the following pages. Rosebery District High School has experienced all of these benefits.

Benefits to students

The merits of any approach to the management of schools must be established first and foremost in terms of benefits to students. Three benefits are offered:

1 The focus of this approach to school management is the student. Successful implementation ensures that all resources — teachers, time, space, facilities, supplies, equipment and services — reflect plans to achieve priorities in programmes for learning and teaching. These programmes represent the school's approach to organising for learning and teaching in implementing policies which have been formulated to achieve goals and satisfy needs. These policies, goals and needs reflect the interests of the school community as well as society at large.
2 There is provision for the involvement of students in the policy-making process, especially through structures such as school councils, as well as in planning for programmes in which students may have a special interest or expertise.
3 The documents described in this chapter will assist students to gain knowledge and understanding of the programmes of the school. It is intended that policies, plans, budgets and evaluation reports be available to all in the school community, including students.

Benefits to the policy group

Collaborative School Management will aid the efforts of those with special responsibilities in the policy process. Such aid is important, given the trend

Figure 3.7 The programme budget for Learning Resources integrating goals, policy, plan, budget and evaluation

---

Purpose
The purpose of the Learning Resource Programme is to provide learning resources for staff and students. More specifically, the purpose is to ensure that:
1   the full range of learning resource services is made available to staff and students in an efficient and effective manner;
2   new and replacement materials are provided to meet ongoing learning needs.

Broad guidelines
1   The Learning Resource Programme is implemented through a Learning Resource Centre.
2   The Learning Resource Centre provides print and non-print materials together with facilities and staff for their housing, maintenance, organisation and use.
3   The staff of the Learning Resource Centre includes a trained teacher who will provide instruction in other aspects of the school programme as well as to all students in the use of learning resources.
4   The trained teacher who is responsible for the programme is assisted by an aide in the maintenance and organisation of the centre.

Plan for implementation
A major evaluation of the Learning Resource Programme last year made use of a specially devised Learning Resource Services Survey to obtain staff and student views on the services and resources offered by the Learning Resource Centre. It revealed a backlog of work associated with the preparation of materials, delays in providing services for a number of teachers and a lack of print materials to provide central support to the mathematics and science programmes. The policy group has assigned a high priority to overcoming these shortcomings during the next year. The following is the plan for implementation with elements of that plan placed in an order of priority:
1   to maintain the service provided by the teacher-librarian at the current level of 0.4 FTE (16 units of time per week);*
2   to acquire and maintain resources at the current level with the exceptions noted below;
3   to reduce backlogs and delays by increasing the library aide's time from 0.5 FTE (20 units) to 0.8 FTE (32 units);
4   to acquire new texts to provide central support to the mathematics and science programmes;
5   to acquire new periodicals in science;
6   to acquire new shelving space for the materials listed in elements 4 and 5;
7   to provide a reserve to meet contingencies throughout the year.

---

*   This school has 40 units or periods scheduled each week, hence a 0.4 Full-Time Equivalent (FTE) teacher is committed to 16 units of time.

Figure 3.7 cont.

Resources required

Planning element (see Plan for implementation)	Teaching staff	Support staff	Supplies	Equipment and furniture	Reserve	Total
1 Teacher-librarian 16 units at $600 per unit	9 600					9 600
2 Acquisition of print and non-print material at current levels			1 045			1 045
3 Library aide 32 units at $250 per unit		8 000				8 000
4 Textbooks for maths and science			500			500
5 Periodicals in science			120			120
6 Shelving space for new materials				500		500
7 Reserve					150	150
TOTAL	9 600	8 000	1 665	500	150	19 915

Evaluation (minor)
A Learning Resource Services Survey will be conducted in July to gather information from staff and students to help make judgements on whether service has improved with the increase in the library aide's time. Other information in the survey, along with information gathered informally, will enable staff of the Learning Resource Centre to monitor the general quality of service provided.

to devolve policy responsibilities to the school level. Eight benefits are offered:

1 The approach integrates the often fragmented approaches to goal-setting, policy-making, planning, budgeting and evaluation in a manner which establishes a clear, unambiguous and continuing role for the policy group in each phase of the management process. The fragmented approaches often encountered in school management may result in *ad hoc*, haphazard decisions on the allocation of resources which do not reflect priorities among policies and plans.

2 Policy is defined in a manner which will be generally accepted by all in the school community. This benefit is particularly important where boards of governors or school councils have a policy-making role; in these instances, teachers are frequently uncomfortable if

policy is defined in a manner which may result in 'parents telling teachers how to teach'. With the view outlined earlier in this chapter, policy provides the framework within which teachers can exercise their professional judgements in the learning-teaching process.

3   The focus on policy for the policy group ensures that the routine aspects of implementation are left in the hands of others. The policy group should not, for example, be involved in passing accounts for payment: the budget of the school is approved once only and expenditure consistent with that budget may occur without further reference to the policy group except for regular financial reporting.

4   The focus of the process is on the primary purpose for the school's existence, namely, learning and teaching. This is appropriate for a policy group whose tasks should enable it to 'see the whole picture' in terms of this primary purpose.

5   All documents are expressed in language which should be readily understood by all members of the school community.

6   Benefits 3, 4 and 5 combine to produce another, namely, the attraction of capable people to serve on policy groups. This benefit is particularly important for boards of governors or school councils where the experience of many schools has been one of difficulty in attracting interest among parents. A lack of interest is understandable if policy groups are preoccupied with routine matters such as correspondence, reports, passing accounts for payment and issues which appear far removed from the classroom. Collaborative School Management makes service on a policy group an attractive investment of time for those who may have been discouraged from such involvement in the past.

7   The approach provides for accountability, with a substantial and readily understood information base on how resources are to be allocated and why, and with a systematic approach to programme evaluation which ensures that the policy group can assess the extent to which policies have been successfully implemented.

8   The approach lends itself to implementation in stages, with the order of implementation and selection of strategies and tactics tailored to the local setting. With most policy groups typically facing heavy agendas for change, the recommended three- to five-year period of adoption has special appeal.

Benefits to the head teacher and other educational leaders

Most of the benefits described for the policy group and for teachers apply to the head teacher and other educational leaders but three special benefits are identified:

1 Collaborative School Management is a systematic approach to policy-making and planning which constitutes a framework wherein the head teacher can exercise his or her role as an educational leader in the school; that is, work with and through others to ensure that goals unique to the school are set, needs are identified, policies are formulated and plans are devised for the implementation of policies. In the policy process, the head teacher may serve as policy initiator/orchestrator, policy analyst/researcher, policy implementer and policy evaluator. As a leader and the executive officer of the policy group, the head teacher invariably has responsibility for ensuring that the process works smoothly. In the planning phase of Collaborative School Management the head teacher has responsibility for one or more programmes but must also act as a co-ordinator, motivator and source of information for others with programme responsibility.

2 Collaborative School Management also provides a framework wherein the higher-order functions of leadership can be exercised, namely, working with and through others to build the enduring school culture which is critically important if excellence in schooling is to be attained.

3 The approach provides a framework within which the development of many educational leaders is fostered through programme teams and the various working parties involved in the policy-making process.

Benefits to teachers

Teachers are, in many respects, the key to successful implementation of Collaborative School Management. They are partners in the policy process, and, for most programmes, have the responsibility for preparing plans for implementation and for carrying out those plans. Eleven benefits are identified:

1 Collaborative School Management gives teachers a role in management which focuses on the primary reason for their employment, namely, the education of children. The role of the teacher in school management is largely unsatisfying if it is limited to the more routine aspects of administration.

2 The approach ensures that all teachers have the opportunity to contribute according to their expertise and stake in the outcomes of the decision-making process. This benefit is assured through the focus on policy-making and planning for programmes which correspond to the way in which teachers organise their time and energy.

3 Distinctions between policy-making and planning are made clear,

thus avoiding many of the uncertainties, ambiguities and conflicts which are often encountered.

4   The approach provides a framework wherein teachers, working in programme teams, can make a substantial contribution to the decisions concerning the allocation of resources in their area of interest.

5   Programme plans and budgets provide a source of information for teachers as far as the work of their colleagues is concerned. This information is frequently not available or is not known. especially in larger schools.

6   A well-implemented system of Collaborative School Management ensures that goals and policies are translated into action. Many well-intentioned goal-setting and policy-making endeavours in the past have resulted in disappointment, if not cynicism, as the results gather dust because of the absence of an approach to school management which ensures that plans and budgets reflect goals and policies.

7   The approach provides a valuable framework for the management of conflict due to the opportunity it affords for collaboration and openness. Commitment is more likely to result when teachers have had the opportunity to collaborate. Heat and hostility in conflict is minimized when teachers have the opportunity to differ on the basis of good information about the interest of others. Much conflict exists because participants lack such information.

8   The openness of the approach and the systematic matching of resources and needs provide teachers with the opportunity to identify areas of overlap and avenues for co-operation. Less systematic, *ad hoc* approaches to school management often result in needless duplication of resources.

9   The approach to Collaborative School Management described in this chapter clearly establishes the worth of teachers as the major resource in the learning process. While caution is advised in costing the services of teachers in programme budgets, the extent of teacher support for the various programmes is readily evident to all in the school community.

10 Collaborative School Management provides an opportunity for many teachers to exercise responsibility. With the current limited opportunity for promotion, this benefit may be seen as fostering job satisfaction as well as commitment to achieving a high degree of school effectiveness.

11 The approach calls for a minimum of writing and paperwork in the light of the recommended maximum length of the various products in the process: one-page policies, two-page plans and budgets, and one- or two-page evaluation reports for each programme. This precision is a contrast to many existing approaches which have seen

writing as a tedious chore when policy, for example, has been loosely defined to include practices and procedures, and school reviews have resulted in massive reports which have frequently been a source of paralysis by their size alone.

The benefits listed above are those which may accrue to schools. Benefits to local, regional, state or national authorities are also evident but are not elaborated here. These include the view that Collaborative School Management as defined in this chapter may well be the best, if not only, means by which much of the rhetoric of decentralisation and school effectiveness can be brought to fruition.

The processes which will allow the various benefits to be achieved are explained and illustrated in Part B of this book. Before turning to these processes, it is useful to examine the alternatives for establishing the composition of the policy group and to note the similarities of Collaborative School Management and other approaches which have been identified in studies of effectiveness and excellence. These matters are considered in chapter 4.

4 Alternatives in Collaborative School Management

No attempt has been made so far to define the composition of the two types of groups — policy and programme —with major responsibilities in Collaborative School Management. Alternative patterns are outlined in the first section of this chapter, with variations from relatively autocratic approaches involving only one person in the policy group, namely, the head teacher, to highly collaborative approaches now making their appearance in the form of school councils or boards of governors. While we see Collaborative School Management as applicable to all educational settings, our preference is for the highly collaborative mode with responsibility for the adoption of policy in the hands of a school council or governing board.

The second part of the chapter contains brief accounts of similarities and differences between Collaborative School Management as described and illustrated in this book, and other approaches. Several aspects of the approach are considered, particularly its consistency with procedures in schools which allocate resources in a highly effective manner as identified in the Effective Resource Allocation in Schools Project, its similarity to contemporary approaches to corporate planning, its contrast with generally discredited attempts in the 1960s and 1970s to establish Planning Programming Budgeting Systems (PPBS), and some interesting parallels with studies of excellence in business and industry as reported in Peters and Waterman's *In Search of Excellence.*

Patterns in Collaborative School Management

A variety of patterns may be adopted in Collaborative School Management, depending on the composition and powers of the group described in chapter 3 simply as 'the policy group'. It is for this reason that the Collaborative School Management Cycle is offered as a framework or model to suit all settings in education.

A Framework for Self-management

A Framwork for Self-management

Levels of collaboration

Figure 4.1 illustrates a range of alternatives, from a relatively low degree of collaboration (Level 1), where the head teacher alone determines educational policy within guidelines provided by the education department or other employing authority, to a relatively high degree of collaboration (Level 8), where policy is determined by the head teacher, staff and community through a formal structure such as a school council or board of governors. The former is now rare in most systems of education, with the more common approach in systems without school councils or boards of governors being Level 4 where the head teacher and senior staff work together to determine policy after seeking information and/or options from staff. The head teacher is legally responsible and held accountable for policy despite the collaborative nature of the arrangement with senior staff.

Some schools provide for collaboration at Level 7, that is, the head teacher and staff determine policy after seeking information and/or options from the community, with the school council or governing board as a formal advisory structure. Other schools offer a degree of collaboration represented by Level 8: the principal, staff and community determine policy with the school council or governing board as the formal policy-making body.

The patterns in Figure 4.1 are illustrative only, with other arrangements evident in some schools. Not included, for example, is provision for student involvement where appropriate. It is acknowledged that there may be a difference between what is preferred or intended and what, in reality, occurs. Legal requirements may stipulate, for example, a high degree of collaboration such as that in Victoria, Australia, at Level 8. In reality, however, the policy group may in some instances be content to accept or 'rubber stamp' a policy which was determined with a pattern similar to that at Level 4 in Figure 4.1.

It should be noted that several policy groups may exist in a school at any one time, each addressing different sets of issues. Different patterns among those listed in Figure 4.1 may be evident. This book is mainly concerned with the 'over-arching' group which is concerned with the educational policies of the school.

A preference for school councils or governing boards

The authors have a preference and a commitment to collaboration at Level 8 in Figure 4.1, that is, for a school council or board as the policy-determining body. In our view, this maximises the benefits set out in Chapter 3, especially in the following respects:

1   All who have stake in the outcomes of schooling have the opportunity to contribute in the policy-making process. At a representative

Figure 4.1 Patterns in school management for collaboration in the policy group

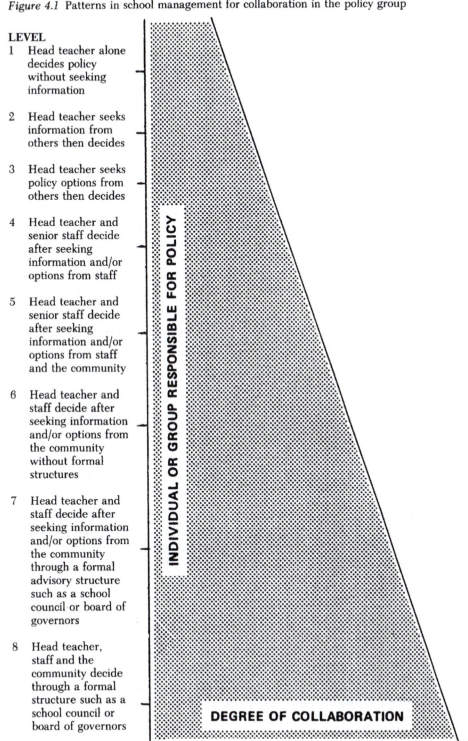

LEVEL
1 Head teacher alone decides policy without seeking information

2 Head teacher seeks information from others then decides

3 Head teacher seeks policy options from others then decides

4 Head teacher and senior staff decide after seeking information and/or options from staff

5 Head teacher and senior staff decide after seeking information and/or options from staff and the community

6 Head teacher and staff decide after seeking information and/or options from the community without formal structures

7 Head teacher and staff decide after seeking information and/or options from the community through a formal advisory structure such as a school council or board of governors

8 Head teacher, staff and the community decide through a formal structure such as a school council or board of governors

INDIVIDUAL OR GROUP RESPONSIBLE FOR POLICY

DEGREE OF COLLABORATION

    level, this contribution is formalized through the structure of the
    school council or board.

2   The closest possible match is fostered between community interests
    and needs on the one hand and school policies and programmes on
    the other. A close match can be assured with a lesser degree of
    collaboration but, all other factors being favourable, this match is
    maximised with a council or board having a policy-determining
    role.

This commitment to a high degree of collaboration does not imply a belief that all schools should seek to establish such a pattern immediately. A school currently providing for, say, collaboration at Level 4, may require five to eight years before collaboration at Level 8 is achieved with efficiency and effectiveness. In Victoria, for example, varying patterns of collaboration involving school councils were established in government schools in 1975. It was not until 1983 that all schools were required to adopt a Level 8 pattern. The approach to Collaborative School Management at Rosebery District High School which is described in chapter 5 evolved over a period of seven years, with Level 8 attained in the last two.

Collaborative School Management without school councils

The detailed explanations and illustrations of Collaborative School Management contained in Part B have Level 8 collaboration as their focus. Schools without councils or boards can, however, utilise this information and follow the guidelines for implementation by using the term 'policy group' as defined in the local setting.

Some Similarities and Differences

This section of chapter 4 notes some similarities and differences between Collaborative School Management as described and illustrated in this book and other approaches. Consideration is given first to its consistency with the criteria for a high degree of effectiveness in the allocation of resources as identified in the Effective Resource Allocation in Schools Project (ERASP).

Criteria for a high degree of effectiveness in the allocation of resources

A well-implemented system of Collaborative School Management satisfies all of the criteria for a high degree of effectiveness in the allocation of resources as identified in ERASP. Details were provided in chapter 2, with

Figure 2.2 listing nine criteria related to the process and three criteria related to outcomes. Now that a detailed explanation of Collaborative School Management has been given in chapter 3, it is useful to match these criteria with what can be accomplished in the various phases of the cycle. Figure 4.2 provides this matching.

It goes without saying that establishing the structures and process for Collaborative School Management will not guarantee the characteristics P1–P9 and O–O3 in Figure 4.2. The approach provides the framework wherein these characteristics can be developed and integrated in the manner described in chapter 3. How this development and integration can be achieved is the subject of consideration in Parts B and C.

Contemporary approaches to corporate planning

Contemporary approaches to corporate or strategic planning are consistent with the process of Collaborative School Management. Particular attention is given in corporate planning to goal-setting, policy-making and long-term planning, that is, the first three phases of the Collaborative School Management Cycle. A corporate plan for, say, a three-year period, may provide a useful framework for the annual policy-making, priority-setting, planning, budgeting and evaluation cycle which was described in chapter 3. This integration of functions leads us to define *corporate planning* as a continuous process in administration which links goal-setting, policy-making, short-term and long-term planning, budgeting and evaluation in a manner which spans all levels of the organisation, secures appropriate involvement of people according to their responsibility for implementing plans as well as of people with an interest or stake in the outcomes of those plans, and provides a framework for the annual planning, budgeting and evaluation cycle.

Corporate or strategic planning is best viewed as a refinement of Collaborative School Management which is well suited to large schools or colleges where a long-term plan prepared in a collaborative manner will serve to give members of the school or college community a sense of purpose and unity in contrast to a feeling of fragmentation and disunity which is often encountered in large organisations. Such a plan will, of course, provide a 'blue-print' for planning over, say, a three-year period and will serve as the starting point in the annual planning and budgeting process.

One of the authors served as a consultant to Devonport Technical College (Tasmania) in the preparation of a corporate plan which served the purposes described above. On the basis of twenty programmes in the college (sixteen teaching departments, three service departments including administration, and a special programmes department), the corporate plan consisted of a document of some twenty-five pages, with a statement of

Figure 4.2 Match between phases of Collaborative School Management and criteria for a high degree of effectiveness in resource allocation

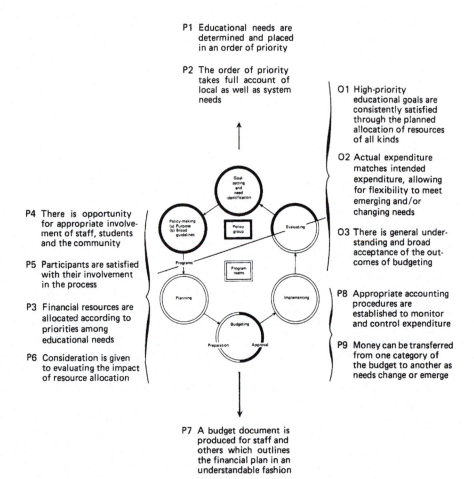

P1 Educational needs are determined and placed in an order of priority

P2 The order of priority takes full account of local as well as system needs

O1 High-priority educational goals are consistently satisfied through the planned allocation of resources of all kinds

O2 Actual expenditure matches intended expenditure, allowing for flexibility to meet emerging and/or changing needs

P4 There is opportunity for appropriate involvement of staff, students and the community

P5 Participants are satisfied with their involvement in the process

O3 There is general understanding and broad acceptance of the outcomes of budgeting

P3 Financial resources are allocated according to priorities among educational needs

P6 Consideration is given to evaluating the impact of resource allocation

P8 Appropriate accounting procedures are established to monitor and control expenditure

P9 Money can be transferred from one category of the budget to another as needs change or emerge

P7 A budget document is produced for staff and others which outlines the financial plan in an understandable fashion

*Criteria identified in Effective Resource Allocation in Schools Project described in Chapter 2. Criteria prefixed P concern the process of resource allocation, criteria prefixed O concern the outcomes of resource allocation.

purpose and priorities for the Division of Technical and Further Education in Tasmania (one page), a statement of purpose, priorities and strategies for achieving key priorities in the college as a whole over the next three years (two pages), statements of purposes, priorities and strategies for achieving key priorities for each programme over the next three years (twenty pages), and a schedule for managing the corporate plan for the next year (one page).

The adoption of a corporate planning approach is thus recommended as an option for larger, more complex settings. However, all who seek theoretical support for Collaborative School Management will be satisfied with the writing of Russell Ackoff, the Daniel H. Silberberg Professor of Systems Sciences at the Wharton School of the University of Pennsylvania. Ackoff is probably the most articulate and respected advocate of the contemporary approach to corporate planning but, as demonstrated below, his views provide strong support for Collaborative School Management as described in this book.

According to Ackoff,[1] the essential difference among alternative approaches to planning is their orientation in time:

> The dominant orientation of some planners is to the past, *reactive*; others to the present, *inactive*; and still others to the future, *preactive*. A fourth orientation, *interactive* ... regards the past, present and future as different but inseparable aspects of the mess to be planned for. It focuses on all of them equally. It is based on the belief that unless all three temporal aspects of a mess are taken into account, development will be obstructed.

Ackoff proposes three operating principles of interactive planning: the participative principle, the principle of continuity, and the holistic principle. In explaining what he terms the *participative principle*, Ackoff contends that 'in planning, process is the most important product ... The principal benefit of it derives from engaging in it.'[2] The following are powerful, thought-provoking illustrations of Ackoff's views in this regard.

> It is through participation in interactive planning that members of an organisation can develop. In addition, participation enables them to acquire an understanding of the organisation and makes it possible for them to serve organisational ends more effectively. This, in turn, facilitates organisational development.[3]
>
> It is better to plan for oneself, no matter how badly, than to be planned for by others, no matter how well.[4]
>
> In interactive planning, plans are not prepared by internal or external planning units and then submitted to executives for approval. Rather, executives engage directly in the planning process. Doing so is one of their major responsibilities. Furthermore,

all those who are normally planned for are also given an opportunity to engage in the process.[5]

... the proper role of professional planners and planning units inside or outside the organisation ... [is to] provide whatever motivation, information, knowledge, understanding, wisdom and imagination are required by others to plan effectively for themselves.[6]

With the *principle of continuity*, Ackoff proposes that planning be a continuous activity rather than discontinuous as in many organisations. He offers two reasons: (a) circumstances change so no plan will work as expected, and (b) values change so the benefits or outcomes sought will change. The implication is that plans should be continuously reviewed and modified as facts and values change.

The *holistic principle* has two parts: the 'principle of co-ordination' and the 'principle of integration'.

The 'principle of co-ordination' states that no part of an organisation can be planned for effectively if it is planned for independently of any other unit at the same level. Therefore, all units at the same level should be planned for simultaneously and interdependently.[7]

The 'principle of integration' states that planning done independently at any level of a system cannot be as effective as planning carried out interdependently at all levels.[8]

When the principles of co-ordination and integration are combined, we obtain the 'holistic principle', which states that the more parts of a system and levels of it that plan simultaneously and interdependently the better. This concept of all-over-at-once planning stands in opposition to sequential planning, either top-down or bottom-up.[9]

The major characteristics of Collaborative School Management can now be listed in terms of the various principles proposed by Ackoff.

1   Policy-making and planning should be considered a continuous process, linking the often unsystematic, fragmented processes which have been the subject of frustration and ineffectiveness in the past ('the principle of continuity').

2   Policy-making and planning at the unit level — 'the programme' — should be considered a component of a comprehensive process for the organisation as a whole — 'the school' ('the holistic principle').

3   Policy-making and planning should be 'all-over-at-once' rather than 'top-down' or 'bottom-up', with appropriate involvement of people at all levels: communication should be multi-directional, flowing up, down and across lines of authority ('the participative principle').

4   Policy-making and planning should take account of past, present and future, recognising the achievements of the past and present by basing many policies and plans on existing practice but antici- pating the desired future by setting other new policies and planning accordingly ('interactive planning').

Parallels with findings in studies of excellence in other fields

The phrase 'in search of excellence' is now widely known because of the book of that name by Thomas J. Peters and Robert H. Waterman, with its subtitle indicating a focus in the private sector in the United States — *In Search of Excellence: Lessons from America's Best-Run Companies.*[10] Those with an interest in excellence in other fields have endeavoured to find parallels in these 'lessons'. What follows is an attempt to find these parallels in Collaborative School Management.

The reader may question consideration of the findings of Peters and Waterman since they do not address issues in education. They are included because many educators have read the book. They are also included because management is a universal process and the lessons for education, particularly for schools, seem to literally leap from the page.

In Search of Excellence was, in many ways, a reaction to the call for sweeping adoption of Japanese approaches to management. Surely, it was argued, we can study the very best practices in our own settings and draw lessons accordingly. Much the same approach was adopted in the Effective Resource Allocation in Schools Project described in chapter 2.

The major findings are listed in Figure 4.3 along with what are proposed as parallels in Collaborative School Management. Peters and Waterman found, for example, that effective companies keep 'close to the customer', providing 'unparalleled quality, service and reliability . . . That comes from listening, intently and regularly.'[11] Collaborative School Man- agement, especially through structures such as school councils or boards of governors, provides for regular appraisal of goals, policies, plans and budgets through the involvement of teachers, parents and students. Effective companies also have a 'bias for action', being 'analytic in their approach to decision-making but are not paralysed by it',[12] avoiding a narrow view of rational approaches to management which often lead to 'paralysis through analysis'. Collaborative School Management is a rational approach to management with a minimum of paperwork and simplicity in language: one-page policies, two-page plans and budgets, one- or two-page evaluation reports. Brevity allows the analysis to be made and changed quickly, keeping the focus on action.

It has been stressed in several places in chapter 4 that the structure of Collaborative School Management alone is no guarantee of effectiveness. At times in education it seems that inappropriate attention is given to

Figure 4.3 Parallels between Collaborative School Management and findings in studies of excellence in business

Findings in business*	Characteristics of Collaborative School Management (CSM)
BIAS FOR ACTION	
Effective companies are analytic in their approach to decision-making but are not paralysed by it: they avoid a narrow view of rational approaches to management which often leads to 'paralysis through analysis'.	CSM is a rational approach to management with a minimum of paperwork and simplicity in language: one-page policies, two-page plans and budgets, one- or two-page evaluation reports. Brevity allows the analysis to be made or changed quickly.
CLOSE TO THE CUSTOMER	
Effective companies provide unparalleled quality, service and reliability ... That comes from listening, intently and regularly.	CSM, especially through structures such as school councils or boards of governors, provides for regular appraisal of goals, policies, plans and budgets through the involvement of teachers, parents and students where appropriate.
AUTONOMY AND ENTREPRENEURSHIP	
Effective companies foster many leaders and many innovators.	Leadership is fostered in CSM, by designating people with responsibility in programme teams. Innovation is fostered through the planned allocation of resources.
PRODUCTIVITY THROUGH PEOPLE	
Effective companies treat the rank and file as the root source of quality and productivity gain ... they do not foster we/they labour attitudes.	CSM, especially with structures such as school councils or boards of governors, brings teachers, parents and students together in a partnership. Teachers as members of programme teams, are recognised and valued as the major resource in the learning-teaching process.
HANDS-ON, VALUE-DRIVEN	
The achievements of effective companies have more to do with their basic philosophy than with their technological or economic resources, organisation structure, innovation and timing.	The structures and processes of CSM will contribute little unless the school has a clearly articulated set of goals and values which give shape to or 'drive' the efforts of all.

Figure 4.3 cont.

STICK TO THE KNITTING

The odds for excellence favour those who stay close to business they know well.

CSM, especially through structures such as school councils, or boards of governors, seeks goals, policies and priorities which match the needs of the school community. Planning identifies areas of over-lap or irrelevance. Frills, padding and empire building are discouraged.

SIMPLE FORM, LEAN STAFF

The underlying structural forms and systems in effective companies are elegantly simple.

Complex committee structures have no place in CSM: a single policy group and a programme team for each programme are all that are required.

SIMULTANEOUS LOOSE-TIGHT PROPERTIES

Excellent companies are both centralised and decentralised, with autonomy pushed down to the shop floor or product development team. On the other hand, they are fanatical centralists around the core values they hold dear.

CSM provdes a framework for the identification of core values by the policy group, with appropriate consultation. Those values are reflected in policies which shape all planning and budgeting. Implementation is the responsibility of members of programme teams.

---

*Findings in business are taken from Thomas J. Peters and Robert H. Waterman Jr. *In Search of Excellence: Lessons from America's Best-Run Companies.* Harper and Row, New York, 1982.

structures. Peters and Waterman found that seven interrelated and interdependent variables require attention if effectiveness is to be attained: structure, strategy, skills, staff, style, systems and, of central importance, shared values.[13] The acknowledged interdependence of these variables is not new: others have stressed, for example, that effective change cannot be made in an organisation merely by changing its structure.[14] Due attention must be given to the adoption of appropriate strategies, the development of appropriate skills, the selection of appropriate staff and the development and acceptance of shared values. These observations apply also to the introduction of Collaborative School Management as will be explained and illustrated in Parts B and C.

Collaborative School Management is not the discredited PPBS

At first sight, Collaborative School Management, especially its programme budgeting component, resembles Planning Programming Budgeting

Systems (PPBS) which were implemented or attempted in the United States and some other countries from the mid-1960s to early 1970s. Such is not the case.

There is now general recognition that PPBS failed for reasons which included excessive attention to the minutiae of budgeting, the excessive paperwork, lack of flexibility, the lack (at that time) of effective, low-cost, computer-based accounting and management information systems, and timelines for implementation which were unrealistic. To these shortcomings may be added an inappropriate emphasis on the specification of performance requirements or criteria for evaluation. PPBS assumed a greater degree or capacity for rational or analytical planning than existed or was possible. In short, PPBS suffered from the 'paralysis through analysis' which is to be avoided if effectiveness along the lines studied by Peters and Waterman is to be attained.

Collaborative School Management differs from PPBS in very significant ways. Indeed, it is in many respects the antithesis. A minimum of paperwork is required: 'one-page policies, two-page plans and budgets, one- or two-page evaluation reports'. Criteria for evaluation are kept simple and are clearly related to learning and teaching.

Collaborative School Management should be no less flexible than traditional approaches to policy-making and planning, with a powerful case for it being more so: priorities which are initially set in the light of need can be quickly reordered as new needs emerge. Finally, Collaborative School Management can and should be implemented in stages over a three- to five-year period, in contrast with the unrealistic efforts at change which often characterised the introduction of PPBS.

Guidelines for Implementation

Part A of this book has been largely concerned with describing and illustrating Collaborative School Management. The context was the concern for school effectiveness, with the approach possessing all of the characteristics which have been described in a project to identify effective approaches to the allocation of resources.

Part B provides descriptions of the process of Collaborative School Management, with detailed guidelines for each phase of the cycle: goal-setting, policy-making, planning and budgeting, implementing and evaluation.

Part B

The Process of Collaborative School Management

5   The Process at Work

This chapter contains a description of collaborative management at work in a school where the policy group is a school council consisting of a chairperson; ten members of the school community; ten members of staff, including the principal (head teacher); and four secondary students, two from Grade 9 and two from Grade 10. In keeping with the usual pattern, programme teams consist entirely of school staff members. Examples are used to illustrate the process at various points in the Collaborative School Management Cycle. These examples are taken from Rosebery District High School.

A description of the setting will be helpful at this point. The township of Rosebery is located on the west coast of Tasmania. The town has developed in conjunction with the mining industry. The school of some 600 students serves not only Rosebery but also the neighbouring Hydro-Electric Commission village of Tullah and the mining town of Zeehan. The school is referred to as a K–10 school as students are enrolled at the age of four years in kindergarten and continue through until the fourth year of high school, year 10. Approximately one-half of the students are of primary age, the other half being of high school age.

At Rosebery there was no conscious decision to adopt or implement Collaborative School Management. An approach to school management evolved over a seven-year period that eventually resulted in the process described in this book. This evolution occurred as the school and community endeavoured to address three major concerns that were evident in 1977. The first of these concerns was a strong desire by the community and staff to be involved in school management. This desire had arisen from problems within the school resulting from new mining developments and subsequent expansion of the mine and town. The school building and planning programme was at first not sufficient to meet the new situation and consequently there was dissatisfaction on the part of all involved.

The second major concern was related to the nature of the curriculum and its suitability to the Rosebery students. Today this idea is expressed as 'the relevance of the curriculum'. Rosebery is an isolated town and the climate is wet and cold. These factors, together with the problems of overcrowding in the school and in teachers' residences and hostels, meant that the school suffered a very high turnover of teachers. Consequently the school was unable to carefully plan courses that were always best suited to students. The curriculum content, of necessity, often reflected the background and experiences of staff rather than the needs of students. Obviously this was a further cause of dissatisfaction.

The third major concern related more to how the school operated as a part of the state system rather than to local problems. Circumstances dictated that systematic planning was impossible because the school never knew early enough, or at one particular time, what resources would be available in any one year. Staff were always being required to plan for some particular quantity and type of resource without knowing the whole situation. On this basis, planning for resources tended to be 'spending' instead of developing plans related to policies and identifying the resources those plans would require. It was also evident that this piecemeal approach to planning and budgeting was not only less than totally effective but an inefficient use of staff time.

In addressing these concerns a collaborative management style was developed which is now well established. This has enabled the development of clear, concise policy statements on important issues, including the curriculum. These policies are developed by collaboration of the staff and school community, thus ensuring relevance and commitment. These policies provide the school staff with a framework for programme planning which leads to the identification of the resources required within programmes. This information forms the basis for the school budget which is then approved by the council if it considers that the budget reflects established policies and priorities. What follows is an outline of the process through which this policy-making, planning and related budgeting occurs.

It is important to realise that Collaborative School Management is cyclical in nature and that the cycle is based on a school year which, in Tasmania, commences in February and concludes in December. It is advisable, therefore, to establish a timetable of events for each year that clearly identifies the actual tasks, those responsible for each task, and the deadline for completion of each task. In this way there can be no misunderstanding by the staff and council members concerned. Figure 5.1 contains the timetable used to prepare the 1985 programme plans and budgets at Rosebery. It should be noted that most of the policy-making and planning occurred during 1984. Each of these tasks will now be considered in some detail, and particular attention given to the roles of the policy group (council) and programme teams (school staff).

Figure 5.1 Timetable for preparation of 1985 programme plans and budgets at Rosebery District High School (school year is February–December)

	Task	Responsibility	Completion
1	Bringing policy up to date	Council	1/6/84
2	Determination of projected enrolments	Principal	21/6/84
3	Identification of programmes and allocation of responsibility	Principal and senior staff	21/6/84
4	Identification and estimation of resources	Principal	21/6/84
5	Preparation of proposed plans and budgets	Programme teams	23/7/84
6	Preparation of summaries of proposed programme budgets	Principal	30/7/84
7	Reconciliation of proposed plans and budgets with estimated resource revenue	Senior staff	9/8/84
8	Adjustment of programme plans and budgets	Programme teams	23/8/84
9	Preparation of summaries of programme budgets	Principal	30/8/84
10	Presentation of programme plans and budgets to school council	Principal	30/8/84
11	Budget approval	Council	Oct-Nov 1984
12	Refinement of budget in light of first enrolments' effect on actual revenue	Principal and senior staff	February 1985
13	Ordering procedures	Programme teams	Ongoing
14	Accounting process	Bursar	Ongoing
15	Evaluation of programmes	Council and programme teams	Late 1985
16	Consideration of programme evaluation	Council	Early 1986

Tasks in Collaborative School Management at Rosebery

Policy-making and the setting of priorities

Policy-making is the primary role of the school council. It is a continuing role because a set of policies can never be established for all time. However, it is necessary at some point for the council to pass to the head teacher and staff a set of policies to serve as the basis for planning for the next school year. Chapter 3 included an outline of the way in which policies concerning substantive issues are based on the philosophy of the school, goals to be achieved and identified needs. The policy on any particular issue states the purposes to be achieved and the broad guidelines by which those purposes can be achieved in a one-page, jargon-free format. The documenting of policies is a lengthy process, but once a set of policies has been established, the work of changing policies in line with new developments or emerging needs is easily accomplished by the council, using techniques described in chapters 6 to 11.

The school council, as the policy group, has the additional task of establishing some priority among policies. This is to aid the later allocation of resources, especially if resources available are insufficient to meet all identified needs. It is unrealistic to expect that all the policies of a school can be placed in an order of priority by the council. Most people may agree that language development should be first in the order but there would be disagreement as to what should be second. Considering that a school might have some forty to fifty policies, the difficulties are clearly evident. The matter is resolved at Rosebery with categories of priority, with these categories described as Priority 1, 2 and 3. Clearly all are important, but Priority 1 policies are more important than Priority 2 policies. Figure 5.2 lists the policies and priorities established at Rosebery to provide for planning for 1985.

The documenting of policies was carried out over a four-year period. It required a concerted effort by the staff and council but now provides the framework for planning by the school. Policy changes can be initiated by any interested party but are undertaken by the council. The policy statements, together with statements of school philosophy, goals and priorities, are collected together in a policy handbook which is updated each year. Copies are given to all members of the council and school staff as well as to members of the community on request. Policy statements are published as a feature in the weekly parent bulletin. Examples of these policy statements are contained in the Appendix.

Determination of projected enrolments

Planning is greatly assisted if the enrolments for the next school year are known to a reasonable degree of accuracy. This information is required to assist in estimating the resource revenue to be available to the school since resources, including staff, are usually allocated to the school according to student numbers. This information also aids programme planning, especially in optional subjects in high school classes. It is not necessary that these predictions be absolutely accurate, but sufficiently accurate (90–95 per cent) to make realistic planning possible.

Programme identification

When policies have been established, then programmes are identified for implementing those policies. Making a new policy can result in an

Figure 5.2 Policy priorities for 1985 at Rosebery District High School

Priority 1	Priority 2	Priority 3
Computer education	Arts and crafts	Art acquisition
Commercial education	Student assessment	Extra-curricular
Excursions	School certificate	activities
Early intervention	Discipline	Foreign language
K–2 General studies	Drama festival	History
3–6 General studies	Homework	Home economics
Language development	Handwriting	House system
Learning to read	Journalism	School assemblies
Technology	Kindergarten and	Canteen
Mathematics	preparatory education	Fund-raising
Physical education	Music	
Pastoral care	Option subjects, 9–10	
3–6 Regrouped language	Preparing for school	
Special education	Presentation Day	
Sport	Your Child's Report	
Technical subjects	Social studies	
Support services	Science	
Budget and planning	Talented children	
Teacher induction	Transition education	
Communications	Visual arts	
Decision-making	School magazine	
School council	Buildings and grounds	
	Community bus	
	Curriculum resource	
	Staffing	
	Book sales	
	Administration	
	Formation of classes	
	School organisation	
	Professional development	
	Public relations	

additional programme just as withdrawal of a policy can result in the demise of a programme. Not all policies have a corresponding programme, although this is usually the case and is easily seen in the examples of mathematics, science and language. However, policies dealing with such matters as discipline, student assessment and reporting to parents, for example, are reflected in a number of programmes. The total set of programmes encompasses all activities conducted by the school. The programme structure is determined by natural divisions in the curriculum

Figure 5.3 Programmes for 1985 at Rosebery District High School

101	Extra-curricular activities	161	7–10 Technical subjects
102	Art acquisition	162	7–10 Visual arts
103	Administration	163	7–10 Home economics
104	Community bus	164	9–10 Commercial subjects
111	Curriculum resource	171	Early Intervention
112	School council	172	K–2 General studies
113	Presentation Day	173	K–10 Special education
114	3–6 Regrouped language		
		181	3–6 General studies
121	K–10 Music	182	Public relations
122	K–10 Physical education		
123	K–10 Sport	191	Cleaning
124	Support services	192	Grounds
		193	Canteen
131	7–10 Social studies	194	Book sales
132	9–10 History		
133	7–10 Transition education	201	Journalism
134	7–10 Note/test production	202	School magazine
		203	Student council
141	7–10 English		
142	7–10 Foreign language		
143	K–10 Speech and drama		
144	Drama Festival		
151	7–10 Mathematics		
152	7–10 Science		
153	K–10 Computer studies		
154	K–10 Talented children		

and the organisational pattern of the school. Each programme involves one or more teachers with a senior member of staff usually being assigned responsibility for the day-to-day operation of the programme. All the teaching staff involved in a particular programme form the programme team which undertakes the planning and budgeting for the programme as well as implementing and some evaluating.

Figure 5.3 is a list of the 1985 programmes at Rosebery. Each programme is given a code which assists in the ordering and accounting procedures. Programmes are grouped according to the staff member responsible for the programme and this responsibility grouping is also indicated by the number code. The actual number of programmes has varied from year to year as a result of policy changes by the council and with different approaches to school organisation.

Identifying and estimating resources

Once policies have been established and programmes identified, it is possible to proceed to the preparation of programme plans and budgets. There are two ways in which to proceed. One is to proceed without any reference to the levels of resources available and for programme teams to prepare plans from the point of view of what is ultimately desirable. This approach can lead to considerable frustration for teachers when later budget-balancing results in extensive 'lopping'. For this reason the preferred approach at Rosebery is to provide programme teams with an estimate of the total resources available to the whole school for the forthcoming year before they prepare programme plans and budget proposals. As it is necessary to commence preparing budgets in June, an estimate is all that can be provided; resources are obtained from various sources and these become known as definite amounts at various times between August of the preceding year and February of the actual school budget year.

It is apparent that by estimating the resources to be available programme teams can plan with realistic expectations, and this certainly aids the process of balancing resources required with resources available. It goes without saying that the accuracy of the estimations is critical to the successful operation of programmes in the planning year. After several years of experience at Rosebery, it has been relatively easy to estimate the income for the forthcoming year with sufficient accuracy for planning purposes.

Figure 5.4 contains details of the estimated resource revenue for Rosebery for 1985. Estimated income is shown in five categories: teaching staff resource, non-teaching staff resource, grants and subsidies, levies and fees, and school activity projects.

Teaching staff and non-teaching staff can be estimated from the predicted student enrolment patterns and from the staffing agreements. As the staffing agreements change from year to year, difficulties can be encountered, but experience has shown that it is possible to predict this resource with sufficient accuracy by carefully considering trends, particularly in government policy. Some would disagree with the inclusion of the staff resource and/or the staff resource being expressed in dollar terms. This development is discussed fully in chapter 13. At this point it is sufficient to say that there is school control of staffing to the extent of determining the composition and nature of the staff within the quota of staff established by the State. In Tasmanian Government schools, this quota can be increased through allocation of Commonwealth Schools Commission funds.

Grants and subsidies are those provided from state sources through the Education Deparment, and those originating from commonwealth sources (mainly through the Schools Commission). These are easily identified and relatively easy to estimate as they are generally based on enrolments and follow well-established patterns of change from year to year.

Levies and fees are those paid directly to the school by parents. They are set by the council as part of the planning and budgeting process within Education Department guidelines, and can therefore be accurately predicted from known enrolment patterns. Profits from school-initiated activities are again easily identified and estimated with reasonable accuracy from past experience.

Reference is made in Figure 5.4 to a colour coding. This is a system used to take account of restrictions placed on sources of income by the state or commonwealth authority. Chapter 7 demonstrates that these restrictions can be accommodated with considerable ease and do not require any significant attention in the planning and budgeting processes.

Preparation of proposed programme plans and budgets

Before explaining the process at Rosebery, we shall discuss the question of who should prepare the plans and budget for each programme. With some thirty to forty programmes required in a reasonably large school, obviously the head teacher cannot do it alone. As the majority of programmes are directly related to children's learning, preparing proposals cannot be the responsibility of the bursar alone. Realistically, the task is best accomplished by those with the expertise in each programme. These may be the teachers who work in a programme area, or, for some programmes, other categories of staff such as those in cleaning and canteen work. The people who work in programmes and who prepare the programme plans and budget proposals are referred to as programme teams.

At Rosebery each programme team usually consists of a senior member of staff and the teachers who work within the programme. In some cases the person responsible for the programme may also be a teacher with particular expertise and/or interest. In programmes involving large numbers of staff, for example, Administration and Pastoral Care, it is possible for a representative group to prepare plans and budget proposals rather than the whole group. The task is organised so that no member of staff is involved in preparing more than three or four programmes. As some programmes vary little from year to year, the task is realistic and major work is only required each year on programmes when there has been a substantial policy and/or priority change.

In considering the preparation of programme plans and budget proposals the next matter to be addressed is how proposals are to be prepared. Programme proposals should conform to a format that has been agreed on; this format will include the details of the main policies concerned, the plan for implementation, resources required and the planned evaluation. A standard format also facilitates comparisons of programmes and quick assimilation by all concerned of the information contained in the programme proposals. It is recommended that programme

Figure 5.4 Summary of estimated resources for 1985 at Rosebery District High School

Type of resource	Classification	Resources predicted	Source by colour code
Teaching staff	1 Principal (Head teacher)	$40 114	
	2 Vice principals	64 736	
	4 Senior masters	121 516	
	1 Infant mistress	28 944	
	1 Senior teacher (primary)	26 689	
	34 Teachers	776 765	
		$1 058 764	
Non-teaching staff	Clerical staff	$40 805	
	Custodial staff	77 802	
	Kindergarten aide	6 642	
	Relief staff (Prof. Dev.)	1 748	
	Support staff	9 136	
	Book-hire aide	1 083	
		$137 216	
Grants & subsidies	Annual requisition	$19 167	Dark pink
	Annual Requisition Grant cash election	4 792	Orange
	Schools Commission	48 000	Dark green
	Excursion & physical education grant	7 000	
	Library grants	3 880	Light pink
	Participation & Equity	3 620	
	Home economics subsidy	85	
	Postage subsidy	628	
	Telephone subsidy	2 500	
		$89 672	
Levies & fees	General levies, K-10	$9 017	Blue
	Specialist levies, 7-10	8 037	Light green
	Book-hire fees, 7-10	4 785	Yellow
		$21 839	
School activities	Book-sale profits	$3 500	
	Canteen profits	2 500	
	Investment account	1 500	
	Gala Day	2 000	
		$9 500	
	TOTAL	$1 316 991	

proposals should always be limited to two typed pages.

At Rosebery a format has been developed that is illustrated in the examples given in the Appendix. Basically, information is provided under the following headings:

Programme name
Purposes
Broad guidelines
Plan for implementation
Resources required
Plan for evaluation
Programme team

The format includes the programme's name and code as well as the initials of the senior member of staff responsible for the programme. Related policies are summarised under 'Purpose' and 'Broad guidelines'. The 'Purpose' is a statement of what the programme intends to achieve and is derived from policy statements. Naturally it is a very succinct statement of intention compared to the original policy statements. The 'Broad guidelines' are a concise description of how the purposes are to be achieved. Again this information is gained from the original policy statements.

Then follows a detailed statement as to how the programme is actually to operate, under the heading of 'Plan for implementation'. This plan is a list of what is going to be done, who is going to do it, when, how often, with what and where. This information is given as a series of planning elements listed in priority order. Under 'Resources required' the planning elements are translated into actual resources and hence to dollars under the headings of 'Staffing', 'Materials and equipment', 'Book hire', 'Travel', 'Services', and so on. The 'Plan for evaluation' follows, with details as to how it is intended that the success or otherwise of the programme in achieving its purposes be assessed. This involves evaluation of both effectiveness of the programme, with respect to the degree of achievement of purposes, and of the efficiency of the programme, that is, the cost value in that achievement. The proposal concludes with a listing of the names of the programme team as a way of recognising the input of those concerned.

A careful study of the format reveals the clear relationship established between the content of policies approved by the school council and planning and resource identification carried out by the staff in the programme teams.

Examples of programme plans and budgets are contained in the Appendix. Those included are Administration, Technical Subjects, and K–2 General Studies. The process of translating policies into programmes through planning and budgeting is the subject of chapter 7.

Experience has shown that the best time to negotiate teaching conditions for staff is during the preparation of proposals. At this time staff are very much aware of the ramifications of their requirements, and are able to balance teaching conditions against developing more desirable programmes for students. Some would argue against this, wanting these negotiations to be completed before the preparation of proposals commences. In any event, the negotiations must be completed before the final reconciliation (balancing) of the budget. However, at Rosebery, where the programme planning and budgeting process and negotiations over teaching conditions proceed together, the context for these decisions, namely, learning opportunities for students, is uppermost in everyone's thinking.

Preparation of summaries of proposed programme budgets

In each programme, planning elements are translated into resources required under different categories of expenditure, for example, 'Staffing', 'Materials and equipment', 'Travel', 'Books', and so on. At the end of each programme budget the expenditure required for each category as a whole is totalled as well as the expected total cost of the programme. Information for all programmes is summarised on one double-page sheet to form the summary of the programme budget. An example of such a summary of a programme budget is given in the Appendix.

The main purpose of the summary is to identify the amount by which the total resources required for all programmes exceeds (or is less than) the resources available. In this way information is provided to aid the reconciliation process which leads to a balanced budget. The summary sheet enables the overall picture to be kept in mind as changes are made to programmes in line with previously established priorities.

Reconciliation of proposed programme plans and budgets with estimated resource revenue

One purpose of the reconciliation process is to balance the budget of resources required with resources available. Another equally important purpose is for the process to act as a check, ensuring that proposals accurately reflect policies and that established priorities among policies are reflected in the resources allocated to programmes. This second purpose suggests the composition of the group that should carry out the reconciliation, namely those members of staff (usually senior members) who are responsible for programmes throughout the school. However, the group or person allocated the task will vary from school to school depending on the approach to management which has been adopted. It could be argued that the reconciliation task belongs to the policy group or council. This could well be so, but it is suggested that the reconciliation is really part of the preparation of the budget; the council is able to make changes as it sees fit during the approval process, with the assurance that any changes must be accommodated within a balanced budget.

Reconciling the differences between proposals and expected income can be difficult unless a systematic approach is adopted. The approach used by the senior staff at Rosebery is described below.

1 All members of senior staff are charged with acting in the best educational interests of the total student body rather than representing sectional interests. In advertisements for senior staff it is stressed that the person, first and foremost, will be part of a senior management team responsible for the total education programme and, second, should have expertise in some particular area.

2 All members are required to be well versed in the details of the proposals before any reconciliation meeting.

3 No 'writer' of a proposal speaks to that proposal in the meeting. There is no selling!

4 There is an opportunity to proceed systematically through the proposals with questions for clarification being addressed to the writer of the proposal. Any questions must be directly answered rather than using the opportunity to 'sell'.

5 It is always emphasised that 'proposals' are being dealt with, and expectation of some change is built up so that the writers of proposals do not see a defence as necessary, and potential conflict is minimised.

Keeping these ideas in mind, the group proceeds to identify relationships between priorities and comes to consensus on the changes needed to achieve a set of programme plans and budgets that accurately reflect established policies and the priorities occurring both between and within policies. It should be noted that in preparing proposals it is necessary to list planning elements in order of priority. This is to assist the reconciling of proposals as indicated above to achieve a balanced budget.

As an adjunct to the reconciliation process, there is an allocation of resources within programmes in keeping with the restrictions placed by the sources concerned. This is the colour-coding system that was described earlier. These source restrictions have not proved to be any real problem. It really means that proposed expenditure on any particular item must come from a legitimate source. For example, a teacher aide to assist teachers with notes and production of tests could not be allocated against levies paid by students. However, the aide could be allocated against Commonwealth Schools Commission funds. Books and expendable items used by students can be allocated against levies. These restrictions do not present problems and can easily be accommodated in the budget process. The only difficulty is in keeping track of whose money has been allocated to which element of what programme. The colour coding on a budget summary sheet takes care of the problem.

Adjustment of programme plans and budgets

Following reconciliation of the programme proposals, it is necessary to make some adjustments to programme plans and budgets so that they can be produced in final form. This task is referred to the programme teams, especially where decisions are made to subtract small amounts from a number of lower priority programmes to achieve the final balance rather than eliminating planning elements from particular programmes. The programme teams in question are then able to make desired changes within their programmes to accommodate these small reductions.

Preparing summaries of programme budgets

When the reconciliation is complete, it is followed by the production of accurate summary sheets. These become particularly useful when the budget is being approved, and in later programme accounting. At Rosebery, the reconciled programme plans and budgets, final summary sheets and an outline of the planning and budgeting highlights are put together in book form and presented to the school council for ratification and approval. All members of the school staff as well as all members of the council are issued with personal copies.

Presentation of programme plans and budgets to the school council

Members of council receive copies of the plan and budget book at least seven days before the council meeting at which they are to be presented. The presentation is undertaken by the head teacher and involves outlining the resources to be available, with particular emphasis on changes from previous years and changes in policies by the council and by state or commonwealth governments. Attention is then drawn to new programmes or programme changes that have occurred as a result of policy-making by the council in the immediate past year. The balancing of the budget is also explained, particularly with reference to the compromises that may have been made between programmes in the light of priorities established earlier by council. Emphasis is given to any new programmes resulting from new policies, including how they have been matched with available resources and the resulting effect on other programmes.

The presentation is concluded with the formal tabling of the document for consideration by the council. After the presentation, questions are expected and answered for clarification of general directions, but the approval process is not commenced until the following council meeting. At Rosebery, this means that one month elapses between the official present-ation and commencement of the approval process which usually takes a further two meetings or more. It is desirable that there be a reasonable period before approval is attempted, so that everyone concerned has time to study the plan and budgets, discuss them with other people in the community and school and generally gain reaction from others while forming their own opinions.

Budget approval by the council

Council's approval of the budget is based on whether the budget as presented is a true and accurate reflection of council policies and priorities. The task is made possible for the council by the preparation and present-ation of the budget in programme form. This means that programme expenditure is clearly related in each programme to a plan for implement-ation, with that plan being clearly related back to the purposes and broad guidelines in the relevant policies. In other words, there is a mechanism that clearly relates planned expenditure to actual policies. This allows the council's role in approving budgets to be realistic.

It is interesting to compare the council's role in this kind of budget approval with what happens when a traditional budget is presented with expenditure related to categories of service (teachers, books, travel, maintenance, and so on), but without any reference to programmes. The difficulty in trying to relate planned expenditure directly to actual policies in the traditional budget form is well known and the validity of a council being given a role in budget approval with a traditional budget system is highly questionable.

When a budget is presented in programme form, a council can undertake the approval process by addressing itself to the following questions:

1 **Are all established policies reflected in the budget?** A 'checking-off' system can be devised to answer this question.
2 **Are the established priorities among policies accurately reflected?** A close examination of the programmes and the programme budget summaries provides the information required. Obviously this task is difficult because qualitative as well as quantitative considera-tions are involved.
3 **Are any policies included that are not endorsed or held by the council?** This question must be addressed as well as the first

question as it could be that activities inconsistent with policies have been included irrespective of the views of the council.

4   **Is there an obvious relationship between the proposed evaluation and the purposes of each programme?** This question is necessary as another responsibility of the council is evaluation. It should approve of the method of evaluating the programme and the relevance of the proposed evaluation to what is to be achieved.

Questions of a similar nature can also be addressed. The outcome of these considerations may be that council decides to make some changes. When the council is satisfied that a true relationship has been established between planned expenditure and policies, then the budget is formally approved. Amended copies are printed and widely distributed as the educational plan and budget for the next school year. It then becomes the role of the head teacher and staff to implement the plans using the resource allocations that have been approved.

No doubt there are questions that spring to mind concerning the approval of the budget by the council. For instance, does this approval process give the council the role of choosing actual text books and specific materials or determining which teacher will teach which class? These tasks are regarded as 'implementation' and therefore the responsibilities of the head teacher and staff. Obviously, what is implementation and what is not requires exploration and definition but these are readily discernible with practice. At Rosebery, specific issues of this nature are usually resolved by referring to the relevant policies, particularly to the broad guidelines within policies.

When the budget has been approved, it is then the task of the head teacher and staff to deliver those programmes to students. We do not intend to address the nature of this learning and teaching although it is the focus of the related processes of policy-making, planning and budgeting that is Collaborative School Management.

Ordering procedures

Approval of the programme plans and budgets well before the commencement of the year allows for the required resources to be ordered and obtained ready for use as required. This task is given to programme teams. Each team is responsible for its own operation both in ensuring that materials are available as required, and in allowing for possible responses to emerging needs for resources thoughout the budget year. These issues are considered further in chapter 8.

The accounting process

Programme planning and budgeting are best monitored from a financial point of view by the development of an appropriate system of programme accounting. This approach to accounting relates income and expenditure not to categories such as materials and equipment or books, nor to sources of funds such as Schools Commission or State equipment grants, but to the actual programmes. A programme team is able to check income that has been received and expenditure from their programme and calculate a balance, taking into account orders forwarded and yet to be received and/or paid for. This information can be compiled for all programmes at regular intervals and presented as a financial statement. At Rosebery, a financial statement is presented at each council meeting. The bursar keeps the accounts and prepares financial statements. From these statements, council is able to ascertain the current financial position and trends for any programme as well as for the school as a whole. It is emphasised that the role of the council is the consideration of such information; council members are not involved in the keeping of books.

As sources of finances are mainly external to the school and are of government or public origin, there is an obvious need for auditing. Naturally it is necessary to consider sources of finances as well as programmes. This can be accomplished by various methods which are outlined in chapter 8.

Evaluation of programmes

Programme evaluation completes the cycle in this approach to Collaborative School Management. A measure of the degree to which the purposes have been achieved gives an indication of the effectiveness of programmes. A measure of effectiveness in relation to the resources required gives an indication of efficiency.

The relevance of evaluation to policy-making and planning demonstrates the joint role of the council, as the policy-making group, and the school staff, as the programme teams. Chapter 9 is devoted to the issues involved in programme evaluation.

At Rosebery, programmes are evaluated in the latter part of each budget year. Evaluation reports are prepared either by the programme teams or by work groups appointed by the council. Reports are limited to one or two pages and presented to the council at the end of the school year.

Consideration of programme evaluations

When the council receives programme evaluations, the real task in evaluation begins. The information contained in the reports must be interpreted and related to the priority placed on a programme. This issue is explored in detail in chapter 9. It is sufficient to say at this point that measures of effectiveness and efficiency are not enough on their own to determine the future of programmes. Related priorities must also be taken into account. For instance, would it be realistic to delete a library programme that is ineffective and inefficient? This question illustrates the point that the real purpose of evaluating programmes is related to goals, needs and policies with subsequent modifications which may lead to enhancing the education provided for students. In this way Collaborative School Management through policy-making, planning, budgeting, implementing and evaluating provides a means for the school and community to successfully share in the management of education to the ultimate benefit of students.

SUMMARY
THE PROCESS AT WORK AT ROSEBERY

POLICY-MAKING

- The council makes policies on substantive issues including areas of the curriculum.
- The council makes policies based on the goals, needs and philosophy of the school.
- The council passes policies to the head teacher (principal) and staff for implementation.

PLANNING

The head teacher and staff plan to implement policies by:

- determining projected enrolments;
- identifying and structuring programmes through which policies can be implemented;
- identifying and estimating resource revenue;
- preparing proposed programme plans and identifying the resources required to implement those plans.

BUDGETING

The head teacher and staff prepare programme budgets by:

- identifying resources required in programmes and estimating their cost;
- drawing up summaries of proposed programme budgets for comparison purposes;
- balancing proposed programme budgets with estimated resource revenue.

The council approves programme plans and budgets if they accurately reflect policies and priorities.

IMPLEMENTING

- The approved programmes provide the educational plan for the school.
- The programmes are implemented within the school through learning and teaching.
- The implementation of programmes is the responsibility of the head teacher and staff.
- Implementation also involves ordering and accounting.

EVALUATING

- The council and the head teacher and staff jointly share the task of evaluating programmes.
- Programmes are evaluated with respect to effectiveness and efficiency.
- Information is provided on which to base decisions concerning future developments to further improve outcomes and experiences for students.

6   *Goal-setting and Policy-making*

Many schools have made pleasing progress in recent years in determining their goals or aims. Some goals and aims are contained in curriculum statements, while others, for the school as a whole, find their place in special documents which are published for staff and community. However, there is no generally accepted model for the policy process for schools. The purpose of this chapter is to provide such a model.

Conceptually, there is lack of agreement on the meaning of the term 'policy', which is often defined either too broadly, in terms of a set of goals or aims or in a statement of belief, or too narrowly, in terms of a detailed specification of a course of action to be followed or a set of rules and procedures. Different views also prevail as to the role which members of staff and the school community may play, especially through structures such as school councils or governing boards. In discussing councils or boards of governors with policy-making powers, some professional educators contend that 'the community does not want such bodies' and 'the community does not have the expertise to serve' while members of the community often have the view that 'we should leave it to the professionals' or 'we do not have the skills'. In our judgement, these views and concerns can be allayed with clear explanations and illustrations of policy and the policy process.

Accordingly, the first section of this chapter is devoted to explaining and illustrating policy, offering distinctions between policy and other terms such as goals, needs, objectives and procedures. The benefits of a systematic approach to policy-making are listed. Then follows a model for the policy process, with guidelines for the development of policy on issues which are contentious as well as those which are not. With these guidelines to follow, it is intended that a school with no written policy can, in two years, establish a substantial policy base which will shape planning and resource allocation.

In terms of the Collaborative School Management Cycle this chapter is primarily concerned with the first two phases: goal-setting and need identification (Phase 1) and policy-making (Phase 2), with the emphasis on the second phase, given the need for policy processes outlined in the first paragraph.

Some clarifications and distinctions

At the outset, it is important to understand what is meant by the term 'policy' and to distinguish policy from terms such as goals or aims, needs, objectives, regulations or rules, procedures, job descriptions and by-laws.

A *policy* is a set of guidelines which provide a framework for action in achieving some purpose on a substantive issue.[1] The guidelines specify in general terms the kind of action which will or may be taken as far as the issue is concerned: they imply an intention and a pattern for taking action. In a school, these guidelines provide a framework, often with some basis for discretion, within which the head teacher, staff and others in the school community can discharge their responsibilities with clear direction. A policy is established to achieve some purpose, which invariably reflects a set of beliefs or values or philosophy on the issue concerned. Not all issues require a policy: action on routine issues can usually be shaped by the formulation of simple procedures. A policy is a more appropriate framework for issues of some substance.

This view of policy is illustrated in the sample policy on homework at the secondary level in Figure 6.1. Homework is clearly an issue of some substance in every school and warrants a written statement of policy to serve as a framework for action. The policy in Figure 6.1 implies a purpose as far as homework is concerned: 'Regular homework. . . contributes to the development of sound study habits.' This statement reflects certain beliefs about the value of sound study habits and the contribution which homework can make to achieving them. Three guidelines are provided, each being mandatory as far as intention is concerned, with the term 'will' used in each instance. It should be noted that each guideline in the policy statement expresses in general terms the pattern for taking action. In the second guideline, we read that 'every child will be assigned some homework on each day of the school week, with at least two days per week assigned for each of language, mathematics and social studies'. The guideline does not, for example, specify how much homework will be assigned in language on each day in year 7: this level of detail is inappropriate in a statement of policy.

A special feature of the illustration in Figure 6.1 is the length of the statement. As noted in chapter 3, we recommend that no policy exceed one page in length. Anything longer often makes the task of writing appear burdensome to busy people who have many responsibilities. Anything longer makes it all the more difficult to change the policy when a need for amendment becomes evident. Anything longer makes it uncertain that

Figure 6.1 Sample statement of policy on homework at the secondary level

SCHOOL HOMEWORK

Purpose

Regular homework is a valuable aspect of the learning process and contributes to the development of sound study habits. Consistent with this belief, homework shall be implemented according to the following guidelines:

Broad guidelines

1   Each child will be assigned homework in each subject on a regular basis.
2   While the amount of homework will vary according to age and learning needs, every child will be assigned some homework on each day of the school week, with at least two days per week assigned for each of language, mathematics and social studies.
3   Teachers will be responsible for reviewing the homework assignment of each child.

Framework for planning and evaluating

members of the school community will read and understand the policy. This one-page statement is also free of jargon: it should be expressed in simple terms so that its intention is clear to all.

With this explanation and illustration in mind, it is now possible to make some distinctions. The guidelines illustrated in Figure 6.1 provide the basis for the preparation of rules and procedures. A *rule* or *regulation* is a statement which directs action, usually by specifying who is responsible for implementing a policy. The preparation of rules is thus the first step in the implementation of policy. A *procedure* is a further specification of who does what, how, and in what sequence, in implementing the terms of a policy. Some rules and procedures may be mandatory, that is, they specify what action *shall* take place, while others may be discretionary, specifying what action *may* occur. These characteristics of rules and procedures are illustrated in Figure 6.2, with sample statements associated with the policy on homework contained in Figure 6.1.

A *goal* or *aim* is not a policy. As explained in chapter 3, a goal is a statement of broad direction, general purpose or intent; it is general and timeless and is not concerned with a particular outcome at a particular moment in time. Goals are often implied in statements of policy; for example, the statement of purpose in the policy on homework illustrated in Figure 6.1 suggests that a goal of the school is 'the development of sound study habits for all students'. Similarly, a *need* is not a policy. As also explained in chapter 3, a need is usually considered to exist if *what is* falls short of *what should be*. In the homework example, *what should be* might be that there should be consistent approaches to the setting and reviewing

Figure 6.2 Sample rules and procedures for policy on homework at the secondary level

---

A SAMPLE RULE ON SCHOOL HOMEWORK
1   The head of each department shall be responsible for ensuring that homework practice in the subject concerned is consistent with the policy.
2   The head of each department is responsible for referring unusual circumstances to the head teacher for resolution.

SAMPLE PROCEDURES ON SCHOOL HOMEWORK
1   The general practice for homework in each department shall be determined annually during planning meetings in the first week of the school year.
2   The practice in each department shall be communicated to parents in the first issue of the school newsletter.
3   In accordance with general practice in the department, each teacher shall establish a schedule and shall determine the manner in which homework is to be reviewed.
4   The teacher may advise parents of the schedule and other details in a special written communication.

---

of homework across the school. *What is* might be an evaluation which revealed inconsistency in practice and some consequent dissatisfaction among parents, teachers and students. Accordingly, a decision was made to formulate a policy on homework. A policy may thus be formulated to help satisfy a need.

An *objective* is not a policy. An objective is a statement of outcome, often expressed in measurable terms, which is to be achieved in a particular period of time. Objectives are often set in association with the implementation or evaluation of policy; for example, an objective for the policy on homework illustrated in Figure 6.1 might be 'At least 80 per cent of a sample of parents surveyed after one year will express a high degree of satisfaction with the time spent by their children on assigned homework.'

Neither *job descriptions* nor *by-laws* can be considered statements of policy. Job descriptions may, of course, arise from policy; for example, the policy on homework illustrated in Figure 6.1 suggests that one statement in a job description for teachers in the school having such a policy may be 'Teachers will be responsible for setting homework in accordance with the policy of the school and for reviewing the homework assignment of each child.' *By-laws* for the operation of meetings of staff, school council or governing board are only related to policy in the sense that they will reflect or describe the manner in which the policy is to be made.

It is evident from the foregoing that a high degree of complexity is possible, even for an issue such as homework, when goals must be established, policy developed and supporting regulations and procedures formulated. Such may indeed be the case, and the policy handbook for a large school offering a diverse programme in a volatile environment may be a very weighty, often-changed document. A small school, on the other hand, offering a relatively straightforward programme in a somewhat stable environment may have a small collection of rarely amended policy-related documents. Despite such contrasts, the policy process in any setting is clearly a very demanding affair. It might be wise to identify the benefits of such efforts before proceeding further.

Benefits of Policy

The benefits of well-written and continuously updated policies may be couched in the following terms.

1   Policies demonstrate that the school is being operated in an efficient and businesslike manner. When policies are written, there is rarely ambiguity with regard to the goals of the school and how the school is to be administered.
2   Policies ensure to a considerable extent that there will be uniformity and consistency in decisions and in operational procedures. Good policy makes 'ad hoc' or whimsical decision-making difficult.
3   Policies must be consistent with those for the system as a whole and with the various statutes which constitute school law. Policies thus add strength to the position of the head teacher and staff when possible legal actions arise.
4   Policies help ensure that meetings are orderly. Valuable time will be saved when a new problem can be handled quickly and effectively because of its relationship to an existing policy.
5   Policies foster stability and continuity: administrators and teachers may come and go but well-written and constantly updated policies remain. Such policies make clear the general 'direction' of the school, and therefore facilitate orientation of newly appointed members of staff of the school, and of the council or governing body, where such a group exists.
6   Policies provide the framework for planning in the school.
7   Policies assist the school in the assessment of the instructional programme. Written and publicly disseminated statements of policy show that the policy group is willing to be held accountable for decisions.
8   Policies clarify functions and responsibilities of the policy group, head teacher and staff. All can work with greater efficiency, satisfaction and commitment when school policies are well known, understood and accepted.

A Model for the Policy Process

This section of the chapter provides, first, an account of the policy process as it is usually experienced. This account is both descriptive and prescriptive: it describes the manner in which policy issues arise, it describes what often does occur and suggests what should occur when a policy response is made. It is a frankly political view of the policy process. Then follow recommendations for policy-making, with separate guidelines for contentious issues and non-contentious issues. The chapter concludes with a special note on the critically important leadership role of the principal.

No extended reference is made here to goal-setting and identification of needs. The reader is referred to chapter 3 where the product and process for each is the subject of description and illustration. Both are the responsibility of the policy group and, in many respects, the process described in the pages which follow may be applied also to the task of making decisions on goals and needs.

A political view of the policy process[2]

Turning now to the process of policy-making, one is immediately struck by the differences when a comparison is made with more routine decision-making. Routine decision-making usually entails a response to recurring simple situations in which objectives are clear and generally accepted. Consequences of alternatives are readily apparent. Policy matters, on the other hand, are invariably associated with a combination of problems. A diversity of interests and preferences may result in vague and conflicting objectives among those who are directly or indirectly involved. This diversity, along with elements of uncertainty and risk, makes it difficult to anticipate the consequences of alternative courses of action. That such a process is highly political is also evident if one accepts that political behaviour arises from disagreement. Participants in the process invariably differ as far as means and ends are concerned.

Policy arises from the various *'desires, wants, needs and demands'*[3] which are expressed in the school community. These may be expressed formally, in meetings of staff or governing bodies, or informally, through casual conversations with policy-makers or those in a position to influence the policy process. Over time, these desires, wants, needs and demands are *'articulated and aggregated'* to the point where attention is warranted: there is enough discussion of an *'issue'* that action must be taken to determine a framework for action. For the homework issue illustrated in Figure 6.1, concerns of parents and teachers at inconsistent approaches to the setting of homework in school may have built up to the point where a resolution calling for the adoption of a school policy on the issue was passed at a meeting of staff or the governing body of the school. Those responsible for making policy then typically engage in a '*search for policy alternatives*', with varying amounts of '*policy research*' and '*communication with constituents*'.

Policy research involves the gathering of information to shed further light on the issue and the alternatives. For the homework issue, this research may involve a study of regulations to determine what is legally permitted, or a reading of texts to clarify the educational justification for the setting of homework. For policy research in general, investigation may extend to many areas including legal (what is allowed), economic (what can be afforded), technological (what is known about the workability of the various alternatives for resolving the issue), political (what is acceptable for individuals, groups and institutions who may have an influence on the adoption and implementation of policy), demographic (what are the implications of trends as far as population is concerned) and socio-cultural (what is valued in the community). At the very least, policy research involves the identification of existing policies which may shape or constrain in some way the policy under consideration.

Consistent with this political view of the policy process, communication with constituents involves the identification of alternatives which are considered desirable and acceptable by the various individuals and groups in the school community. For the homework issue, this information might be gathered through meetings called for the purpose, or through surveys to determine the views and preferences of parents. The various alternatives for action are then the subject of 'assessment' and 'choice', according to criteria which may be classified as *desirability* ('Will this alternative resolve the issue, achieving the benefits intended with minimal harm in the area under consideration or in other areas?'), *workability* ('Can this alternative be implemented with the available resources of personnel, time, facilities and money?') and *acceptability* ('Will this alternative be accepted by those who will be affected by the policy or who will be required to implement the policy?').

The political nature of the process is evident throughout this account; that is, disagreement may occur at any point in the process on the ends which are being sought or on the means by which these ends are to be achieved. A successful policy will result if this political process is effectively managed and the three criteria of desirability, workability and acceptability are satisfied.

Readers will readily identify instances from their own experience where this process has been evident and where it has been absent. The process may occur quickly, over a few hours or even in a few minutes when policy must be determined quickly. In general, however, the process will require time if appropriate attention is to be given to consultation ('communication with constituents').

Investigation of policies which have failed has highlighted the importance of a process such as the one described. Five out of eight reasons for policy failure which were identified in a recent study[4] refer to flaws or omissions in this process. The reasons for policy failure were identified as follows.

1   The issues which gave rise to the policy were not clearly understood or were poorly defined. The policy which resulted was simply unrelated to the real issue.

2   The people involved in the implementation of the policy were not, in general, those who articulated the issues in the first place or those who were involved in the formulation of the policy.

3   The policy itself was weak. Its philosophical basis was unwarranted, its objectives or intended outcomes were unclear and it was vague about the means by which the outcomes were to be achieved. In other words, the problem, the solution and its execution were poorly defined. The anticipated consequences were not expressed in terms which were measurable.

4   An insufficient number of policy alternatives were considered.

5   Questions of feasibility were not addressed adequately.

6   The implementation strategy was deficient in one or more ways: the leadership style was inappropriate; organising, co-ordinating and communicating were inadequate; groups or units required for implementation were poorly structured; resources were insufficient; the process was not controlled or monitored.

7   The weakness in implementation stemmed from the basic issue of administrative responsibility: inattention to specification of responsibility through regulations or rules and lack of direction through procedures resulted in the policy tending to 'slip between the cracks'.

8   Over time, circumstances changed: issues changed, different conditions in the environment emerged, new actors or constituents appreared.

Policy on policy-making

Each school should develop an approach to policy-making which takes account of the process described above. This approach is, in effect, a 'policy on policy-making' or a 'blueprint' for the policy process. Formulating a policy on policy-making should, of course, be one of the first tasks of the policy group. Such a policy will require procedures for its implementation in the same manner as policies in general. The policy and associated procedures should be communicated to all in the school community who may have a role or an interest in policy-making. The same benefits for policies in general outlined earlier in this chapter apply also to the policy on policy-making.

What follows is a recommended approach which might form the framework for a school's policy on policy-making.

Getting started: identifying and classifying the issues The recommended approach assumes that the school currently has no written statements of policy and that there is an interest in building a base of written policies which reflect (a) satisfaction with current practice and (b) a determination to attend to those current practices which are unsatisfactory. Three tasks are recommended: identifying, classifying and scheduling the issues.

The first task is for the policy group to list by title the issues for which it would like to have written policies. This may be done in a short brainstorming session, adding, where appropriate, to a list which may have been prepared in advance by a member of the group. Initially there should be no restriction placed on the inclusion of an issue: if only one member of the group feels an issue is important enough to warrant a written statement of policy then it should be included. As with the classification of goals set out in chapter 3, policies may be established in four areas: (i) policies related to outcomes for students, which may also be described as curriculum policies; (ii) policies related to learning experiences for students, which may also be described as instructional policies; (iii) policies related to the provision of resources to support teaching and learning; and (iv) policies related to the management of the school, including issues such as discipline and reporting on pupils' progress to parents. The list of issues may be quite large, exceeding fifty for a large school such as a P–12 institution, or small, typically being less than twenty for a small primary school.

In the classification described above, it should be emphasised that a curriculum policy is not a curriculum. This distinction is particularly important in establishing the role of policy groups such as school councils or governing boards which include parents. We believe that it is appropriate for all school policy groups, including school councils, to formulate policy in areas of the curriculum, but working out the details of the curriculum itself is the responsibility of professional educators who are trained for the purpose. It should be recalled that a policy is a framework consisting of a statement of purpose and broad guidelines: parents and teachers alike, with students where appropriate, can and should make a contribution to establishing the framework.

The initial attempt to list areas for policy-making need not be exhaustive. Other titles will be added as the need arises, or annually when a review of policy is conducted. For a policy group which is getting started in this manner, it is suggested that this task be accomplished in the first or second meeting of the year. For example, the first meeting of the school year may be an organisational meeting at which new members are welcomed, interests are identified and committees are established. The second meeting may have as a major agenda item the listing of areas for policy-making in the manner described above. This list should be refined prior to the third meeting at which time the second task suggested, classifying, might be completed.

Each issue in the list of areas for policy-making should be classified as either contentious or non-contentious. A contentious issue is one for which there is major disagreement, conflict or dissatisfaction with current practice. A non-contentious issue is one for which there is general satisfaction with current practice. A different approach is used to formulate policy, depending on whether the issue is contentious or non-contentious. As described in more detail below, written policy for non-contentious issues may be formulated by a simple documentation of existing practice in the format which is agreed for statements of policy. For contentious issues, it is generally suggested that a working party be established to prepare options for consideration by the policy group. The task of classifying issues as contentious or non-contentious may be completed at the same meeting as the initial listing, or at the next meeting when a timetable for policy-making is prepared.

The task of classifying issues as contentious or non-contentious should not, in itself, become a contentious issue. In general, a brainstorming approach may be used: if at least one member of the policy group considers the issue contentious then it should be classified as such. An order of priority is established among contentious issues in the manner outlined below and issues for which only a small number see a need for change may be addressed later in the schedule for policy-making than those for which there is general agreement on the need for change. A useful rule of thumb is to regard an issue as contentious where any doubt exists. The process which is recommended for making policy on contentious issues will soon reveal the extent of dissatisfaction with current practice.

The third task is to establish a timetable for policy-making. This task will involve the setting of priorities among the issues which have been identified. Policy-writing for the non-contentious issues can be spread over one or more years. Since there is general satisfaction with current practice, there is no special urgency in documenting that practice. Writing up to four each month in the manner described in the next section is a reasonable schedule which will enable written policies on up to forty issues to be prepared over a ten-month period. The policy group may wish to establish some order of priority among the non-contentious issues.

A different schedule is required for preparing policy on contentious issues. These will require a substantial degree of consultation, since there are differences as far as ends and/or means are concerned and options must be prepared. In general, a policy group can expect to approve no more than three to five such policies each year. This will require the setting of some priorities among the contentious issues. Combining the approaches for contentious and non-contentious issues, it is evident that some careful scheduling will be required if the task of preparing a policy base is to be completed over a one- or two-year period. It will, of course, be necessary to revise this schedule as new needs and priorities emerge.

With identification, classification and scheduling of issues in the three tasks set out above, the stage is set for policy-making over the aforementioned period of one or two years. This may seem a somewhat leisurely approach to policy-making but an analysis of the amount of time available for the policy group suggests otherwise. Consider a governing body, for example, which meets ten times a year. The first meeting is usually set aside for orientation and organisation; the final meeting is usually devoted to review and social activities. Meetings must generally take place in evenings to enable working parents to attend. Evening meetings generally cannot commence before 7.30 pm, and, as experience has demonstrated, little effective decision-making can occur after 10 pm. Given that a minimum of thirty minutes must be set aside for minutes, correspondence and reports, there are at most two hours on each of eight occasions during the year when the whole policy group can devote its energies to policy-making: a total of sixteen hours a year. Actually, the amount of time is much less, since the Collaborative School Management Cycle calls for the policy group to consider and approve plans for the allocation of resources and to plan and consider the outcomes of evaluation, as well as making policy. This analysis suggests that the policy group must adopt an approach to policy-making which must be highly efficient as well as effective, with extensive use of delegation and such devices as working parties. The guidelines which follow are intended to meet these twin goals of efficiency and effectiveness in policy-making.

Making policy on non-contentious issues A simple five-step process is recommended for writing policies on non-contentious issues. The process calls for documenting existing practice in an agreed format according to a schedule over a one- or two-year period. The recommended process is outlined here.

   1   **Share the task of writing different policies among members of staff and others with expertise in the area under consideration.** For policy on mathematics, for example, the senior teacher with responsibility for mathematics should be invited to document the existing approach to the teaching of mathematics. For policy on excursions, a teacher who is frequently engaged in this approach to learning may perform the task. A parent may be involved in preparing the policy statement on issues such as reporting on pupils' progress to parents or on communication with parents. In general, these responsibilities should be dispersed widely to minimise the workload. With, say, thirty policies to prepare over a two-year period, the involvement of fifteen people means that an average of two policies per person is required, or one per person per year, an easy task given that one is merely documenting existing practice.

   2   **Each person involved in the writing of policy should be provided with a good example to serve as a guide.** The sample policy on homework in

Figure 6.1 might be useful in this regard. This example should make clear that a well-written policy should have the following characteristics:

- a maximum of one page in length;
- a brief statement of purpose which may be derived from goals or aims established earlier or contained in curriculum statements; and
- freedom from jargon and technical language, so that the policy can be read and understood by everyone in the school community.

3.   **A draft statement should be shared with others who have knowledge of the area under consideration.** For example, the senior teacher responsible for mathematics should distribute the draft among other teachers of mathematics who might suggest changes to ensure that the statement matches as closely as possible the general understanding of existing practice. Drafts of policies which apply to the school as a whole should be widely distributed for critical reaction in the same manner. One approach which ensures a minimum of paperwork is to post the draft policy on a staff noticeboard with an invitation to make suggestions for change which can be written directly on the draft. The aim of having a statement which matches existing practice should be made clear to all.

4   **Refined statements of policy should be submitted to the policy group in batches according to the timetable established earlier.** If those responsible for the statement have correctly documented existing practice, it should be expected that the policy group will readily give its approval. If it does not, the policy may be returned for amendment and resubmission. It may be that, on reading the proposed statement of policy, members of the policy group express disagreement on whether the purpose and/or guidelines are appropriate. In this case, the policy issue has moved into the domain of the contentious and it may be necessary to refer it to a working party for further investigation and the preparation of options. It is emphasised, however, that the policy group is not merely a 'rubber stamp' in the matter of policy on non-contentious issues; responsibility for adoption of the policy remains with the policy group. But the need for efficiency in the process as well as effectiveness points to the wisdom of sharing the task of drafting statements of existing practice among as large a group as possible.

5   **Once adopted by the policy group, the policy should be disseminated as widely as possible.** The statement should, of course, be included in a policy handbook which is retained by all members of the policy group and which should be made available to all members of staff and others involved in the implementation of policy. The regular channels of communication should be used in ensuring that all members of the school community are aware of policy. One practice which is recommended is the inclusion of one-page policy statements as 'centrefolds' in regular parent bulletins, with the policy selected according to issues which are important at different times of the year. For example, the policy on homework might be published early in

the year and that concerned with reporting on pupils' progress disseminated shortly before reports are issued.

Policy-making for contentious issues Policy-making for contentious issues
is clearly a more demanding and time-consuming activity since there is disagreement on the appropriateness of existing policy or on the ends and/
or means of resolving emerging issues. A ten-step process is recommended.

1   **A maximum of three to five policies a year is a target** to set for
policy-making on contentious issues, given the complexity and time-
consuming nature of the process.

2   **A working party should be established** to make recommendations
on the policy which should be adopted. Policy on policy-making should
preclude adoption at the meeting at which the issue is raised: time is
required to analyse the issue and identify options in the manner outlined
below. The working party or task force approach is considered to be a more
effective way of carrying out the process than reliance on a 'policy
subcommittee' to which all matters of policy are referred. Aside from the
special demands which dependence on a subcommittee of fixed membership will produce, it is important to share the tasks of policy-making to take
account of the contributions which different people can make.

3   **A maximum of six to eight people is recommended** for each working
party. A larger number will impair the working atmosphere of the group,
introducing formalities and limiting flexibility. Wherever possible, a smaller
number should be appointed to the working party whose responsibilities
are to analyse the issue, carry out policy research, communicate with
constituents, and identify possibilities for consideration by the policy
group.

4   **The working party should be composed of people with relatively
high levels of both expertise and stake in the issue concerned.** People with
expertise are generally those with special training and/or experience in the
issue. People with stake are generally those who will be required to
implement the policy or whose lives will in some way be affected by the
policy. For policy on homework at the secondary level, most teachers and
some parents will have high levels of expertise; teachers, parents and
students will have a high level of stake in the outcome. In most cases the
number of people with high levels of stake and expertise will exceed the
recommended maximum of six to eight people to be appointed. In these
instances it will be necessary to appoint or elect representatives of those
with high levels of expertise and stake.

Some readers may be concerned that the working party approach is
unnecessarily restrictive as far as the opportunity for collaboration is
concerned. As noted in paragraph 5 below, the working party should
consult more widely in carrying out its responsibilities and will, of course,
be limited to preparing options for consideration by the policy group which

is, after all, a collaborative body in the manner defined by the Collaborative School Management Cycle.

5   The working party should gain information from a wide range of individuals or groups with expertise or stake in the issue. Figure 6.3 provides a useful set of guidelines for the manner in which people should be involved.[5] People who have relatively high levels of expertise but relatively low levels of stake should be consulted in the policy research stage when information is sought to help clarify the issue, identify options and explore the likely consequences of those options. Since these people have special training and/or experience in the issue they are likely to make useful contributions at this point. People without special expertise but who will be required to implement the policy should be consulted to obtain their views on the merits of the various options.

A variety of methods may be chosen for consultation, ranging from informal conversations over a cup of coffee to special meetings called for the purpose, or surveys of members of the school community. The most effective approaches to the calling of meetings or the conduct of surveys are those which avoid a general invitation to all members of the school community but concentrate instead on systematic sampling by invitation. The 'shot-gun' approach rarely brings a representative sample or even a large number of people. Many schools have become sceptical of community involvement because meetings are attended by 'just a few of the same old faces'.

A recommended approach for larger schools is to divide the school community into a number of representative samples; for example a school with 100 families might be divided into five samples of twenty families, each of which is representative in terms of grade level and geographic location. A different sample might be invited to attend a meeting for each policy issue. Personalised invitations usually draw high levels of response, so over the course of a year when policy must be made on; say, five issues, it is possible to involve all families. It will, of course, be necessary to make this approach known to all members of the school community so that they will all appreciate that failure to receive an invitation does not mean that appropriate consultation is not occurring; their turn will come soon on another issue. Some schools using this approach may also wish to issue a general invitation to all, as well as the personalised invitation to a representative sample. Similar approaches may be used in distributing questionnaire surveys. It is not necessary that all in the school community receive a questionnaire; distribution to a representative sample will suffice. One additional suggestion related to questionnaire surveys concerns their length. A maximum of one page is recommended; anything longer will reduce the number of responses.

The suggestions made above are intended to provide for appropriate consultation without making repeated demands on busy people, whether they be teachers, parents or students. 'Decision saturation' may be

Figure 6.3 Alternatives for involvement for different levels of stake and expertise

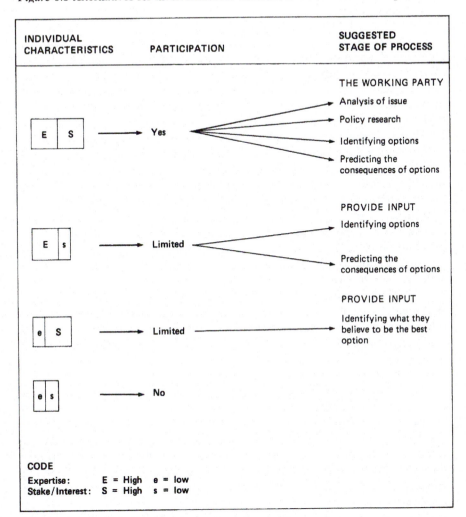

encountered if efforts are made to involve all in the school community in all decisions all of the time.

6   Perhaps the most significant departure from traditional practice is our recommendation that **the working party should prepare at least three options for consideration by the policy group.** Past reliance on discussion papers and committees has usually meant the presentation of a single recommendation. Further, with the traditional reliance on parliamentary procedure, what usually occurs is the presentation of the single re-commendation, the moving and seconding of a formal resolution for adoption, and an ensuing debate in which participants speak for or against the motion, often with a plethora of confusing amendments. Meetings often

become sharply polarised, with high levels of conflict and the inevitable winners and losers.

If options are prepared which reflect the range of views as far as ends and means are concerned, then all members of the policy group see elements of a potential policy to which they can give their support. The aim in discussion is to mix and match these elements until a policy can be put together which is not only desirable and workable, but is also acceptable to as large a number of people as possible. This is, of course, the process of building consensus and an effective way to manage the conflict which is usually inevitable in policy-making on contentious issues. These approaches to the management of conflict are explored further in chapter 12.

It seems that more and more organisations are moving to this approach to achieve not only high quality decisions through the careful examination of alternatives but also more acceptable decisions through the building of consensus. Decisions by cabinet in most states or countries now require ministers to prepare options for consideration by their colleagues. The preparation of options does not preclude the identification of a preferred course of action, but in general it is recommended that this be avoided in order to increase the chances of a consensus being built.

7   **The working party should have a good illustration of a policy statement** to assist in the writing of the various options. The example on school homework in Figure 6.1 may prove useful. Each option should conform to the criteria described in more detail earlier in the chapter, that is, each option should:

- be a maximum of one page in length;
- include a brief statement of purpose and broad guidelines as to how those purposes are to be achieved; and
- be free from jargon.

Options will vary in different ways. The purposes for each may be the same but with different guidelines. Alternatively, the options may reflect different purposes as well as having different guidelines. The Appendix contains an illustration of three policy options on the issue of special education.

One simple technique is recommended for small groups engaged in the task of drafting policy. It may be used at any point in the process when policy options are to be prepared. The need for this technique arose from the difficulties inevitably encountered by small groups endeavouring to draft a statement word by word. The process is frustrating for those whose involvement results from their expertise in the issue under consideration: they are pleased to share their ideas but are either unwilling or unable to spend more than a few minutes on the technical task of writing a policy. It is recommended that each working party appoint a recorder at the drafting stage whose task is to listen to the free flow of ideas contributed by other members of the group and then to paraphrase or summarise these ideas in a concise statement of purpose or in a series of broad guidelines. What is written can be read back to members of the group who may then suggest refinements or amendments. This technique can also be used in the preparation of policy for non-contentious issues when this task is undertaken by a group.

8   **The outcome of initial deliberations by the policy group will usually be a rough outline of policy** containing a number of elements and suggestions for change as far as statements of purpose and guidelines are concerned. It will be necessary to refer this rough outline to the working party or to the executive officer of the policy group for refinement of the policy before it is presented to the next meeting of the group.

9   **After the outline has been refined, it should be adopted as a routine matter** at the next meeting of the policy group, though further amendments may be raised when members have the opportunity to see the proposed final form in the agenda papers. This further amendment should be accepted as an often inevitable and continuing part of the political process.

10   **Once adopted, the policy should be disseminated** in the manner described in paragraph 5 of the process outlined for policy-making on non-contentious issues: everyone in the school community should have the regular opportunity to read and understand the policies of the school.

Figure 6.4 provides a checklist of the characteristics of a good statement of policy which may serve as a further guide to those involved in the process.

The Role of the Head Teacher

The critically important role of head teachers in highly effective schools was made clear in chapter 2. Findings in the Effective Resource Allocation in Schools Project reveal that thirteen of fifty-five criteria employed in ERASP to identify highly effective schools are highly dependent on the head teacher if they are to occur in Phase 1 (goal-setting and need identification) and Phase 2 (policy-making). The thirteen criteria are:

The collaborative nature of the process

D1   There is a high degree of involvement of staff in the development of school goals

D2   There are high levels of teacher involvement in decision-making at the school.

D3   There are high levels of community involvement in decision-making at the school.

CL18 There are high levels of cohesiveness and team spirit among teachers.

P4   There is opportunity for appropriate involvement of staff, students and the community in the process of resource allocation.

Figure 6.4 Characteristics of a good policy statement

A GOOD SCHOOL POLICY

1 A good school policy is based on a clear statement of belief or purpose and arises from goals which have been adopted for the school. ☐

2 A good school policy contains guidelines which provide a framework for achieving clearly stated purposes on a substantive issue. ☐

3 A good school policy tells what is wanted of units or individuals in the school. ☐

4 A good school policy tells why certain things are wanted of the units or individuals in the school. ☐

5 A good school policy provides a clear basis for the preparation and implementation of rules and procedures. ☐

6 A good school policy provides positive direction for teachers and administrators, but does not, and should not, prescribe methods for arriving at an end result. ☐

7 A good school policy permits administrators and teachers to make interpretations in such a way as to adjust for changing conditions without making any basic changes in policy. ☐

8 A good school policy provides a standard for evaluating performance. ☐

9 A good school policy on an issue is a statement which does not exceed one page. ☐

10 A good school policy is free of jargon, being written in a style which is readily understood by all members of the school community. ☐

Goal-setting and policy-making

CU1   The school has clearly stated educational goals.

CU2   The school has a well-planned, balanced and organised programme which meets the needs of students.

CU3   The school has a programme which provides students with required skills.

CL1   The school has a set of values which are considered important.

CL6   There are expectations at the school that all students will do well.

CL8   The head teacher, teachers and students have high expectations for achievement.

P1   Educational needs are identified and placed in an order of priority.

P2   The order of priority takes full account of local as well as system needs.

In terms of the policy process itself, the head teacher's role for all kinds of policy group may be best described as a policy initiator, policy orchestrator, policy analyst, policy researcher, policy implementer and policy evaluator. In the role of policy initiator, the head teacher is a leader: the effective head teacher takes the lead in sensing the need for policy, and, using expertise and experience, proposes options through participation or consultation with working parties. In the roles of policy orchestrator, analyst and researcher, the head teacher facilitates contributions from interest groups, works with members of staff and others to analyse the nature and consequences of the various alternatives, and generally provides information to the policy group which may assist in the formulation of policy. The precise nature of the role will, of course, vary according to leadership style and circumstance. A more detailed examination of leadership in the self-managing school is contained in chapter 11.

SUMMARY
THE POLICY-MAKING PROCESS

IDENTIFICATION AND CLASSIFICATION OF ISSUES

The policy group:

1. lists by title issues for which it would like to have written policy;
2. classifies issues as either contentious or non-contentious according to the extent to which there is major disagreement on, or dissatisfaction with, existing practice;
3. establishes a timetable for policy-making, with a different approach for contentious and non-contentious issues.

FOR NON-CONTENTIOUS ISSUES

DOCUMENT EXISTING PRACTICE AS FOLLOWS:

1. Share the task of writing different policies among members of staff and others with expertise.

2. Provide a good example for policy-writers to follow:
   - one page long;
   - statement of purpose and broad guidelines included;
   - free of jargon.

3. Refine draft policies on the basis of critical reaction from those who have experience in or knowledge of the issue.

4. Submit refined policies to the policy group in batches for adoption or further refinement.

5. Disseminate policies regularly to all in the school community.

FOR CONTENTIOUS ISSUES

PREPARE OPTIONS AS FOLLOWS:

1. Set a maximum of 3–5 policies per year.
2. Appoint a working party for each issue.
3. Have a maximum of 6–8 people in each working party.
4. Appoint to the working party people with both stake and expertise.
5. The working party should gain information from a wide range of individuals and groups with expertise or stake.
6. Formulate at least three options to help build consensus.
7. Each option should be based on a good example as far as format is concerned.
8. Elements of consensus should be refined in a well-written statement.
9. Adopt the policy.
10. Disseminate the policy.

ROLE OF THE HEAD TEACHER

- Policy initiator
- Policy orchestrator
- Policy analyst
- Policy researcher
- Policy implementer
- Policy evaluator

---

7   *Planning and Budgeting*

Planning and budgeting involve translating policies provided by the policy group into programmes for students. This task is carried out by the head teacher and staff in programme teams. For each programme this involves developing a plan for implementation which is an outcome of the relevant policies. Summaries of the purposes of the programme and the broad guidelines by which these purposes are to be achieved are presented with the plan to demonstrate the relationship between policy-making and planning. The resources required to implement the plan as a learning programme for students are then identified. These resources are costed to form a programme budget. An outline of a plan for programme evaluation is also provided, indicating how the effectiveness and efficiency of the programme might be ascertained. Planning and budgeting for a programme can then be described as:

1   using relevant policies, identifying and summarising the purposes to be achieved in the programme;
2   using relevant policies, identifying and summarising the broad guidelines by which the purposes are to be achieved;
3   preparing a plan for implementation that will ensure the programme is consistent with the broad guidelines;
4   identifying and costing the resources required in the plan for implementation;
5   preparing a plan for programme evaluation.

Before proceeding to consider these tasks in detail, it will be useful to illustrate each task with an example from a specific programme. A Special Education Programme from a school catering for primary and secondary children has been selected. The actual policy on special education is not reprinted in this chapter but is given in the Appendix. In Figure 7.1 the purposes of the programme have been clearly stated.

These purposes refer to the kinds of student for which the programme is designed, the diagnosis of their problems, and the determination of

Figure 7.1 A sample purpose for special education

PROGRAMME: Special Education

1. **Purpose**: We aim to have all children achieve their full potential in all areas of development during their school years. We recognise, however, that some children fail to achieve their potential due to some specific disability which affects their capacity to learn. A purpose of the Special Education Programme is to identify these children, determine the nature of their disability and to devise and implement plans to overcome the disability where possible.
   A further purpose of the programme is to identify children who have a very low potential, and have great difficulty in learning, and then to assist these children to achieve their potential by designing individual programmes for them and providing the necessary intensive help.

Figure 7.2 Sample guidelines for special education

PROGRAMME: Special Education

2. **Broad guidelines**: Children with specific disabilities or generally low learning potential will be identified through consultation amongst the relevant people. Fundamental to the programme is the philosophy that children should remain part of their peer group in as many respects as possible, and that by its very nature, special education requires a highly individualised approach to achieve maximum benefits. Those who design the teaching programme must, therefore, ensure that the programme is appropriate for each individual. A programme could involve extraction as part of a group, or a totally individualised programme to operate within the normal classroom.
   The main thrust of the programme will be towards the younger children in need of special help so that problems can be overcome or reduced as early as possible. It is recognised, however, that older children can need special education, and that this need should be met if possible.
   It is vital that opportunities are provided for close liaison between the special education teachers and the classroom teacher of each child involved.

---

corrective actions. The broad guidelines by which the purposes are to be achieved are summarised in Figure 7.2.

The broad guidelines indicate in a general way how the children will be identified. They also highlight the need for these students to remain part of their peer groups. Their learning difficulties, and how these difficulties are to be corrected, are approached by taking into account the individuality of each student. The broad guidelines also bring out the need to focus the programme on the younger students involved. The plan for implementation enabling the purposes to be achieved within these broad guidelines is shown in Figure 7.3.

This plan provides for the employment of the equivalent of 1½ full-time special education teachers and indicates the space needed by the staff and students involved. The work of associated staff is also indicated. The

Figure 7.3 A sample plan for implementation of a Special Education Programme

---

PROGRAMME: Special Education

3. **Plan for implementation**
   3.1 The equivalent of one full-time and one half-time special education teachers will be employed.
   Three rooms will be provided as teaching areas for extraction purposes, at least two of which will also be set up as resource centres for special education materials.

   3.2 Senior staff will supervise the programme.

   3.3 A part-time aide will be provided for the programme to assist in the preparation of learning materials.

   3.4 Sufficient materials and equipment will be provided for the effective operation of the programme, including structured language and maths materials, manipulative equipment, art and craft supplies, and part-purchase of an additional large-print typewriter.

   3.5 Additional stocks of appropriate reading materials will be provided to enhance the effective operation of the programme, particularly in the areas of high interest/low ability reading material for upper primary and lower secondary students, and teachers' resource material.

Figure 7.4 A sample plan for minor evaluation in special education

---

PROGRAMME: Special Education

5. **Evaluation (minor)**
   Keeping individual records for each child will provide the basis for evaluation reports. These reports will be given to teachers and parents although their form will vary according to the situation.
   The criteria used to determine children in need of the programme may also be used to measure the progress of the total group and the programmes effectiveness.

---

type and nature of materials to support the work of the teachers and students are outlined. These include a variety of materials specifically related to the field of special education. It should be noted that it is planned to give special attention to material needs for an identified age-group of students. This is clearly a priority for the allocation of resources for the year in question.

Further details of the resources required to support the plan in its implementation are given in Figure 7.5.

In the 'Resources required' section, the teaching, supervision and aide staff components of the plan are set out in greater detail and the respective costs calculated. The costs of the required support materials and books are also detailed. The plan for the later evaluation of the programme is given in Figure 7.4.

Figure 7.5 A sample listing of resources required for a Special Education Programme

PROGRAMME: Special Education

4. Resources required

Planning elements	Teaching staff	Non-teaching staff	Materials & equipment	Books	Services
4.1 Teaching units provided by special education staff 37 units × $595/unit	22 015				
Related units of Planning, Marking and Organization (PMO) 9 units × $595/unit	5 355				
4.2 Senior supervision of the programme by infant mistress 2 units × $738/unit	1 476				
4.3 Provision of teacher aide services to develop support materials 2 hrs × $7.22 × 40 weeks		577			
4.4 Support items for students' use			750		150
4.5 Books for students and staff to use, including a special focus for 1985				300	
	$28 846	577	750	300	150

Programme total = $30 623

The plan for evaluation refers to information-gathering throughout the year and reporting to parents and other teachers. It also indicates a way in which this information may be of value when looking at the programme's effectiveness and efficiency in meeting the needs of the children concerned.

All sections of the Special Education Programme's plan and budget are brought together and shown in completed form in Figure 7.6. It should be noted that the actual presentation gives further details of senior responsibility for the programme and lists the members of the programme team. All these staff work in the programme and it is their professional role to

Figure 7.6 A sample programme plan and budget for a Special Education Programme

---

PROGRAMME: Special Education   RESPONSIBILITY: M.S.   CODE: 173

---

1. **Purpose:** We aim to have all children achieve their full potential in all areas of development during their school years. We recognise, however, that some children fail to achieve their potential due to some specific disability which affects their capacity to learn. A purpose of the Special Education Programme is to identify these children, determine the nature of their disability and to devise and implement plans to overcome the disability where possible.
A further purpose of the programme is to identify children who have overall a very low potential, and have great difficulty in learning, and to assist these children to achieve their potential by designing individual programmes for them and providing the necessary intensive help.

---

2. **Broad guidelines:** Children with specific disabilities or general low learning potential will be identified through consultation amongst the relevant people. Fundamental to the programme is the philosophy that children should remain part of their peer group in as many respects as possible, and that by its very nature, special education requires a highly individualised approach to achieve maximum benefits. Those who design the teaching programme must, therefore, ensure that the programme is appropriate for each individual. A programme could involve extraction as part of a group, or a totally individualised programme to operate within the normal classroom.
The main thrust of the programme will be towards the younger children in need of special help so that problems can be overcome or reduced as early as possible. It is recognised, however, that older children can need special education, and that this need should be met if possible.
It is vital that opportunities are provided for close liaison between the special education teachers and the classroom teacher of each child involved.

---

3. **Plan for implementation:**
   3.1 The equivalent of one full-time and one half-time special education teachers will be employed.
   Three rooms will be provided as teaching areas for extraction purposes, at least two of which will also be set up as resource centres for special education materials.

   3.2 Senior staff will supervise the programme.

   3.3 A part-time aide will be provided for the programme to assist in the preparation of learning materials.

   3.4 Sufficient materials and equipment will be provided for the effective operation of the programme, including structured language and maths materials, manipulative equipment, art and craft supplies, and part-purchase of an additional large-print typewriter.

   3.5 Additional stocks of appropriate reading materials will be provided to enhance the effective operation of the programme particularly in the areas of high interest/low ability reading material for upper primary and lower secondary students, and teachers' resource material.

Figure 7.6 cont.

---

4. Resources required:

Planning elements	Teaching staff	Non-teaching staff	Materials & equipment	Books	Services
4.1 Teaching units provided by special education staff 37 units × $595/unit	22 015				
Related units of Planning, Marking and Organisation (PMO) 9 units × $595/unit	5 355				
4.2 Senior supervision of the programme by infant mistress 2 units × $738/unit	1 476				
4.3 Provision of teacher aide services to develop support materials 2 hrs × $7.22 × 40 weeks		577			
4.4 Support items for students' use			750		150
4.5 Books for students and staff to use, including a special focus for 1985				300	
	$28 846	577	750	300	150

Programme total = $30 623

---

5. **Evaluation (minor):** Keeping individual records for each child will provide the basis for evaluation reports. These reports will be given to teachers and parents although their form will vary according to the situation.

The criteria used to determine children in need of the programme may also be used to measure the progress of the total group and thus the effectiveness of the programme.

Programme team:
Liz Brient   Michele Davison   Trudy Drukin   Marilyn Spinks   Carol Titley

---

prepare the plan and budget as a reflection of the policy made by the policy group. As well, it will be the responsibility of this team to implement the programme following approval and adoption of the plans and budget.

Linking Policies to Programmes

The example of the Special Education Programme illustrates the view that policies are translated into educational programmes for students through planning and budgeting. In this illustration the programme can be directly linked to the policy. However, this link from policy to programme cannot always be easily made even though it is fundamental to the collaborative approach. Policy-makers need to have evidence that their policies are being implemented and without directly linking policies to programmes, such evidence can be hard to find.

The problems involved in linking all policies to programmes can be illustrated by considering the definitions of policies and programmes and then considering further examples. Policies are statements about substantive issues, including the curriculum, that contain the purposes to be achieved and the broad guidelines by which they can be achieved. Policy statements are prepared about such issues as mathematics, language development, social science, physical education, assessment of students, discipline, and reporting to parents. Programmes are natural divisions of the curriculum that reflect how the school is organised and how teachers work and children learn. Just as the set of policies will differ from school to school, so will the set of programmes. Some policies will link directly to programmes; for example, the policies on mathematics and physical education will be reflected in Mathematics and Physical Education Programmes, respectively, in most schools. However, this will not always be the case with all curriculum-related policies in all schools.

In a secondary school there may be programmes for the areas of language and social science, as direct outcomes of their respective policies, because these programmes are taught by specialist staff. However, these same curriculum areas are usually approached in a different manner in the primary schools. With the emphasis on language in these schools, it is unlikely that planning for separate Language Development Programmes and Social Science Programmes will really reflect how the children learn and how the teachers work. In primary schools, it may, therefore, be necessary to consider having groups of curriculum-related policies linked to age-grade programmes of a general nature, such as prep-to-year-2 General Studies, and year-3-to-4 General Studies. These programmes reflect how the school is organised. Curriculum policies reflected across all age-grade programmes provide the basis for continuity and co-ordination. There will, of course, be some programmes clearly linked to specific policies in both types of schools. Physical Education and Music are possible examples. Experience has shown that the highest degree of effectiveness is achieved if no particular teacher works in more than three specific curriculum-related programmes. Naturally all staff work in programmes such as Administration and Pastoral Care.

In linking policies and programmes, it is also necessary to consider such policies as assessment of students, discipline, and reporting to parents. These policies are rarely reflected in specific programmes within the school but relate to how programmes operate.

It can be seen that the linking of policies to programmes is possible, but there is an obvious need for these links to be clearly identified and demonstrated to all concerned. The teachers in the programme teams require this information to ensure that they are using the appropriate information for their programme planning. The policy group requires this information to check that policies are being implemented and to enable a realistic approach to budget approval to be adopted.

Ways of linking policies to programmes

The simplest way to achieve the link between policies and programmes is to identify a programme structure for the school and then to list the relevant policies for each programme. In most cases one of the policies will be the key policy for the programme. Two examples of this approach are shown in Figure 7.7. One example concerns a secondary school, while the other relates to a primary school. It should be noted that the relevant policies are listed for only one programme in each case. A secondary school may have thirty or more programmes, and primary schools may have eight to twenty-five programmes, depending on the size of the school. This method of demonstrating the links between policies and programmes is therefore only appropriate in small schools because the information must fit on only one page so that it can be understood at a glance. The fact that many policies are linked to more than one programme in all schools suggests that the information can be represented in grid. A sample approach for primary schools is shown in Figure 7.8. This example does not attempt to show all possible programmes and policies for a primary school; it only attempts to indicate how the links between policies and programmes might be represented. Different schools need to approach this issue in different ways to suit their own situations but we consider that, irrespective of the philosophy of the school and its approach to organisation, its programme structure and links with policies can be shown in this way. It is emphasised, however, that the way programmes are organised across the policy areas will be different for each school.

Another approach to demonstrating the links between policies and programmes is shown in Figure 7.9. This approach is probably more applicable to secondary schools where the relationship between curriculum policies

Figure 7.7 An illustration of the policy-programme link

PRIMARY SCHOOL	HIGH SCHOOL
PROGRAMME: Years 3 to 4	**PROGRAMME: Years 7 to 10**
Language Development	**Technical Subjects**

RELATED POLICIES   RELATED POLICIES

*   P–6 language development   *   Technical Subjects

   P–6 creative writing   7–8   manual arts

   P–6 oral language   9–10 wood work

   P–6 written language   9–10 metal work

   P–6 spelling   9–10 technical drawing

   P–6 handwriting   9–10 technology

   Reading for enjoyment

   Assessment of students   *   Selection of optional subjects

                              Assessment of students' homework

*   Key Policy   The School Certificate

                              Discipline

                              Formation of classes

                   *   Key Policies

---

and programmes is more clear-cut because of the ways in which these schools are organised. The example shown actually refers to a school which encompasses kindergarten, infant, primary and secondary education in the one integrated setting. Policies and programmes are clearly identified and the relationships between them are indicated by circles at intersecting points on the grid. The key relationships for each programme are shown by a triangle rather than a circle.

Linking policy priorities and programme priorities

The various approaches considered demonstrate the relationships between policies and programmes to assist in planning and budgeting. But a further aspect of this relationship needs to be considered. It is recommended that the policy group determine priorities for policies and assign each policy a specific priority rating. This rating assists the programme teams when they are planning and budgeting. When a relationship between policy and respective programme priorities has been established, it is possible to allocate resources to programmes in accordance with the policy group's priorities.

    If each policy were reflected in its own specific programme, this relationship would be easily identified. However, with some policies reflected in several programmes and with the different policies concerned with any one programme belonging to different categories of priority, the

Figure 7.8 Sample policy-programme links in a primary school

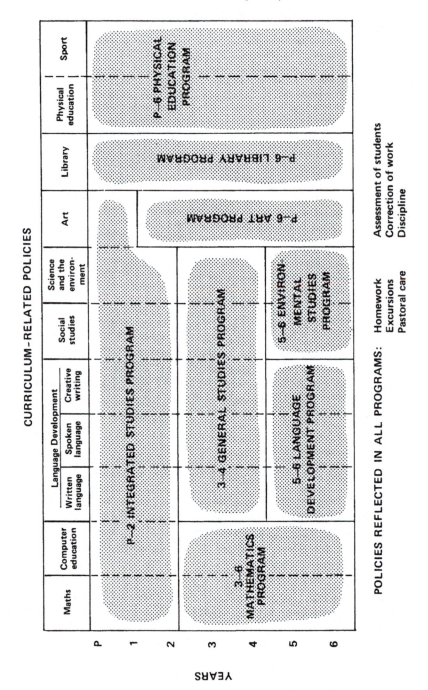

Figure 7.9 A sample policy-programme grid

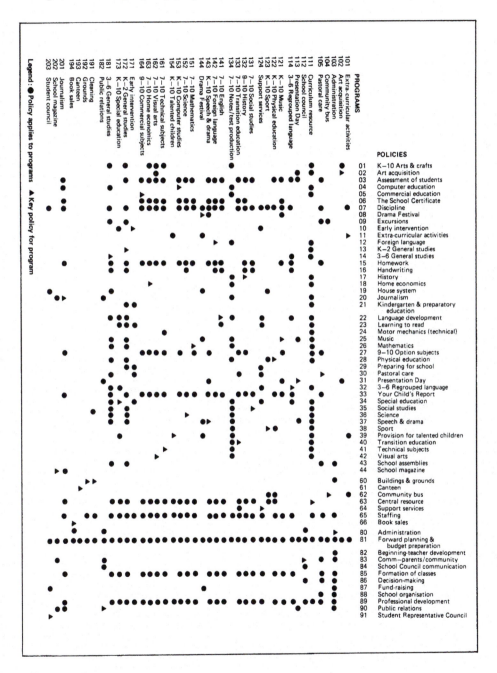

situation is not quite so clear. The problem can be resolved by assigning the same priority to a program as to its key policy.

Plans and Budgets

Format for presentation of programme plans and budgets

It is recommended that a common format be adopted for the presentation of all programme plans and budgets. An example is shown in Figure 7.10. This example will be referred to in detail later in the chapter. It should be noted that information is provided under.the following headings:

Purpose
Broad guidelines
Plan for implementation
Resources required (budget)
Evaluation
Programme team

For various reasons, formats will differ from school to school but using a standard format within any one school has certain advantages. A standard format greatly assists readers because they know where to look in any programme for specific information 'somewhere within the plan and budget'. This clear placement of related information also assists in making comparisons between programmes as information is provided in parallel form. The common format can also be used to 'define the task' for the programme teams involved in the planning and budgeting in that it is quite clear as to what information is to be provided and how it is to be provided.

Whatever the actual format adopted by any school it is strongly recommended that all programme plans and budgets be limited to two printed pages or less in their presentation. This has two main advantages. It limits the amount of writing and allows anyone involved with a programme to understand the whole plan at the one time. This speed and ease of appraisal is beneficial to members of the programme team and policy group.

Preparing the plan and budget

The first task in preparing a programme plan and budget is to provide a summary of the information contained in the relevant policies. This is provided under the headings of 'Purposes' and 'Broad guidelines' in keeping with these two key aspects of a policy. The 'Purposes' section contains a succinct summary of the intentions of the programme. The 'Broad guidelines' section contains a summary of the most important guidelines by which the purposes can be achieved.

Figure 7.10 A sample format for plan and budget proposals

SCHOOL: PROGRAMME: RESPONSIBILITY: CODE:	4 RESOURCES REQUIRED
1 · PURPOSE	
2 BROAD GUIDELINES	
3 PLAN FOR IMPLEMENTATION	EVALUATION
page 1	page 2

It could be argued that the summarisation of this information and presentation in the programme plan is unnecessary because it is available in complete form from the policy documents or the School Policy Handbook. However, the summarised presentation serves two purposes. Firstly, the task of preparation ensures that the members of the programme team are familiar with the relevant policy statements. They have used the policy-programme relationships and priorities as the starting point for programme planning. Secondly, when the programme plan is complete, no one is able to appraise the plan and budget without immediate reference to the relevant policy information. This approach in presentation continues the link between policy-making and planning.

The 'Plan for implementation' details what is going to be done, who is going to do it, when, how often, with what and where. This plan is a direct outcome of the broad guidelines. It is developed as a series of planning elements and these planning elements are listed in order of priority. This approach is an aid later in the process when the budget is 'balanced': if all the resources required by a programme cannot be provided, then those least important to the operation of the programme will be the ones omitted.

The planning elements identify the 'Resources required' to implement the plan successfully. The identification of these resources and the estimation of their cost represent the programme budget. The identification of the resources required and their costing is carried out separately for each planning element. The costing for each element is indicated against categories of expenditure such as teaching staff, non-teaching staff, travel, materials and services, and totals calculated for each category of expenditure for the whole programme. Accuracy in both identifying and costing the resources required for each planning element is necessary. Programme teams can be assisted in the tasks of identifying the resources required by the design and use of checklists that can be applied to each planning element. At the same time staff need access to information on updated costs for the various types of resources.

A sample checklist to help identify resources required for the planning elements is shown in Figure 7.11. The checklist enables the programme team to answer a series of questions concerning each planning element that relate to the resources that might be required. Schools can design such checklists to suit their own purposes. Sample questions in a checklist may include:

1 What are the staff requirements to implement the element?
2 Staff development? Will relief or emergency teachers by required to facilitate this development?
3 What are the material and equipment requirements of the element?
4 Does the element require the provision of new books?
5 Will students or staff need to travel?
6 What services are needed? Copier? Telephone?

Figure 7.11 A sample checklist for identification of resources required

Details of planning element	Staff requirements	Professional development	Materials & equipment	Books	Travel	Services	Reserve

A SAMPLE CHECKLIST FOR IDENTIFICATION OF RESOURCES REQUIRED

7 Is it prudent to set aside a reserve to cater for unforeseen circumstances?

With 'Resources required' identified and costed, the next task to be addressed is programme evaluation. Information is provided in this section as to how the effectiveness and/or efficiency of the programme might be measured. Information on effectiveness and efficiency alone is not sufficient for judging educational programmes. Information relating to priorities and values is also important. Figure 7.11 contains a summary of the most important guidelines by which the purposes can be achieved.

The presentation of the programme plan and budget is completed by the section listing the members of the programme team. This recognizes that there is 'ownership' and 'commitment' to the plan by the team members.

Further examples of programme plans and budgets

An example of a K–2 General Studies Programme is shown in Figure 7.12 using the format that has been described. The key policy relating to this programme is contained in the Appendix. It should be noted that the 'Purpose' and 'Broad guidelines' statements are summaries of the policy and clearly indicate what the programme is designed to achieve and how, in general terms, this is going to be done.

The 'Plan for implementation' identifies groups of children and therefore the staff required. The nature of the curriculum areas involved is also indicated. Further planning elements list the supervision of the programme, requirements for materials and equipment, and the need for assistance from a teacher aide. The necessity for assistance from aides in other classes and in preparing learning materials is identified in another element. Later elements identify special equipment requirements for that year and the need for professional development with a special focus for the teachers concerned in the programme.

'Resources required' are costed separately for each element. Teaching services units are calculated and costed along with units of supervision involving a senior member of staff. It is not necessary to actually 'cost' teachers, although many choose to do so. This aspect of programme budgeting is fully considered in chapter 13. Attention is drawn to Items 4.3, 4.6 and 4.7 which all involve materials and equipment. Even though the sums involved are substantial ($4,350, $900 and $450) the actual materials and equipment are not specified in detail. It is considered the role of the specialist staff to select the actual items as required and as needs emerge throughout the year once the budget has been approved.

An example of a Technical Programme for years 7 to 10 is shown in Figure 7.13, again using the format for presentation described earlier. The key policy relating to this programme is contained in the Appendix. The similarity between the nature of the planning elements in this programme and the previous programme should be noted. The first element lists the curriculum areas involved, numbers of classes and time allocated. Parallel information in 'Resources required' is used to identify the teaching staff required. An interesting aspect of this programme is Element 3.6 which relates to the purchase of a large item of equipment as part of a continuous replacement system. The lathe is to be purchased over a two-year period with $2,000 being set aside in this, the first of those two years.

The nature of the planning task

The planning tasks carried out by the programme teams can be described as (a) collecting and interpreting information from the policy statements and priorities, and then listing a series of elements that will allow the programme to work; (b) identifying the resources that will be required; and (c) costing these resources. Most of these tasks are already done by teachers but the work is often approached in a fragmented manner. Programme planning and budgeting as part of Collaborative School Management' ensures that maximum benefit is gained from the time staff spend planning, by integrating the planning in a careful way with the other aspects of school management and by completing the overall planning task at the same time each year.

Writing the programme plan and budget can present difficulties for programme teams but experience has shown that, as with policy-writing by groups, the task is best approached by appointing one member of the programme team as recorder. While the other team members raise, discuss, discard and adopt ideas, the recorder does not participate directly but concentrates on writing down a simple, clear statement of the plan being developed by the others. If a number of meetings are held, then this role can be passed around. Eventually a written plan is produced for all to consider and then to modify and/or adopt. As with policy-making, the use of appropriate language is important. The completed plan must be free of jargon, and easily understood not only by the team involved but also by the policy group and other members of the school community. A major outcome of programme planning and budgeting is a series of simple, brief, clearly written plans and budgets for all programmes throughout the school that are available to all. This openness of information not only creates awareness in staff of the overall school operation but builds trust among all concerned.

Approval of the plans and budgets

With the completion of plans and budgets for all programmes, it is possible to produce a programme budget summary for the school. An example of this summary chart is given in the Appendix. This summary identifies amounts

Figure 7.12 A sample programme plan and budget for K–2 General Studies

---

ROSEBERY DISTRICT HIGH SCHOOL   **1985 BUDGET**

PROGRAMME: K–2 General Studies   **RESPONSIBILITY: M.S.**   **CODE: 172**

---

1. **Purpose:** K–2 General Studies embraces the following curriculum areas — language, maths, science, social studies, art, music°, speech and drama°, and physical education°. (°Complementary to the specialist services provided.)
   The purpose of the programme is to use, and integrate where possible, the above curriculum areas, with a particularly strong emphasis on language, as a basis for development of each child as a whole person — taking into consideration his or her potential for physical, intellectual, social and emotional growth.
   A further purpose of the programme is to cater for the individuality of children. Thus it will take into account, and build on, the learning that has already taken place prior to the child entering school, and will continue to allow learning to proceed at the pace best suited to the individual child.

2. **Broad guidelines:** Fundamental to the nature of the K–2 General Studies Programme is the concept of children as learners through direct experience; hence the teaching programme will reflect an activity-centred approach which takes into account the interests and capabilities of the children and provides related 'real' experiences. These experiences, to be most beneficial, must take place in an environment which provides a sense of security for the children and at the same time is stimulating and dynamic.
   The children's day will be designed to provide a balance appropriate to the level of development between (a) all curriculum areas; (b) individual and shared experiences. The emphasis will move gradually within K–2 from mostly individual activities to an equal balance of individual and shared activities.
   Parents will be encouraged to be closely involved in their children's education through the most appropriate means. This will vary according to different family circumstances.

3. **Plan for implementation:**
   3.1 Children will be divided into five teaching groups on the basis of chronological age, as follows:
   kindergarten — 1 × 45 children (approximately)
       prep — 1 × 23 children (approximately)
       year 1 & 2 — 3 × 23 (approximately)
   Each group will be allocated a teacher and provided with a classroom adequately furnished for the numbers.
   Each teacher will take responsibility for teaching all curriculum subjects. As an adjunct to the daily classroom programme, P–2 will have specialist teaching time allocated in the areas of physical education and music/drama for three units per class per week.
   3.2 Senior supervision of the programme will be provided.
   3.3 Each teacher will be provided with a wide range of materials and equipment (classroom-based) so that the K–2 programme can fulfil its purpose of catering for individual differences, and integration of curriculum areas.
   3.4 A part-time aide will be employed specifically for kindergarten to assist the teacher and to take a major responsibility for organising the weekly parent–child sessions.
   3.5 A part-time aide will be provided in the P–2 area and will be used by teachers either to assist in the classroom or to prepare learning materials.

3.6 An allocation of money for minor materials will be provided to allow special class projects such as cooking or photography to proceed.

3.7 Special provision will be made for 1985 with respect to materials and equipment to continue to bring maths resources up to a level which will enable programmes to proceed as planned.

3.8 A professional development programme will be devised which will focus on developing teacher skills in the area of reading.

3.9 An extraction system will be devised to assist teachers with students.

4 Resources required:

Planning elements	Teaching staff	Non-teaching staff	Relief days	Materials & equipment	Minor materials	Services	Reserve
4.1 Teaching groups K: 1 × 28 = 28 units P–2: 4 × 27 = 108 units total = 136 units 136 × $595/unit	80 920						
Related units of Preparation, Marking and Organisation (PMO) 34 + 4* units × $595/unit	22 610						
4.2 Infant Mistress supervision 6 units × $738/unit	4 428						
4.3 Materials and equipment				4 350		150	300
4.4 Kindergarten aide 23 hours/week		6 642					
4.5 P–2 Teacher aide 10 hours × $7.22 × 40 weeks		2 888					
4.6 Minor materials for class/teacher use 5 × $30 × 3 terms					450		
4.7 Maths equipment				900			
4.8 Professional development 5 days relief			380				
4.9 Extraction system teaching: 4 units	2 380						
PMO: 1 unit	595						
	$110 933	9 530	380	5 250	450	150	300

(* Additional PMO units to reduce teachers' loadings.) Total = $126 993

5 Evaluation: (minor)

Evaluation of the programme will be largely subjective in nature and will monitor the development of concepts, skills and attitudes in the curriculum areas listed earlier, through a system of weekly reviews, child studies, checklists and reporting to parents in both the verbal and written form.

Programme team:	Sharon Ansell	Kim Jansson	Cheryl Murray
Trudy Durkin	Margaret Johnson	Marcell Norton	Marilyn Spinks

Figure 7.13 A sample programme plan and budget for 7–10 Technical Subjects

---

ROSEBERY DISTRICT HIGH SCHOOL   **1985 BUDGET**

PROGRAMME: 7–10 Technical Subjects   **RESPONSIBILITY: P.B.**   **CODE: 161**

---

1. **Purpose:** Technical Subjects can be defined as a programme incorporating wood work, metal work, technical drawing and technology for years 7–10. The programme will allow students the opportunity to develop knowledge and understanding of a wide range of materials, tools, equipment and processes unique to the area. Courses will be concerned with identifying and developing those areas of technical knowledge and skill that will be of assistance to the individual in both a vocational and recreational sense.

2. **Broad guidelines:** The programme will be activity-based. Children will be given the opportunity to think creatively through participation in the design of projects. Children will be encouraged to look at and analyse their work critically, and this will lead to further development of communication skills. Constant reference to and explanation of safe working practices will be a feature in all aspects of the programme. The sequence and detail of the tasks undertaken will be organised according to the level of co-ordination and expertise displayed by the individual. The logical result of this practice will be reflected in the levels offered in years 9 and 10 where the options offered allow specialisation to occur.

3. **Plan for implementation:**
   3.1 Students in years 7 and 8 will be divided into four groups and each group will study two units each of manual arts and technical drawing. Students in years 9 and 10 will be offered metal work, technology, wood work, and technical drawing as options. Year 10 classes will be allocated four units. Year 9 classes will be allocated three units and four units if on the same line as advanced mathematics.
   3.2 Provide supervision for four units per week.
   3.3 Provide materials and equipment for classes.
   3.4 Duplicate notes and testing materials and print relevant texts for students' use.
   3.5 Provide minor materials required to operate the programme.
   3.6 Through a major equipment replacement programme over two years, purchase a metal lathe of suitable size and quality to enable all the operations required of it to be performed.
   3.7 Provide two relief days to enable staff to participate in seminars or inter-school visits.
   3.8 Telephone charges in relation to ordering of materials and equipment.

---

4 **Resources required:**

Planning elements	Teaching staff	Relief days	Materials & equipment	Minor materials	Services

---

4.1 Teaching groups
   7–8 manual arts
   8 × 2 units = 16 units
   7–8 technical drawing
   8 × 2 units = 16 units

9–10 metal work
5 groups = 18 units

9–10 wood work
5 groups = 18 units

9–10 technology
5 groups = 17 units

9–10 technical drawing
4 groups = 15 units

total = 100 units

100 units × \$595/unit	59 500				
Preparation, Marking and Organization (PMO) 25 + 4* units × \$595/unit	17 255				
4.2 S.M. supervision 4 units × \$738/unit	2 952				
4.3 Materials and equipment			5 200		
4.4 Duplication service					1 200
4.5 Minor materials				500	
4.6 'Hercus' 2 600 metal lathe			2 000		
4.7 Teacher development		152			
4.8 Telephone					100
	\$79 707	152	7 200	500	1 300

Total = \$88 859

(* Additional PMO units to reduce teachers' loadings.)

5 **Evaluation (major)**
1   Identify inadequacies and problem areas as an outcome of discussion on the purpose and nature of the programme.
2   Identify those areas of the programme that have been very successful in meeting the needs of individual students.
3   Consider the results of year 10 students on self-moderation tests in wood work and metal work.

Programme team:

Craig Allen	Peter Bradley	Ron Kamphius
Phil Parish	Allan Snare	Steve Tammens

required for expenditure in categories for each programme. These categories include teaching staff, travel, book materials and services. It is then possible to calculate the total expenditure required for the school in each of these categories and finally the total cost required for the operation of the school. A comparison of this figure with the previously determined total of resources to be available to the school usually shows a deficit of funds available and the necessity for reconciliation of 'resources required' with 'resources available' to achieve a balanced budget. It is surprising how close the difference can be in schools with only limited experience of preparing programme budgets and where the programme teams know the total resources to be available to the whole school before the planning and budgeting task is commenced. In one such school in 1984 the difference was $40,000, with total resources amounting to $1,123,072. In the same school in 1985 the difference was $3,900 with total resources amounting to $1,316,991. Irrespective of the size of the difference between 'resources required' and 'resources available' it is necessary to make a reconciliation and to achieve a balanced budget. This is easily accomplished by carrying out the following process.

1   Check all programmes to ensure that planning and costings are realistic and in line with policies, and make adjustments accordingly.
2   Identify the lower-priority programmes and remove some of the lower-priority planning elements within those programmes. This process could be modified for higher-priority programmes.
3   Achieve a final balance by subtracting minor amounts from lower-priority programmes and requiring the relevant programme teams to make adjustments within their programmes accordingly.

It can be seen that this task is not undertaken in a way that could be misinterpreted or treated with suspicion or even hostility by those involved. In all cases reference is made to previously established priorities both between and within programmes. The desirability of all information being available to all concerned in school management, and in an easily understood form, is again emphasised.

The question of who carries out the budget reconciliation will be addressed by different schools in different ways. It might appear to be an obvious role for the policy group and this could quite easily be the case, but it is a task most easily undertaken by a relatively small group of people. This could be the senior staff of the school, the head teacher or the finance committee. It is not necessarily a task for a finance committee: although the task is to balance money, the real decisions being made concern the curriculum. In general, we recommend that the task be undertaken by the head teacher and senior staff of the school. It is relatively unimportant, however, because the reconciliation only provides the base for budget approval which is clearly designated as a role for the policy group.

An important part of programme planning and budgeting is the policy group's approval of the budget. It is at this point in the cycle that the policy-makers clearly have responsibility for ensuring that programme plans and budgets accurately reflect established policies and priorities. The process is the same, irrespective of the composition of the policy group. Changes are made and the balanced budget maintained to produce a set of educational programmes proposed by teachers, judged to be in line with accepted policies and finally adopted for the forthcoming year. This set of educational plans is then in place to guide the learning of students and the work of teachers.

8   *Implementing*

Policy-making, involving the identification of purposes and the broad guidelines through which those purposes are to be achieved, provides the framework for planning and budgeting. The preparation of programme plans and budgets by the head teacher and staff, and the subsequent consideration and approval of these programmes by the policy group, provides a set of educational plans to guide work in the year ahead. The 'Implementing' phase of the Collaborative School Management Cycle has learning and teaching as its focus. This learning and teaching is guided by programme plans and is supported by resources allocated to the programmes. Learning and teaching and the related use of resources require supervision and day-to-day control or facilitation. The scope of this chapter is not to explore and discuss learning and teaching (although this is the most important aspect of implementation), rather it is to consider programme facilitation in some detail. This is undertaken by considering first, the nature of programme facilitation, and second, roles of the various participants.

Facilitating programmes involves supervising, providing support, staff development, accounting and monitoring progress in achieving purposes. Monitoring progress in Collaborative School Management is considered separately in chapter 9.

The supervision of programmes can be described as working with teachers to ensure that the activities occurring within the programme are in accordance with the programme's broad guidelines and plans and are directed towards achievement of the programme's purposes. Providing support involves supplying resources relating to materials, equipment, travel and services. This is accomplished by anticipating requirements, selecting appropriate materials and ordering to ensure supply at the time required. It follows that the supply of materials should be monitored through accounting, inventory control and auditing.

Staff development is another important part of facilitating programmes and ensuring their success. Collaborative School Management is constantly changing with consequent changes to programmes. Often these programme changes may not be overtly dramatic, but changes in emphasis and changes to some aspects of programmes must be made. Irrespective of the degree of change, it is still necessary to ensure that the staff implementing the programme are totally aware of these changes and have acquired the knowledge, skill and attitudes to accommodate the new ideas when they provide relevant learning activities for students. This can only be achieved by making staff development a fundamental part of programme implementation.

With this understanding of programme facilitation as an aspect of implementation, it is now intended to explore the facilitating role of the participants in Collaborative School Management. Although it is emphasised that learning and teaching are the most important aspects of implementation it must be remembered that these activities are unlikely to succeed unless appropriately supported and facilitated.

Roles in Implementation

The role of the policy group in implementation

Implementing concerns learning, teaching and facilitating. The policy group thus has a limited, if any, role in programme implementation. Does the policy group want to keep books, pay bills, select items of equipment, and undertake the related activities? Does the policy group want to supervise the work of teachers, select and/or design learning activities for students and undertake staff training? The first group of tasks are best undertaken by staff appointed for that purpose, or in the case of selecting and ordering, best undertaken by those who have to use the items. The second group of tasks are obviously those associated with the professional work of teachers and educational administrators who have the training and expertise necessary to undertake these tasks successfully. Some policy groups have attempted to undertake tasks relating to teaching and the supervision of teaching but usually with less than satisfactory results. Some groups have concentrated on providing resources and accounting. The result has been that group members have been tied up with tedious, time-consuming tasks, and staff have been frustrated by unnecessary delays in procuring supplies. Obviously there is a role for the policy group in monitoring expenditure from budget allocations but this can be accomplished by giving the policy group financial statements on a regular basis.

These issues make it necessary for policy groups to analyse their role carefully, taking into account the amount of time at their disposal and the relevance of the tasks they want to set themselves. In previous chapters we have emphasised the important role that the policy group can play in Collaborative School Management, through goal-setting, identification of needs and policy-making. These are the major tasks that provide the directions and framework for school development. As noted in chapter 6, a policy group may meet ten times a year with only two to three hours of effective meeting time on each occasion. With two meetings required for elections and end-or-year activities, it is likely that there are only eight meetings for business purposes. If half-an-hour is required at each meeting to deal with minutes, correspondence and financial monitoring, there are only about sixteen hours left. Surely this time is required for policy-making, reviewing, evaluating and planning for the future rather than for passing accounts for payment and determining which make of photocopier to acquire for the school.

The role of the head teacher in implementation

The role of the head teacher in implementation is twofold. Firstly, the head teacher is responsible to the policy group for the implementation of programmes. Secondly, the head teacher provides leadership to the' programme teams to ensure effectiveness of implementation. This involves providing support to programme teams, encouraging, boosting morale, motivating, communicating, liaising, ensuring that there is co-ordination between programmes, problem-solving and trouble-shooting. Research and experience emphasise the decisive part that the head teacher has to play, by exercising this leadership, in ensuring the success of all programmes.

As well as general responsibility for the implementation of all pro-grammes, the head teacher is usually the facilitator or has specific responsibility for key programmes such as Pastoral Care of Students and Administration. The head teacher ensures that activities in these pro-grammes are directed towards the programmes' purposes and are within the programmes' guidelines, plans and budgets. Depending on circum-stances the head teacher may also work as a team member in a specific learning programme related to his or her background and training as a teacher. This is highly desirable, because it allows the head teacher to demonstrate professional competence and skill in teaching. Consequently, the head teacher can continue to establish credibility and concern for the real task of the school — learning and teaching. Related roles for the head teacher in implementing programmes are concerned with professional development and assessment of staff. The importance of staff development to the successful implementation of programmes has been considered earlier. It is important for the head teacher to take the lead in this task and to ensure that staff are provided with meaningful opportunities to up-date their professional skills in line with emerging needs of students and related programme developments.

The role of the programme team in implementation

The programme team has responsibility for implementing programmes through learning and teaching. Team members are assigned this responsibility in their capacity as professionally trained teachers with both specific and general areas of expertise. Using their training, background and experience, members of programme teams must select and/or design learning activities for students, present those activities to students, involve students in those activities in the most appropriate way, and assess individual students' success. This selection, design, presentation, student involvement and assessment takes place in the context of the policies established by the policy group. These tasks relating to student learning are also carried out in the context of the plans and budgets approved by the policy group as outcomes of the policies.

Turning now to facilitation and, in particular, to programme supervision, it can be seen that the head teacher must delegate responsibility for individual programmes to a particular member of each programme team. In some cases this will be a member of the staff specifically appointed to the school for the purpose, such as a senior member of staff, or a teacher appointed within the school by some agreed means. Although someone from the programme team is appointed supervisor, it is emphasised that the decisions relating to major matters concerning the team are the responsibility of the team as a whole, in line with the collaborative approach for management of the school. There is, however, a need for someone to exercise responsibility and give direction on a day-to-day basis. In many ways the relationship between the person with responsibility for a programme and the other team members is similar to the relationship between the head teacher and the staff as a whole. The supervision and day-to-day control exercised by one member of the team need not lead to conflict because all members are involved in the major decisions relating to their programme. It is a part of the supervisor's job to ensure that all team members participate in this way.

The supervisory role of the staff member responsible for a programme also involves ensuring that the team initiates activities that are in accordance with the broad guidelines and plans of the programme and are directed towards achievement of the programme's purposes. This is best achieved by ensuring that these ideas are to the forefront when activities are being designed and selected, rather than being used as criteria for measuring the appropriateness of activities at a later stage. Supervision at this level also includes determining the learning activities for students, planning ways to involve students in learning activities and determining methods for assessing individual students' success. It follows that the staff member responsible for a programme has a similar role to play in staff development, to ensure that programme initiatives respond to the emerging needs of students.

Another aspect of the supervisory role for each programme is ensuring the supply of materials and services. This has often been difficult for teachers due to frustrations resulting from delays with supply, so that teachers have continually had to request supplies, not knowing whether requests will be met. When programme planning and budgeting are introduced not only are these frustrations for teachers eliminated, but also the time wasted by staff and others is reduced. In programme planning and budgeting, plans are prepared and the associated resources in support of those plans are identified and costed. In implementation, therefore, it is appropriate to give control of selection and ordering of materials and services to the programme teams. This selection and ordering can then take place within the framework of the plans and budgets that have been approved. It is appropriate that the material resources should be selected by those who have to use them and ordering by the programme team eliminates many areas of frustration and saves time.

In this way the programme team is able to anticipate needs for materials and to order in advance to ensure supply. It is also able to keep in mind the need to meet demands for resources that could emerge as the year progresses. It is then possible to satisfy those demands without unnecessary reference to others, and the elimination of the 'shopping-list' mentality enhances the professional status of all concerned. Of course it must be accepted that the programme team has to monitor expenditure on programme budgets. This does not present a problem and can be accomplished by having the bursar advise programme teams and prepare financial statements for programmes at regular intervals. These financial statements for programmes also provide the policy group with information which can help the group to monitor the financial situation of the school. It must be remembered that the 'essence' of supplying materials and services is ensuring that the required resources are where they are needed, when they are needed, with the minimum amount of fuss and unnecessary involvement of others. This is accomplished by the 'user selects, orders, and pays principle'. In this context 'pays' means authorising the bursar to pay.

The role of the bursar in implementation

The role of the bursar in programme implementation is threefold: (1) through involvement in one or more programme teams, (2) by providing support to all programmes and (3) through responsibility for the accounting process. It is intended in the following pages to consider each of these roles in some detail and to give examples of how particular tasks can be completed. It is recognised that some schools do not have a bursar or a registrar and that in these schools the tasks described are variously undertaken by the head teacher, office assistant and other members of staff.

The bursar is usually directly involved with one or more programmes, usually those which facilitate and support learning programmes. These include cleaning, ground development and building maintenance, canteen, book sales and administration. In the case of the first four examples named it is likely that the bursar will also exercise a supervisory role. This supervision is exercised in the same way as described for those teaching staff with delegated responsibility for educational programmes. The involvement of the bursar in the Administration Programme is in providing support to all programmes and financial accounting for the school as a whole.

The bursar supports all programmes by aiding the supply of resources. This support consists of giving advice, helping to place orders as required, co-ordinating orders between programmes, and dispersing materials within the school. Advice to programme teams includes information about comparative costs for similar items and information about sources of supply: availability, back-up services and reliability. It is also important for the bursar to support programmes by giving regular advice and information about expenditure in relation to programme budgets, so that budgets are not exceeded and expenditure is in keeping with any statutory restrictions placed on sources of finance.

Although it makes sense, that programme teams should initiate orders for materials and may in fact 'write them out', it makes further sense that these orders be forwarded from the school through the bursar. This saves time for the programme team and allows the bursar the opportunity to suggest alternative sources of supply, items and makes of items. It also allows the bursar the opportunity to co-ordinate the supply of materials between programmes if this opportunity has not already been recognised by programme teams. In this way savings can be made for the programme involved.

Receiving and dispersing materials to programmes is also a responsibility for the bursar. It is often a source of confusion and frustration to teachers that materials are received but incorrectly dispersed, or that there is competition for materials ordered for the whole school. Systems can be devised and operated by the bursar to solve these problems and to facilitate supply. An example of such a system is set out below.

A sample procedure for the supply of materials A sample procedure for the supply of materials makes use of codes in the following manner.

1 Each programme is given a three-digit code. The first two digits indicate the staff member responsible for the programme. If the same staff member is responsible for more than one programme, then those programmes will have the same two digits at the beginning of their respective codes. The third digit of the code will enable differentiation between programmes for which that person

Figure 8.1 Sample coding system for budgeting and accounting

PROGRAMME CODES

101	Extra-curricular activities	151	7–10 Mathematics
102	Art acquisition	152	7–10 Science
103	Administration	153	K–10 Computer education
104	Community bus	161	7–10 Technical subjects
105	Pastoral care	162	7–10 Visual arts
111	Curriculum resource	163	7–10 Home economics
112	School council	164	9–10 Commercial subjects
113	K–10 Music	171	Early intervention
114	3–6 Regrouped language	172	K–2 General studies
121	Presentation Day	173	K–10 Special education
122	K–10 Physical education	181	3–6 General studies
123	K–10 Sport	182	Public relations
124	Support services	191	Cleaning
131	7–10 Social science	192	Grounds
132	9–10 History	193	Canteen
133	7–10 Transition education	194	Book sales
134	7–10 Teacher support services	201	9–10 Journalism
141	7–10 English	202	School magazine
142	3–10 Foreign language	203	Student council
143	K–10 Speech and drama	211	K–10 Talented students
144	Drama Festival		

CODES FOR SOURCES OF FUNDS
(Fourth digit of order code)

Annual Requisition Grant (State) — Cash Grant	0
Commonwealth Schools Commission	1
General levies	2
Specialist subject levies	3
Book-hire fees	4
Participation and Equity Grant	5
Library grants	6
Excursion grant	7
Department subsidies	8
School-initiated activities	9

---

is responsible. An example of such a coding system is shown in Figure 8.1.

2 Sources of funds used by programmes are listed and assigned a one-digit code as in Figure 8.1.

3 Each programme team is issued with an order book which must be used for all orders. For each order, a four-digit order code consists of the three-digit code for the programme and a fourth digit indicating the sources of funds.

Orders are completed and coded in this way by programme teams. For example, referring to the codes in Figure 8.1, an order coded as 1524 would indicate an order placed for the 7–10 Science Programme intending to use funds from Book Hire. A copy of the order is retained by the programme team and two copies are passed to the bursar. The bursar checks that items ordered could be legitimately paid for, according to statutory restrictions, from the funds indicated by the fourth digit of the code. In the example, a check would be made that the items ordered could be charged against funds for textbook hire. When the check is completed, one copy of the order is forwarded to the supplier and the other filed for reference. Suppliers automatically transfer order numbers, in this case including the programme code, to packing slips and invoices. A quick check of the packing slip when items are received enables the items to be speedily delivered to the programme concerned.

Accounting   In the implementation of programmes, the bursar is also responsible for the accounting. The accounting includes paying accounts, keeping financial records as a means of providing financial statements at appropriate intervals, ensuring that audit requirements are met and that the necessary information for audit purposes is kept, and monitoring the cash flow of the school. Accounts can be paid by the bursar without reference to the policy group, if those accounts are in keeping with the programme budgets approved by the policy group. The audit provides assurance that financial practices are in keeping with the wishes of the policy group and with statutory restrictions. The order-code system described previously provides for payment of accounts without reference to the programme for which an order was placed, because the fourth digit in the code indicates the source of the funds to be used.

The bursar's financial records and financial statements require further consideration at this point. Traditionally these activities have been directed towards an analysis of information along lines of expenditure (for example, equipment, book materials, and travel), and/or according to the sources of funds. The statements thus provided would be of little value for monitoring by programme teams and the policy group. Traditional statements do, however, satisfy normal audit requirements. There is a need to rethink how financial statements are prepared for audit purposes so that they can be useful to all concerned. A system of 'programme accounting' can easily be developed to meet these purposes. An example of a monthly summary statement for a school's system of programme accounting is shown in Figure 8.2. To produce this summary, financial records are kept on a programme-by-programme basis. The source of funds involved in the programme transactions can be identified by coding systems or by using different colours in recording the amounts involved. Computer programmes are available to assist in this task.

Another part of accounting is monitoring the school's cash flow to

Code	Programme	Budget estimates	Balances b/f 1983	Receipts to date	Total receipts	Payments	Balance to date
101	Extra-curricular activities	$ 1 400	—	1 400	1 400	674	726
102	Art acquisition	400	—	375	375	165	210
103	Administration	18 581	4 825	11 299	16 124	14 772	1 352
104	Community bus	—		12 943	12 943	12 542	401
111	K-10 Sport	2 390		2 390	2 390	1 675	715
112	Support services	200		200	200		200
113	K-10 Physical education	2 100	2	2 100	2 102	870	1 232
114	Regrouped language	850		800	800	373	427
121	K-10 Music	1 890		1 890	1 890	1 552	338
122	Curriculum resource	9 465	23	9 263	9 286	4 668	4 618
131	7-10 Social studies	3 350	17	3 300	3 317	1 419	1 898
132	9-10 History	900		850	850	343	507
133	Transition education	5 990	1 827	5 990	7 817	2 258	5 559
134	7-10 Note/test production	2 865	29	2 865	2 894	1 957	937
141	7-10 English	415	—	415	415		415
142	7-10 French	530		530	530	191	339
143	7-10 Speech & drama		305	903	1 208	291	917
144	Drama Festival	2 145		2 056	2 056	578	1 478
151	7-10 Mathematics	6 432		6 236	6 236	3 244	2 992
152	7-10 Science	796		726	726	80	646
153	K-10 Computer studies	8 820	792	8 820	9 612	6 906	2 706
161	7-10 Technical subjects	1 716	376	1 716	2 092	1 437	655
162	7-10 Visual arts	2 820	514	2 820	3 334	2 541	793
163	7-10 Home economics	7 300	4	7 300	7 304	7 047	257
164	9-10 Commercial subjects	200		200	200		200
171	Early Intervention	6 150	78	5 925	6 003	3 017	2 986
172	K-2 General studies	1 000	—	1 000	1 000	302	698
173	K-10 Special education	5 594	3	5 162	5 165	1 867	3 298
181	3-6 General studies	4 275		4 275	4 275	4 200	75
191	Cleaning	950		475	475	186	289
192	Grounds						
193	Canteen		—	25 533	25 533	23 572	1 961
194	Book sales	1 100	—	9 082	9 082	8 278	804
201	Journalism	900	10	919	929	628	301
202	School magazine	406	41	1 480	1 521	4	1 517
203	K-10 Talented children		—	430	430	—	430
			8 846	141 668	150 514	107 637	42 677*

Reconciliation:

Cheque account as at 3/8/84	$23 898
Investment account	20 000
Less unpresented cheques	1 783
Plus cash in hand	562
	$42 677*

N.B.:
1 Salary components of programmes are not included.
2 Balances for programmes 193 and 194 excluded stock in hand.

Figure 8.2 A sample programme summary: financial statement for period ended 3/8/84

ensure that an overall credit balance is maintained; at present this is a statutory requirement for most schools. Such monitoring can lead to the identification of periods of high credit balances which allow short-term investments to be made to the school's advantage. In some schools this can be predicted to such an extent that this source of revenue can be included in the annual budget.

The role of the treasurer of a policy group such as a school council or board of governors should be clarified. Obviously there is no need for the treasurer to be involved in bookkeeping because all funds available to the school are budgeted at the one time and recorded through the accounts kept by the bursar. The treasurer's job is to ensure that appropriate statements are prepared and presented to the policy group. This would also occur with the auditor's reports. The treasurer should present these reports and be able to answer questions and/or carry out specific investigations on request.

In summary, consideration in this chapter of the implementation of programmes according to approved plans and budgets has shown how this task can be expedited and monitored using the expertise within the school to full advantage. This allows the policy group to give its full attention to reviewing overall progress and investigating possible developments to meet the future needs of students.

SUMMARY
IMPLEMENTING

WHAT IS IMPLEMENTATION?

- Implementation of programmes primarily concerns teaching and learning. It involves:
  selection and design of learning activities for students;
  presentation of those activities to students;
  involvement of students in the activities in the most appropriate way;
  assessment of individual student success.
- The policies, plans and budgets provide the framework for the implementation of programmes.
- In programme implementation, teaching and learning are facilitated by supervision, provision of support, staff development and accounting.
  Supervision ensures that activities are in accord with programme purposes, guidelines and plans.
  Provision of support involves supplying materials and services.
  Staff development ensures that implementation is appropriate to the emerging needs of students.
  Accounting provides information for the monitoring of programme expenditure.

WHO IS RESPONSIBLE FOR IMPLEMENTATION?

- Implementation of programmes is primarily a role for the head teacher and staff of the school.
- The head teacher as the chief executive of the school is responsible for the implementation of all programmes.
- The staff in programme teams are responsible for the implementation of specific programmes in their professional capacity as teachers.
- Responsibility for day-to-day organisation and supervision of specific programmes is delegated to senior or other members of staff.
- Programme teams are responsible for selecting and ordering their own material resources and services.
- The bursar is responsible for programme accounting and the monitoring of the cash flow of the school.

9 *Evaluating*

In Collaborative School Management, goal-setting and policy-making, resulting in statements of purpose and broad guidelines, provide the framework for planning and budgeting. Educational plans are produced and the related allocation of resources enables learning and teaching to proceed in accordance with the intent of the policy group. It follows that evaluation of programmes, based on the original goals and policies, be undertaken to complete the management cycle and to provide information on which to base new policies or make modifications to existing policies or practices. In this chapter the nature of programme evaluation is explored and an approach is outlined that is both desirable and workable in the school setting.

The Nature and Purpose of Programme Evaluation

It is not intended to provide a comprehensive view of school-level evaluation or even of programme evaluation in this chapter. The purpose is to consider programme evaluation in the context of the Collaborative School Management Cycle and to provide broad guidelines for a cyclical approach which seems well suited to the self-managing school. References are provided which will assist the reader who seeks a more detailed account of the techniques of evaluation.

Some definitions and distinctions

It is helpful to establish the nature of evaluation before proceeding. Definitions of the process abound, but the authors take the traditional view that 'the primary purpose of evaluation has been to provide decision-makers with information about the effectiveness of some programme, product or procedure. ... Despite differences in the conceptual frameworks used by practitioners there has been basic agreement about the decision-making role of evaluation.'[1] We also take the view that information that provides the basis for decision-making may be either quantitative, involving measurement, or qualitative, and that value-judgements are at the heart of decisions. This is illustrated in the following 'equation':[2]

EVALUATION

IS

QUANTITATIVE DESCRIPTIONS

(Measurement)

AND/OR

QUALITATIVE DESCRIPTIONS

(Non-measurement)

PLUS

VALUE JUDGEMENTS

When viewed in this way, it is evident that evaluation occurs continuously in the instructional and management process.[3] This was acknowledged in chapter 3 in our initial description of Collaborative School Management. In this regard, it was noted, the Collaborative School Management Cycle as illustrated is misleading in that it suggests evaluation follows implementation and precedes goal-setting and specification of needs. Our main concern in chapter 9 is, however, the kind of evaluation which does follow implementation of a programme. Such evaluation may, of course, be based on information gathered for other purposes, including classroom testing.

We find the distinction between formative and summative evaluation helpful in describing the recommended approach to programme evaluation in Collaborative School Management. Based on a distinction offered by Scriven in the context of curriculum development:

> The main purpose of formative evaluation is to improve the instructional methods and materials so that greater pupil learning will result. The main purpose of summative evaluation is to appraise the overall effectiveness of a curriculum programme.[4]

With adaptation as described in the pages which follow, the reader will find similarity between these purposes for formative and summative evaluation and our recommendations for minor and major evaluation.

A foundation in Collaborative School Management

Many of the difficulties encountered by schools in programme evaluation are alleviated beforehand with the adoption of the Collaborative School

Management Cycle. From the experience of the authors, a major difficulty has been to ascertain what one is trying to do, so that one can then attempt to discover whether in fact one is actually doing it. Here is the first benefit of Collaborative School Management: at least there is a clear statement of the actual purpose of the programme. As this statement of purpose is easily traced back to documented statements of policy, there is further detail and description of what the programme is endeavouring to achieve. In this way the first step in the evaluation process is quite easy.

Often, the second step in evaluation is discovering how achievement is meant to occur, so that if achievement is not occurring, it might be possible to discover why. On a similar basis, if achievement is occurring, and one knows how this is being brought about, then such knowledge may assist in improving similar programmes. Again, Collaborative School Management offers a benefit in this regard as there are clear and detailed statements of the broad guidelines by which the programme operates and detailed plans related to the implementation of the programme.

It is possible to go even further and say that evaluation usually involves the gathering of information on the resources required for implementation so that the desirability of the programme can be ascertained from a cost point of view. Resources which could be 'saved' or 'available for redistribution' if the programme is curtailed may be identified readily. Again, this information is provided beforehand through the approach to Collaborative School Management outlined in this book.

Policy-making, programme planning and budgeting thus facilitate evaluation because the base-line information is readily available. Time can therefore be devoted to measuring the outcomes of the programmes. The evaluative task becomes realistic, rather than a task in which large amounts of time are spent casting around, wondering what one is really trying to measure.

The realistic and achievable nature of programme evaluation is further illustrated by considering questions which are typically posed during the process. A sample list of questions is provided in Figure 9.1. The first three questions, which are usually the most difficult, have already been answered. The time allowed for evaluation can then be directed to obtaining and interpreting information to guide future developments. Even so, the time involved is an issue requiring further consideration.

The Time Problem

Even with three facets of evaluation addressed before the actual commencement of a programme evaluation, the time involved is substantial and is not usually available. Schools have traditionally been involved in curriculum design, implementing learning programmes and student assessment. With the continuing pressure to complete this work, often with

Figure 9.1 Sample questions in programme evaluation

1	What are the purposes of the programme?	**REFER** TO RELEVANT POLICIES
2	How are these purposes to be achieved?	**REFER** TO BROAD GUIDELINES IN POLICY AND PROGRAMME PLANS
3	What are the costs associated with the various facets of the programme?	**REFER** TO PROGRAMME BUDGETS
4	What information should be collected on which to base an assessment?	
5	How should this information be collected?	
6	On the basis of the information, how effective and efficient is the programme?	
7	How do the estimates of effectiveness and efficiency relate to priorities?	
8	What further action is required?	

shrinking resources, there is great difficulty in allocating scarce time for programme evaluation. Perhaps it is time to realise that allocating scarce time to evaluation will greatly facilitate and improve curriculum design and the implementation of learning programmes.

Another aspect of the time problem is that it may not be possible to achieve the educational purposes in a single budget year. It may only be possible to achieve these purposes over a period of years.

For these reasons, a cyclic approach is best, wherein only a few programmes are evaluated in depth each year: there is a selection of programmes to suit the time available. This limits the size of the task for any one year and a schedule can be drawn up to include all programmes over a number of years. Individual programmes can be arranged on the schedule to reflect the time required for programmes to become 'productive'. This is especially important with the introduction of new programmes or following major modification to existing programmes. This aspect of evaluating school programmes has often been neglected and pressures have been imposed to evaluate before it can realistically be expected that results will be forthcoming. This situation is often observed in special programmes funded by government grants. A submission involving a new programme is approved and the programme commenced. In less than twelve months an evaluation is required. If the programme seeks the achievement of worthwhile goals, including attitudinal changes, then it cannot be expected that results will be forthcoming in less than two or three years. It is often argued that the evaluation required in the first and early years can only be an evaluation of the manner in which the programme is progressing; that is, a type of formative evaluation in the distinction offered earlier. This is not made explicitly clear to the school involved, however, and pressure is often felt in the schools to 'find results' or funding may discontinue. There may be too high an expectation for short-term returns rather than looking for worthwhile gains in the long term, and exercising patience.

Another issue related to time and programme evaluation is the desirability of clearly establishing policies and programme plans and budgets before endeavouring to evaluate programmes. For this reason it is probable that a school instituting the approach will not attempt to evaluate programmes in depth until the third or fourth year. By that time, the desirability of evaluating programmes is usually obvious to all concerned. An approach to cyclic programme evaluation in a school using Collaborative School Management is outlined in the next section.

Cyclic Programme Evaluation

In a cyclic approach to programme evaluation, all programmes are evaluated annually. In a large school, however, it is suggested that only one-fifth of the programmes be evaluated in depth each year in a major evaluation. In that year the other four-fifths of the programmes receive minor evaluations that are far less demanding in terms of time. In this way the evaluative process is a continuing one and all programmes are thoroughly reviewed on a five-year basis. In a small school with fewer programmes, a three-year cycle might be appropriate. A sample cycle of programmes for major evaluations in a large K–10 school is shown in Figure 9.2.

Minor evaluations are usually subjective in nature and focus on indicators of success. They are not time-intensive and therefore do not normally involve instrument design, administration and interpretation. The evaluation is prepared in written form by the programme team and may be presented to the policy group by the head teacher or a person with responsibility for the programme.

Major evaluations are usually objective in nature and are conducted in some depth. The use of evaluation instruments and/or professional expertise from outside the school and community is usually considered. Evaluations are prepared in written form and include recommendations for change and future action. Evaluations are carried out by people appointed by the policy group and may involve members of the programme team, parents and students. Evaluation reports may be presented to the policy group by the head teacher or a person with responsibility for the programme.

Figure 9.2 Cycle of programmes for major evaluation

1984: Year 1
103 Administration
111 K–10 Sport
122 Curriculum resource
133 7–10 Transition education
141 7–10 English
171 Early intervention
193 Canteen
*   Communication with our
      parents and community
*   School organisation

1985: Year 2
104 Community bus
114 3–6 Regrouped language
131 7–10 Social science
151 7–10 Mathematics
161 7–10 Technical subjects
191 Cleaning
201 9–10 Journalism
*   Discipline
*   Preparing Your Child for School
*   Certification of standards

1986: Year 3 `
101 Art acquisition
112 Support services
142 7–10 French
152 7–10 Science
163 7–10 Home economics
173 K–10 Special education
181 3–6 General studies
192 Grounds
211 K–10 Talented children
*   The budgeting process
*   Your Child's Report

1987: Year 4
113 K–10 Physical education
132 9–10 History
144 Drama Festival
153 K–10 Computer education
162 7–10 Visual arts
194 Book sales
202 School magazine
*   Curriculum policy
*   School assemblies
*   Homework

1988: Year 5
101 Extra-curricular activities
121 K–10 Music
134 7–10 Note/test production
143 K–10 Speech and drama
164 9–10 Commercial subjects
172 K–2 General studies
*   Option subjects
      — provision and selection
*   Excursions

1989: Year 6
103 Administration
111 K–10 Sport
122 Curriculum resource
133 7–10 Transition education
141 7–10 English
171 Early intervention
193 Canteen

The cycle of major evaluations shown in Figure 9.2 includes some without programme codes: for example, Option Subjects — Provision and Selection, in 1988. These refer to evaluation of policies that do not involve specific programmes but may influence several or all programmes in some way. Other examples are Discipline (1985) and Homework (1987). As major policy statements they should be evaluated and are therefore included in the cycle. Of course the list of programmes to be evaluated will be extended from time to time as new policies are adopted. Some may be removed.

Although the cycle for evaluation may be adopted by the policy group, circumstances may arise which necessitate some programmes being evaluated in depth before the year intended. Provision may be made for this and a major evaluation can be brought forward by a decision of the policy group. Such a need could arise from a recommendation put forward in a minor evaluation. It is recognised that, should this occur, there is a need to 'delay' for a further period a related programme where the minor evaluation indicates little or no reason for concern. This 'balancing' ensures that the workload of those involved remains realistic and achievable. In this respect it should be noted that in Figure 9.2 related programmes are not scheduled in the same year. Related programmes are those likely to involve the same staff members, for example: 151 7–10 Mathematics (1986), 152 7–10 Science (1986), and 153 K–10 Computer Education (1987).

These are all ways of keeping the task achievable as far as workload is concerned. Similarly, the reporting of evaluations has been considered in this context, and reports of minor evaluations should be limited to one printed page and major evaluations to two printed pages. Reporting and presentation will be considered later in this chapter.

Collection and interpretation of information

With a framework established for realistically accomplishing programme evaluation in schools, attention is now given to gathering and interpreting information. The distinction between major and minor evaluation is also important in these matters.

In the general area of information-gathering and interpretation, evaluations often go astray. There can be a 'mad rush' to gather all sorts of information by many different means without any thought to what information should be gathered and how this information can be gathered with minimum effort. Of course, the situation becomes quite clear to those involved when an attempt is made to interpret the information. The great bulk of information may defy interpretation and no doubt many have read or attempted to read evaluations of this type. In deciding upon what information is required, consideration should be given to collecting the information in such a way and in such quantity that it can be readily interpreted and therefore used to plan future developments.

While considering information-gathering and related issues, it is useful to return to the questions for programme evaluation raised earlier in Figure 9.1. The answer to the first question will consist of a list of the broad guidelines and plans for the programme. A decision must then be made as to which purposes and plans will be the focus of the evaluation: time will invariably prohibit consideration of them all. This is where realistic school programme evaluations will differ from 'research' evaluation, and the two should not be confused. Previous experience may suggest purposes or plans as being particularly in need of consideration. Attention can then be given to identifying the nature of the information required and the most appropriate way to gather that information, keeping in mind the time and other resources available to undertake the task.

Conducting a minor evaluation

In conducting a minor evaluation it should be remembered that such evaluations usually:

- are subjective in nature;
- focus on indicators of success;
- are not time-intensive;
- concentrate on assessing effectiveness of implementation;
- result in a report presented on one page.

This type of evaluation usually requires the staff involved to meet on just two or three occasions for short periods (perhaps one hour) to carry out the following tasks:

1 Review the policies and plans of the programme.
2 Identify and record success indicators.
3 Identify and record areas of concern.
4 Provide comments and recommendations for future action.
5 Prepare a written report on these issues.

A sample report of such a programme evaluation is given in Figure 9.3, for a Special Education Programme. The policies and programme plans and budget related to this sample programme are contained in the Appendix. These should be read in association with the evaluation. It should be noted that indicators of success usually draw on information which is readily available. Areas of concern are usually related to implementation. Comments and recommendations are usually derived from areas of concern.

It could be argued that such an evaluation carried out by the staff implementing the programme is of little value, but it must be remembered that the staff concerned have carried out the evaluation of their work as part of their professional responsibility. As well, if evaluation reports for all programmes for any year are published together in some form or other, then the 'openness' of such information tends to ensure that a 'fair assessment' of each programme is made. In the example shown, the format adopted by the school requires staff to provide information on 'Success indicators' and 'Areas of concern'. This elicits a balanced view of progress within the programme.

Figure 9.3 A sample programme evaluation (minor) report

PROGRAMME: Special Education   RESPONSIBILITY: M.S.   CODE: 173

EVALUATION REPORT FOR 1984
This report should be read in conjunction with the policy and programme plan for special education. Resources were allocated to implement fully the programme plan.

SUCCESS INDICATORS

1   Many teachers have indicated that the Special Education Programme is assisting them to deal more effectively with children who have special needs in the classroom. This has been particularly evident since the increase in provisions for special education at the beginning of this year.

2   Parent-teacher interviews conducted under the regular schedule have indicated strong support for the programme.

3   A number of children on the programme show evidence of increased self-esteem and ability to cope with learning tasks.

4   A small number of children in the early childhood area are likely to be coping well enough in the near future to come off the programme.

AREAS OF CONCERN

1   There has been insufficient time for classroom teachers to consult with special education teachers on the progress of children.

2   Some classroom teachers are unaware of the need to consult, so that work can be followed up in the classroom.

3   Some children with problems 'slip through' and are put on the programme too late, due to lack of continuity in monitoring their progress as they cross from one grade to another.

4   There are problems with the supply of books needed for teachers' resources due to:
    (a) lack of opportunity to select appropriate materials;
    (b) delays by suppliers in meeting orders.

COMMENTS AND RECOMMENDATIONS

● Senior staff need to create opportunities where possible for classroom teachers to consult with special education staff.

● Special education staff need to make themselves available at department meetings so that they can make teachers aware of the resources available. This includes resources in the form of support materials, and information about learning-teaching processes which take place through the individualised programmes.

● Better liaison is needed between senior staff of the different grade areas to ensure that provisions for special education give continuity for particular children when they cross grade levels.

● The school should budget for professional development time so that special education staff can visit language and special education resource centres where they can select suitable materials and either purchase them or borrow them.

Prepared by members of the programme team.

Conducting a major evaluation

The characteristics of a major evaluation are as follows:

- it is objective in nature if possible;
- it is in-depth;
- it requires an appropriate commitment of time;
- it may involve expertise from outside the school and community;
- it may involve extensive collection of information;
- it may include assessment of co-ordination outside the immediate grade area and in other programmes;
- it is carried out by a group appointed by the policy group, and may include teachers, parents and others;
- it focuses on the extent to which programme purposes have been achieved;
- the report is presented on two pages.

When the evaluation group has been appointed, the task can be described as a number of steps.

1 Review the policies and plans of the programme.
2 List the purposes of the programme.
3 List the key aspects of the broad guidelines and plans.
4 Identify which purposes and/or planning aspects are to be the focus of the evaluation.
5 List the kind of information that will be required as the basis for judgements.
6 Identify methods for collecting information required.
7 Select a method (or methods) appropriate to the task, taking into account information required, and time and other resources available.
8 Collect the information required.
9 Interpret the information obtained in relation to the programme focus and the programme in general.
10 Prepare an evaluation report for the policy group.

Once the focus of the evaluation has been agreed upon, the nature of the information required needs to be carefully considered. A characteristic of major evaluations is that they are objective wherever possible. That is, judgements should be based on clearly defined criteria and/or quantitative measures. This requirement emphasises the need to include 'wherever possible' in relation to the objectivity of major evaluations. Many stated purposes in education are by their very nature subjective and can only be evaluated subjectively. As well, time constraints on the evaluation group may prohibit objective evaluations in all cases. Those involved should be prepared to accept subjective evaluations in some cases as long as the evaluation is prepared and conducted in a professional manner. Some would argue that such evaluations can be suspect and/or inconclusive, but in schools, evaluations that are objective where possible, or otherwise subjective, are preferable to no evaluation at all. Although there may be some initial concern as to the validity of subjective evaluations, this is usually overcome once the benefits of regular evaluation are demonstrated.

Some Approaches to the Collection of Information[5]

Observation

If observation is considered, attention must be given to who is going to do the observing, when, and how the information gained is to be made available to the evaluation group. It might be decided that 'outside expertise' is required for this task or perhaps the members of the group can undertake the work and then share their findings. Irrespective of the decision made, it is apparent that observation as a method of gathering information is expensive as far as time is concerned.

Interviews

Interviewing as a method of gathering information can also be expensive as far as time and people are concerned because there is an obvious need to involve a relatively large number of people in order to gain a fair representation. Techniques such as telephone interviewing can be employed to solve the problem of bringing many people together at the same time and place. An interview sheet can be constructed with a set of prepared questions to assist the information-gathering and to aid in reporting back. The interview technique has the advantage of allowing for follow-up and clarification of responses as well as noting the actual responses.

Face-to-face interviews can be efficiently conducted by forming groups. The related problem of gaining a representative group to interview can be overcome by employing appropriate techniques. Families associated with the school can be randomly divided into groups with, for example, twelve families in each group. The families in any particular group can then be personally invited to come to a meeting for a specific purpose. People thus invited are more inclined to participate than when a 'general' invitation is used. As well, a different group of families can be invited to participate for different programme evaluation or policy reviews. The whole school community can become involved in the review, over time, with this approach. It also ensures that the information gained on a particular issue is representative and not just a particular concern or point of view.

Questionnaires

Questionnaires are often favoured as a method of gathering information as they do not require 'face-to-face' meetings and can be aimed at a large audience. Unfortunately their over-use, inappropriate use and poor design has led to their being generally held in disfavour. Many parents as well as teachers despair at yet another questionnaire requiring hours of writing responses. The response rate is understandably low and the validity of the information gained may be questioned on the grounds that only those with a particular view to push actually make a response. However, the fact remains that properly prepared and administered questionnaires can successfully gather information. The following points may be helpful.

1   Keep it short: have no more than one page of carefully thought out questions that are right to the point.
2   Make it easy to respond: instructions need to be clear and the response method easy to follow.
3   Make it easy to return the information: arrange to collect the responses or at least provide a stamped, self-addressed envelope.
4   Give an incentive to return the information: this can often be accomplished by restricting the target group to a representative sample and by indicating that questionnaires have only been forwarded to a certain number of families.

Attention to these points can ensure that information is obtained from an audience that is representative. This enhances the validity of the information.

Techniques for information-gathering and their relative advantages and disadvantages are subjects for further study. The scope of this book does not lend itself to further consideration of these areas, but emphasis is given to the need to carefully consider how information is gathered if it is to be of value in the evaluation task.

Preparation of Evaluation Reports

When the information-gathering task is completed, the evaluation group can relate the information to the focus of the programme evaluation. The group should be in a position to decide whether purposes have been achieved and to what degree guidelines and plans are effective and efficient. Based on this interpretation, the group is then able to make recommendations for future action. This may take the form of recommending that policies and programmes be modified or even that a programme be eliminated. On the other hand, the recommendations may confirm the effectiveness of existing policies and reinforce present practices.

It is the task of the evaluation group to carry out the programme evaluation, but the information gained and the recommendations made are usually considered and acted upon by the policy group. It is therefore necessary that the results and recommendations are reported in an effective and efficient manner. This need is often neglected in evaluation work and lengthy reports are prepared which explain in fine detail the methods employed and information gathered. The recipient often fails to reach the recommendations at the end. This leads to frustration for all concerned, especially those who prepared the report. There is a need to document the actual work involved in the evaluation and this may be lengthy, but it only needs to be available if requested. What is required immediately is a short, succinct report that effectively summarises the findings of the evaluation group and highlights recommendations for future action.

For these reasons it is recommended that major evaluation reports should be no longer than two printed pages. Further, it is recommended that an agreed report format be adopted that defines and highlights the important aspects of the report. A similar need and approach has been identified and described for programme plans and budgets.

An example of a programme evaluation consistent with these recommendations is contained in Figure 9.4. It is a report of a major evaluation of a Special Education Programme. Related policies and plans are contained in the Appendix. It should be noted that the report briefly states how the evaluation was conducted and then immediately highlights inadequacies and problem areas. Then follows a summary of the successful outcomes that have also been identified. Attention is then directed to recommendations for further action and these are clearly related to the information gathered.

A comparison of this two-page major evaluation report can be made with the one-page minor evaluation report in Figure 9.3. The minor evaluation did not attempt to gather information in a systematic way but relied on the opinions of those directly involved. This is reflected by

Figure 9.4 A sample programme evaluation (major) report

PROGRAMME: Special Education   **RESPONSIBILITY: M.S.**   **CODE: 173**

INTRODUCTION

For this year the Special Education Programme was upgraded to provide an increased teacher component (1.5 teachers as compared to one teacher in the previous year). In evaluating the results of this programme the evaluating group held a series of informal meetings with all teachers concerned, interviewed the guidance officer and speech pathologist connected with the school to ascertain objective indications of progress or otherwise of the children concerned, and interviewed a representative sample of parents who have children involved with the programme. Child studies, with names removed to ensure anonymity, were also made available to the group. The findings of this evaluation are summarised below.

INADEQUACIES AND PROBLEM AREAS IDENTIFIED

1   The lack of ready access to some support staff (particularly guidance officer and speech pathologist) means that there are sometimes lengthy delays in obtaining information on which to base individual programmes.
2   One parent interviewed was confused about the provision of 10 hours of teacher aide time (provided from an external source) to cater for mobility of the physically handicapped, and thought that this provision was teacher time to assist in overcoming intellectual handicap.

3 A very small minority of children show evidence of 'opting out' of the normal classroom, preferring the special education situation all the time probably due to the greater feeling of security.

4 Children are sometimes not identified as being in need of special education until they are too old for their problems to be overcome.

5 There is insufficient time for classroom teachers to consult with special education teachers on the progress of children, and in some cases teachers are unaware of the special education resources available.

SUCCESSFUL OUTCOMES OF THE PROGRAMME

1 Many teachers have indicated that the Special Education Programme is assisting them to deal more effectively with children who have special needs in the classroom as they are given help with implementing individualised programmes developed out of the work. The special education teachers do this with the children concerned. This feeling of receiving increased support is directly attributed to the increased provision.

2 A number of children on the programme are showing evidence of increased self-esteem and ability to cope with learning tasks. Tests administered (refer guidance officer) give objective evidence of this.

3 A small number of children in the early childhood area are likely to be coping well enough in the near future to come off the programme. This reinforces the benefits of early identification of children with problems and of early intensive help.

SUMMARY AND RECOMMENDATIONS

1 There is little if anything that can be done about the amount of the guidance officer's and speech pathologist's time provided to the school. The group feels that it is worth noting, however, that as yet the Special Education Programme is in its infancy and that as the special education staff become more confident in their task of dealing with a wide range of disabilities and learning problems, the lack of ready access to support staff should be less of a problem.

2 The confusion that became evident about the nature of the provisions for special education for particular children points out the need for improved liaison between staff and parents. Consideration should be given to increasing the frequency of parent-teacher interviews with respect to children in the Special Education Programme.

3 Particular staff members should be nominated to undertake special pastoral care of the small minority of children having unusual difficulty in coping with the normal classroom situation, particularly in the secondary years.

4 The need to identify children early and the benefits of early intensive help, as previously outlined, underline the need to continue the main thrust of the programme towards the early years. It is essential that continuity in monitoring children 'at risk' throughout the school is further developed and maintained.

5 Senior staff should create opportunities where possible for classroom teachers to consult with special education staff. The special education staff should make themselves available to department meetings so that they can make teachers aware of the resources available. This includes resources in the form of support materials, and information about learning-teaching processes which take place through individualised learning programmes.

Prepared by the Evaluation Group including members of the policy group and programme team

---

reporting on 'success indicators' and 'areas of concern' rather than the 'inadequacies and problem areas identified' and 'successful outcomes of the programmes' in the case of the major evaluation. The ramifications of the recommendations for future action are evident in both cases.

The comparison of the minor and major evaluation reports draws attention to the difference between these two approaches to programme evaluation and their respective uses as the basis for future development. These aspects are highlighted in the comparative chart in Figure 9.5.

Evaluations and Future Action

Evaluations undertaken by subcommittees or working parties provide information and recommendations for future action but the decision to take such future action rests with the policy group if the recommendations concern policy matters, or with the head teacher and staff if they relate to implementation. This highlights the respective roles in Collaborative School Management and the shared role in evaluation. The role of the policy group concerns evaluation of whether its policies are being achieved. It is

Figure 9.5 Comparing the characteristics of major and minor evaluations

MAJOR EVALUATIONS	MINOR EVALUATIONS
1 All programmes included on a cycle over a period of years.	1 Carried out in all non-major years for all programmes.
2 In-depth considerations requiring an appropriate commitment of time.	2 Not time-intensive.
3 Objective in nature if possible.	3 Subjective in nature.
4 A search for programme outcomes and identification of inadequacies and areas of concern.	4 Give a general indication of success and areas of concern.
5 Focus on the purposes to be achieved by programmes.	5 Related mainly to implementation of programme.
6 Usually involve the employment of simple information-gathering techniques.	6 Rely on informed opinion.
7 Include co-ordination with similar programmes in other grades (or schools).	7 Focus is within the programme.
8 Carried out by a group including parents, programme team and others as appropriate.	8 Carried out by the programme team.
9 TWO-page printed report.	9 ONE-page printed report.
10 Report presented to policy group.	10 Report presented to policy group.
11 Can lead to substantial policy and programme changes.	11 Can lead to changes in planning and implementation or to bringing forward scheduled major evaluations.

understandable that the policy group will be very much concerned with major evaluations. In the conduct of major evaluations it is likely that the policy group will appoint a convenor, parents, members of the programme team and others, to actually carry out the review. A period of time will also be stated during which it is expected that the work will be carried out. With some five to ten major evaluations a year for a large school, it can be appreciated that this activity will comprise a major portion of time for the policy group.

The review material provided by evaluations still requires a decision to act from the appropriate group. Measures of effectiveness and efficiency by themselves do not provide sufficient information on which to base judgements with respect to future action. Of necessity this information must be considered in the context of policy and programme priorities. Can a highly effective but inefficient programme with a low priority be allowed to continue without modification? Can an ineffective and inefficient programme with a high priority be scrapped? The combinations and permutations are interesting to consider and this work of the policy group will result in many debates. Judgements based on values are to be expected.. These debates already exist in our schools but are usually not based on comprehensive information and often remain unresolved. It is not suggested that programme evaluation is easy but the net result of the approach outlined in this chapter is a system of continued modification and improvement of educational programmes to better meet the emerging and ongoing needs of students.

Refinements

The approach to programme evaluation outlined in this chapter provides a framework for the self-managing school to begin the process. It is acknowledged that a number of years may be required before all staff and others see the need for and are fully committed to programme evaluation and have developed the basic knowledge and skills. Once this foundation has been established, attention may then be turned to refining the approach, especially as far as the careful selection of indicators is concerned. With increasing interest at government level in efficient and effective use of resources, it is likely that this refinement will be requred in all schools in the near future.

In the context of programme evaluation, an *indicator* is an attribute of a programme, a measure of which is utilised in making judgements about the worth of the programme. Such attributes may be related to inputs, such as resources required to maintain the programme; processes, such as aspects of teaching and learning; or outcomes, such as results on tests of achievement. The measures may be what we described earlier in the chapter as subjective, such as the perceptions of teachers or parents as to the effectiveness of a programme, or objective, such as frequency of use of a service or results on tests.

In this chapter we have made general reference to effectiveness ('the extent to which programme purposes have been achieved') and efficiency ('the cost value of a programme in relation to the outcomes which have been attained'). For example, as far as effectiveness is concerned, consideration must be given to the particular attributes for which information will be gathered to make judgements about the extent to which programme purposes have been achieved. An illustration of the selection of indicators is provided in Figure 9.3 in the report of a minor evaluation for a Special Education Programme. The 'Success Indicators' in the report reveal that information was gathered about the judgement of teachers as far as effectiveness is concerned, frequency of use of special education services, support of parents for the programme, number of children showing evidence of increased self-esteem and ability to cope with learning tasks, and number of children who will be able to return to the regular programme.

While indicators will generally be concerned with effectiveness and efficiency, other considerations such as equity ('extent to which programme is available and accessible to those who need or desire it') may also be important. For example, information may be gathered about the number of students who are served by a programme compared with the number of students who have needs which can be met through participation in that programme.

It is evident that programme evaluation can become quite sophisticated and demanding as far as choice of indicators and selection of approaches to measurement are concerned. Our experience has been that schools will move to this level of sophistication, with the involvement and commitment of teachers, once a basic framework such as that outlined in this chapter has been established and all who are involved see the value of programme evaluation in the management cycle. Setting expectations which are too high in the early stages may be counter-productive as far as commitment is concerned.

SUMMARY
EVALUATING

WHAT IS PROGRAMME EVALUATION?

- In programme evaluation, measures of effectiveness and efficiency are sought.
- Programme effectiveness is a measure or estimate of the extent to which programme purposes have been achieved.
- Programme efficiency is a measure or estimate of the cost value of a programme or an aspect of a programme in relation to the outcomes which have been attained.

WHY IS PROGRAMME EVALUATION DESIRABLE?

- Programme evaluation may lead to the modification of existing polices and establishment of new policies to better meet the ongoing and emerging needs of the students.
- Programme evaluation may lead to improvements in the planning and implementation of programmes to the benefit of students.
- Programme evaluation assists in the process of allocating resources to the areas of greatest student need.

IS PROGRAMME EVALUATION POSSIBLE?

- Programmes can be evaluated on a cycle of major and minor evaluations.
- A schedule of major evaluations can be drawn up so that each programme receives a major evaluation once in a set number of years.
- All programmes can receive a minor evaluation in non-major years.
- Major evaluations are in-depth, objective if possible, focus on the achievement of the programme's purpose and are presented in a two-page report.
- Minor evaluations are subjective in nature, not time-intensive, concentrate on assessing the effectiveness of programme implementation, and are presented in a one-page report.

Part C
Making It Work

10 Getting Started

Part C provides guidelines for 'making it work'. At this point it is intended that the reader will have acquired a broad understanding of Collaborative School Management from Part A, and will be convinced of the contribution it may make to school effectiveness and self-management. Part B provided a step-by-step account of how each phase of the Collaborative School Management Cycle may be implemented. The reader may have reached Part C accepting the desirability and acceptability of the approach but with a host of questions as to its workability. How does a school start the process? Will such a systematic approach provide sufficient flexibility for the school to respond quickly and appropriately to needs as they arise? Will conflict be fostered by providing a framework for collaboration? How does one plan for the allocation of the major resource in the teaching process: teachers? No doubt many more questions must be answered before the reader is satisfied.

Chapter 10 provides sample strategies for implementing the approach at the school level and for the support of schools on a system-wide basis. Chapter 11 demonstrates how the approach may be used as a framework for leadership and the management of change, addressing many of the concerns which are often expressed in schools about these issues. Chapter 12 provides guidelines for the management of conflict in schools, demonstrating how the Collaborative School Management Cycle is itself a valuable framework for dealing with conflict. Chapter 13 is concerned with the allocation of staff in schools.

Chapter 14 provides answers to questions which are commonly asked about the approach, with the authors drawing on their experiences in the school setting and in seminars and consultations associated with its introduction.

Some Critical Considerations

Time

The first consideration of many who have contemplated the introduction of the Collaborative School Management Cycle has been time. At first sight there appears to be a lot of paperwork: a policy handbook for the school, the annual programme plan and budget, and regular evaluation reports. *'We don't have the time.' 'We are already overwhelmed by paperwork and demands for continuing change.'* In our judgement, a well-implemented approach to Collaborative School Management will not add to the paperwork and will not add new tasks to what is already being done and should be done. The concerns about time were addressed in the following terms in Part B:

- Paperwork is kept to a minimum with policies on one page, each programme plan and budget on two pages, each evaluation report on either one page (minor evaluation) or two pages (major evaluation) and each questionnaire survey on one page.
- Responsibility for policy-making and planning is shared, with staff, for example, contributing in programme teams according to their area of expertise.
- A period of three to five years is taken to implement all phases of the Collaborative School Management Cycle, with each phase being smoothly integrated into the management of the school.
- The focus on learning and teaching means that all activities in the Collaborative School Management Cycle are, or should be, carried out at present in one form or another; for example, curriculum policy exists in many schools but is 'buried' in quite large curriculum documents. We recommend extracting and refining policy information.

The strategies in the pages which follow ensure that these four outcomes will be achieved, thereby alleviating the concerns about time.

People

People's reactions are also to be considered. Many head teachers and others have grown weary of what they see as sheer inertia if out outright resistance to the introduction of change in their schools. In many cases this unwillingness to embark on further change has been due to the use of inappropriate strategies for change in the past.

Enough is known about attempts to introduce change on a large scale in an organisation to make three general statements about people which need to be taken into account when a strategy for the introduction of

Collaborative School Management is being devised. What follows is a summary of this knowledge.

1   Individuals pass through different stages in adopting an innovation. Some pass through these stages more quickly than others, while some emphasise one stage more than others. The innovation may be rejected at any stage and may be rejected after an initial decision to adopt. Rogers[1] has identified five stages: awareness, interest, evaluation, trial and adoption. These stages will be evident in the adoption of Collaborative School Management.

2   Individuals fall into different categories when classified according to rate of adoption. Rogers[2] has identified five categories: innovators, early adopters (who usually include opinion leaders), early majorities, late majorities and laggards. Head teachers and teachers who volunteer to embark on Collaborative School Management will include many who may be considered innovators. Opinion leaders may be expected to show interest in the approach shortly thereafter, providing they are assured of its desirability, workability and acceptability.

3   Change in an organisation is effected by breaking the equilibrium between driving forces which tend to move the organisation in the direction of change and restraining forces which tend to maintain the status quo. To break this equilibrium, Lewin[3] advocates as a first priority the reduction or removal of restraining forces. A second priority is changing the direction of restraining forces. A third priority is the strengthening or addition of driving forces; earlier action along these lines may lead to an increase in the strength of the restraining forces. Following the Lewin approach in the introduction of Collaborative School Management, the first step in the reduction or removal of restraining forces might include the provision of accurate, understandable information to remove misconceptions, or the provision of information about the anticipated levels of resources to help schools commence the planning process.

A Sample Strategy for Getting Started in Schools

The three statements set out above suggest a number of features which will be common to all strategies for the introduction of Collaborative School Management in a school. What follows here is a sample which will require three to five years for full-scale implementation. It assumes that the head teacher or, in the case of a school having a council or board of governors, the chairperson, is the catalyst for action.

A ten-step strategy

1 Introduce the change to the policy group and staff by explaining and demonstrating its nature and purpose: there is no need to 'sell' the approach. Reassure all concerned that adequate time will be allowed for its introduction.

2 The policy group should determine the timetable for implementation.

3 Do not introduce the different phases of the approach to all programmes at the same time. For example, there is no need to establish goals for each programme at the same time; there is no need for programme plans and programme budgets to be prepared for the first time in the same year.

4 Invite volunteers to prepare programme plans and programme budgets for a few programmes in the first year, allowing time for integrating this work with other tasks and for consultation.

5 Set priorities for policy-making in the first year with a small number of high-priority contentious issues addressed along with a relatively large number of non-contentious issues.

6 Programme planning and budgeting may be extended to all programmes in the second year, with time allowed for the activity, including the use of an in-service day for adequate information-gathering and consultation.

7 The policy base may be completed in the third year.

8 The programme planning and programme budgeting process may be refined in the third year.

9 Programme evaluation need not be addressed in the early stages. A cyclical approach to major and minor evaluation among programmes may be commenced as late as the fourth year, with volunteers again invited to initiate the process.

10 Programme evaluation may be extended to all programmes in the fifth year.

A minimum of paperwork and jargon

It is recommended that schools adhere strictly to guidelines for minimum paperwork:

1 Policy statements: a maximum of one page.
2 Programme plans and budgets: a maximum of two pages.
3 Report of a minor programme evaluation: a maximum of one page.
4 Report of a major programme evaluation: a maximum of two pages.
5 Surveys of members of school community: a maximum of one page.

All documents should be free of jargon so that they can be read and understood by all members of the school community.

An educational role for the policy group

Meetings of the policy group should be organised to reflect a concern for educational goals, policies, budgets and evaluation. Time devoted to minutes, correspondence, operational matters and non-educational issues should be kept to a minimum. The following strategy may be a useful guide to action, especially when the policy group is a school council or board of governors.

1 Meetings in term 1 may be concerned with refining goals and policies and setting priorities for policy-making for the year. Working parties should be established to develop policy options for contentious issues. In later years this work will be an outcome of considerations of programme evaluation prepared towards the end of the previous year. Policies and priorities among programmes should be communicated to staff.

2 Meetings in term 2 may be concerned with receiving reports from working parties and adoption of policy for the forthcoming year. Staff of the school may be engaged during this time on the preparation of programme plans and programme budgets, taking account of the policies and priorities among programmes received from the policy group.

3 Meetings in term 3 may be devoted to consideration of programme plans and programme budgets prepared by staff. These will be adopted if they are consistent with policies and priorities established earlier by the policy group. Inconsistencies should result in further work and resubmission. Some time may also be devoted to participating in working parties undertaking programme evaluations.

Where to start in the cycle

The Collaborative School Management Cycle which is recommended in the book consists of the following phases:

- Goal-setting and need identification
- Policy-making
- Planning
- Preparation and approval of the budget
- Implementing
- Evaluating

The rational or logical approach to the introduction of programme budgeting is to ensure that goals are identified and written, and policies formulated and documented, before programme plans and budgets are prepared. Our experience has been that such an approach is rarely followed when systematic approaches to policy-making and planning are introduced. Participants can become frustrated and impatient when large amounts of time are devoted to goal-setting or policy-making in isolation from other activities.

For programmes which are currently operating well there may be no written policy. A programme plan and programme budget may be prepared on the basis of this unwritten policy, with documentation of the policy occurring in the following year. A different approach must, of course, be used for programmes where there is no written policy and which are not running well or where there is conflict. In this case, the unwritten policy is clearly contentious and a systematic approach to policy-making should establish a desirable, workable and acceptable policy prior to programme planning and programme budgeting.

The point is that the approach to Collaborative School Management should be tailored to the circumstances. Over time, of course, the Collaborative School Management Cycle will be in full operation. After three to five years a highly systematic approach should be evident in the way new issues are addressed in the policy-making and planning process.

The need for continuous orientation

Members of the policy group may be elected or appointed annually. Head teachers and other staff may frequently change. It is necessary to build in provision for continuous orientation to the process and product of Collaborative School Management if a high degree of efficiency and effectiveness is to be attained. This is best done on a school-by-school basis, with support given as necessary from the central office of the system. Collaborative School Management will rarely just happen, either in a school or in a system of schools. The strategy described in the last section for introducing the cycle in schools assumed that the head teacher or chairperson of the policy group adopted a leadership role to get things started. This section of the chapter suggests a strategy for answering the question '*How does a system of education get schools started on Collaborative School Management?*' Essentially, we offer here a strategy for the central support of Collaborative School Management. A sample strategy is set out in some detail.

Some guiding principles: the 'stepping stone' strategy

The work of Rogers and Lewin was cited earlier in the chapter when people's reactions to change were discussed. What follows here is a simple five-step approach, described by Havelock[4] as a 'stepping stone' strategy, which also takes account of these concerns. It assumes that administrators in education wish to see the introduction of Collaborative School Management in all schools and that some initial trialling has been conducted with the support of heat teachers', teachers' and parents' organisations as appropriate. For government schools in Victoria, Australia for example, this was initially done as part of a comprehensive strategy for the introduction of school-level programme budgeting. In Britain, it may be done in association with government intents to give governing bodies and head teachers control of their own budgets.

1 Introduce Collaborative School Management to all schools in one or more regions at an introductory seminar. The invitation to attend should set out in simple language the nature and purpose of the process.

2 Call for schools to volunteer to begin the process. Schools accepting the invitation will usually be led by people who may be described as innovators. Provide psychological and technical support to these schools to encourage them to become skilled in Collaborative School Management so that they can subsequently demonstrate it to others.

3 Work next with individuals and groups who are potential, but still inactive, resisters. Respond to their questions and concerns. This is the stage at which there should be widespread dissemination of information to remove misconceptions about the approach. 'Protect' the innovators at this stage: they may lose heart without continuous psychological and technical support.

4 Now bring the approach to the attention of those who may be considered 'early adopters': these may include opinion leaders. Allow them to see Collaborative School Management in operation. Encourage them to talk with resisters or would-be resisters once they are 'on side'.

5 Finally, encourage opinion leaders to implement Collaborative School Management and enlist their aid in introducing the approach to remaining schools. At the very least, secure their public support and commitment or place them on key committees or working parties.

Goals for central support

Most systems of education now rely on staff located in a central or regional office to provide support for schools. The detailed strategy for support which is suggested in the following pages reflects six goals which are consistent with the guiding principles in the 'stepping stone' strategy. These goals are as follows.

1   Provide all support staff with details of Collaborative School Management.
2   Ensure a co-ordinated effort among support staff who are supporting other endeavours which may be integrated in Collaborative School Management (for example, school effectiveness or school improvement programmes).
3   Provide technical and psychological support to schools which commence the process.
4   Ensure that people in all schools have a sound understanding of Collaborative School Management *before* being invited to adopt the approach.
5   Ensure that all schools commence the process over a three-year period, with a significant number involved in the first year.
6   Provide continuing support to all schools as implementation proceeds.

The sample strategy

The following is a sample strategy for achieving the goals set out above. It is acknowledged that other strategies may suit particular settings and that there are a variety of approaches to implementing each strategy.

1. **Informing all central staff**

    • An information session for senior officer (Chief Education Officer, Superintendent, Director) should be arranged as soon as possible. The special characteristics of the approach will be stressed, especially the links identified in goal no. 2, above.
    • A seminar is then organised for all regional staff, with the senior officer playing a major part.
    • All central staff consider ways in which they can support the implementation effort. Related activities should be planned and explicitly incorporated in the work schedules of staff in the manner described below.

2. **A co-ordinated effort by central staff**

    • A small, broadly based working party of those concerned with the support of schools should jointly plan the strategy for support. One officer should be designated as having responsibility for the formation and operation of the working party, and the senior officer of the system should be a member *ex officio*.
    • Members of the working party should meet regularly to share information concerning the different activities, and make regular reports to the senior officer.
    • Joint or team efforts by members of the working party will enable

schools to see and experience activities which link, say, initiatives in programme budgeting with developments related to school improvement.

3. **Support for innovators**

- Regular meetings of head teachers who are 'the innovators' will be valuable. Conference telephone calls will be useful in country areas to discuss problems and solutions. This acknowledges that head teachers are vital to the success of implementation.
- Technical assistance should be provided as required: helping schools determine what to do, how to do it, when to do it and how to acquire resources to do it.
- Positive feedback, encouragement, and support in the face of negative comments by others will help.

4. **Informing all schools in the system**

- A simple information sheet to all schools which describes the approach is a minimum.
- System seminars, involving key people, can be used to highlight the efforts of innovators.
- Use newspaper reports and bulletins about progress of innovators.
- Stress that Collaborative School Management is an integrator of school management processes and a framework for coping with major changes which have occurred at the school level in recent years.

5. **Develop system resources**

- Prepare seminar materials and workship packages containing samples of what has been accomplished by innovators in the system.
- Identify innovators who can provide further special assistance to schools who indicate their wish to adopt the approach in the second or subsequent years.

6. **Ensuring system-wide adoption with significant numbers in the second year**

- Following the dissemination effort, form an advisory committee of opinion leaders, influential people, representatives of interest groups and key people from trial schools to plan adoption throughout the region. Membership of this committee should be widely publicised.
- Call for more volunteers to start in the second year. Ask all schools to declare the year in which they will start. Give priority to securing the involvement of opinion leaders among schools.
- Organise further seminars for schools starting in the second year.

> Make use of personnel who are innovators but, again, give priority to securing the assistance of opinion leaders.

7. Continuing support for all schools

- See paragraph 3, but networks of school-based personnel will be required.
- 'Late adopters' or 'laggards' will need special encouragement and assistance.
- Every resource should be pressed into service at this time.

Still more questions

This chapter has been concerned with the strategies for getting started. Other issues must be addressed throughout the implementation effort and these are discussed in the remaining chapters of Part C: Leadership and Management of Change (chapter 11), Management of Conflict (chapter 12), Management of the Staff Resource (chapter 13) and, dealing with a host of other questions which will arise (chapter 14).

SUMMARY
GETTING STARTED

GETTING STARTED IN A SCHOOL

- Take three to five years for full implementation.
- Start at any point in the Collaborative School Management Cycle:
    Goal-setting and need identification
    Policy-making
    Planning
    Budgeting
    Evaluating
- Integrate Collaborative School Management with existing approaches: do not allow it to become yet another change which is a burden to all.
- Use the 'stepping stone' strategy:
    (a) call for volunteers, then
    (b) reassure sceptics and support volunteers, then
    (c) extend to include opinion leaders, then
    (d) involve all programmes.

GETTING STARTED IN A SYSTEM

- Senior officers must give visible support.
- Use a 'stepping stone' strategy for schools.
- Make it a team effort: all central staff having contact with staff are agents for change.

---

11 *Leadership and Management of Change*

This chapter is concerned with two broad issues for the self-managing school which has adopted or is considering the adoption of the approach we describe as Collaborative School Management. As far as leadership is concerned, the reader might ask about the leadership role of the head teacher and others who may have leadership responsibilities. What scope is there for the exercise of leadership in an approach which deals largely with management processes? What scope is there for the leader with a vision for the school and who wishes to secure commitment to that vision by all in the school community? As far as change is concerned, the reader might ask about the extent to which there is opportunity for flexibility in an approach based on policy-making and planning for a number of discrete programmes which reflect 'how the school is organised and how teachers work and children learn'. How can change be accomplished when a need is indicated?

The purposes of this chapter are to describe how leadership may be exercised, indeed enhanced, as a school moves toward self-management through the collaborative approach, and to demonstrate that the Collaborative School Management Cycle is a useful framework for the management of change.

Leadership

Recent studies have painted a much broader picture than was previously evident in the literature about leaders and leadership. Earlier attempts to identify the attributes of effective leaders resulted in a short list which included sense of responsibility, concern for task completion, energy, persistence, risk-taking, originality, self-confidence, and capacity to handle stress, to influence, and to coordinate the efforts of others in the achievement of purpose.[1] Attempts to develop theories of leadership resulted in the identification of the two well-known 'dimensions' of leadership:

concern for accomplishing the tasks of the organisation and concern for relationships within and among members of the organisation. Contingency theories of leadership have described how various patterns of task and relationship styles or behaviours are more effective in some situations than in others.[2] Despite their validity, these theories have not had a major impact on practice and have generally failed to excite the practitioner.

There is now, however, a far richer body of knowledge winning the confidence of scholars and practitioners alike. This has been achieved with more expansive, multi-disciplinary study of organisations and leaders rather than what had become an increasingly narrow focus on a small number of measurable variables in research conducted within the framework of a single field of inquiry. In this section of the chapter, we give attention to two important aspects of this contemporary view of leadership, namely, vision in leadership and the fostering of leadership. We demonstrate how both aspects are enhanced through Collaborative School Management.

Vision in leadership

The importance of vision is a recurring theme in studies of effectiveness and leadership in education as in other organisations. Bennis and Nanus describe a vision as 'a mental image of a possible and desirable future state of the organisation ... as vague as a dream or as precise as a goal or mission statement ... a view of a realistic, credible, attractive future for the organisation, a condition that is better in some important ways than what now exists'.[3] The vision of a head teacher may be a dream expressed in written form as our school will be a learning centre in the community, where every child will enjoy coming to school and will acquire a broad array of knowledge, skills and attitudes, including the basic skills, and where parents and other members of the community can engage in educational programmes for their personal improvement and enjoyment'. The vision may, alternatively, be a more precise statement of mission: 'our students are presently performing far below those in schools in comparable social settings on tests of basic skills: we aim to come in the top ten among these schools on system-wide tests of achievement'.

Having vision alone is not, of course, sufficient for effective leadership. Recent studies have highlighted the importance of the leader gaining the commitment of others to that vision and then ensuring that it shapes the policies, plans and day-to-day activities in the organisation. Values are important as are the meanings which are attached to the behaviour of leaders and to day-to-day activities. Starratt combined all of these perspectives in a simple, eloquent model for leadership as the 'communal institutionalising of a vision':

- The leader's power is rooted in a vision that is itself rooted in something basic to human life.

- That vision illuminates the ordinary with dramatic significance.
- The leader articulates that vision in such compelling ways that it becomes the shared vision of the leader's colleagues, and it illuminates their ordinary activities with dramatic significance.
- The leader implants the vision in the structures and processes of the organisation, so that people experience the vision in the various patterned activities of the organisation.
- The leader and colleagues make day-to-day decisions in light of that vision, so that the vision becomes the heart of the culture of the organisation.
- All the members of the organisation celebrate the vision in ritual, ceremonies and art forms.[4]

The approach we describe as Collaborative School Management is offered as a framework within which this view of leadership can be realised in a school. While a school community will welcome the appointment of a head teacher who has a general vision for schools which is suited to that community, it is evident that this vision must be adapted to the setting and must win the commitment of others if it is to be brought to reality. The collaborative processes described throughout the book suggest the manner in which this might be accomplished. Most important, however, is the view that this shared vision, however developed, be then embedded in the structures and processes of the school so that it then shapes the everyday activities of teaching and learning. The Collaborative School Management Cycle provides a model for this process: the shared vision will shape the selection of goals and needs which, in turn, will shape policies, programmes, priorities, plans, patterns of resource allocation, approaches to teaching and learning, and special considerations in ongoing approaches to programme evaluation.

Fostering of leadership

It was suggested in chapter 6 that the head teacher may exercise a number of roles in the policy-making process. These included policy initiator, policy analyst, policy researcher and policy evaluator. These roles may, of course, be assumed by others who exercise leadership in the school. Collaborative School Management fosters many leaders in teams for programme planning and in working parties on policy-related issues.

Further insights in relation to the fostering and distribution of leadership in the school may be gained by examining recent literature on the links between leadership and excellence in education. Sergiovanni, for example, suggests the existence of five leadership 'forces', each of which 'can be thought of as the means available to administrators, supervisors and teachers to bring about or preserve changes needed to improve schooling'.[5]

These forces, with illustrations of Collaborative School Management involving the head teacher and other leaders, are as follows:[6]

Technical   Technical leadership is concerned with sound management techniques. Examples include the capacity to plan, organise, co-ordinate and schedule to ensure optimum effectiveness and efficiency. With Collaborative School Management, the head teacher has a special responsibility to ensure that the technical aspects of leadership are in place. Each management technique will be required of those who exercise leadership in programme teams.

Human   Human leadership involves the harnessing of available human resources in ways which include building and maintaining morale, encouraging growth and creativity, providing support for staff and encouraging participatory approaches to decision-making. Collaborative School Management provides opportunity for the exercise of these approaches to leadership by the head teacher as well as by leaders of programme teams.

Educational   Educational leadership involves the use of expert knowledge about education and schooling. Examples include the capacity to diagnose student needs, develop curriculum, provide supervision and conduct evaluations. Educational leadership thus defined pervades the school in Collaborative School Management, with every teacher having the opportunity to work with colleagues to determine the particular needs of students and then devise ways of meeting these needs, including the setting of priorities and identification of required resources. Such leadership for the school as a whole is required of the head teacher.

Symbolic   Symbolic leadership involves focusing the attention of others on matters of importance to the school. Examples include touring the school, visiting classrooms, presiding at ceremonies, knowing students and providing a unified vision for the school in the manner described in the first section of the chapter. In Collaborative School Management, the head teacher has the critically important role of focusing the attention of staff and others in the school community on the importance of the various phases of the management cycle, each of which is important in 'institutionalising' the vision for the school.

Cultural   Cultural leadership involves the building of a unique, strong school culture which studies have shown to be so important if excellence is to be attained. Examples of cultural leadership include frequent public reference to the characteristics of the school and its mission in the community, the socialisation of new members, telling stories, maintaining myths and rewarding those who reflect the culture. In Collaborative School Management, the head teacher plays a special leadership role, working with the policy group and others to build and maintain the culture of the school, introducing new members of the school community to the processes and importance of the various phases of the management process, and drawing everyone's attention to successes and significant people who have made a contribution to establishing and achieving school goals.

Sergiovanni offered one view which is of particular interest. He believes that the five leadership forces can be arranged in a hierarchy. Technical and human leadership forces are important but alone are insufficient for the achievement of excellence. Adding educational leadership achieves more but it is only with the addition of symbolic and cultural leadership that a school can attain excellence. Sergiovanni also suggested that highly successful leaders recognise the importance of 'leadership density', referring here to 'the extent to which leadership roles are shared and the extent to which leadership is broadly exercised'.[7] The leadership role of the head teacher is thus critically important in the self-managing school but leadership among others is also necessary, and it is fostered through Collaborative School Management.

Management of Change

Recent studies[8] of leadership have also shown the importance of the leader having a vision of the process of change. It is evident that the Collaborative School Management Cycle provides a model which might be included in such a vision. Its central feature is the management of change: all of the explanations and illustrations offered in Part B were concerned with the identification of needs, the setting of goals and priorities, the establishment of programmes through which these needs will be addressed, the allocation of resources, implementation through teaching and learning and the support of teaching and learning, and ongoing approaches to programme evaluation. In this section of the chapter, we give special consideration to four aspects of change resulting from shifts in internal priorities, the determination of policy in new areas, the re-ordering of policy priorities, and decreases or increases in school funding reflecting shifts in external priorities. Attention is given in each instance to the manner in which Collaborative School Management can facilitate the process of change in a self-managing school.

Policy shifts

Policy shifts may occur when the policy group perceives needs and acts accordingly. For example, a policy shift of this nature occurred in one school's excursion or field trip policy. In past years, it had been policy to enable students to acquire living skills in a variety of outdoor environments, and to develop these skills in a systematic way over a period of time. But more and more students were leaving the quiet isolation of this school and moving to the larger centres. This development resulted in a modification to the policy so that students are now required to develop urban survival skills as well as skills related to remote, rural life. The resultant change will be either an increase in time allocated to excursions at the cost of something else, or a lower standard of rural survival skills for students.

Policy shifts can also occur when central authorities perceive changes in needs or desirable outcomes and react accordingly. The ramifications for the school are similar to those described.

Changes that occur because of policy shifts need to be considered. Rewriting the policy statement in line with the perceived new needs is the easiest part. The difficulty comes in redesigning what students will do to achieve the new purposes or guidelines, and in allocating appropriate resources for resulting activities. Even this can be accomplished with time and thought, but then problems may arise when the ramifications for other student activities and for resource users are discovered. Attempts are often made to accommodate policy shifts by devising new activities but these attempts often fail or are less than satisfactory because of problems which may arise in other areas.

It is suggested that Collaborative School Management can provide a mechanism to assist in coping with shifts in policy by directly linking policies and resource allocation in programme planning. A policy shift can be accommodated by totally rethinking the implementation plan for the related programme and allocating or reallocating resources accordingly. This can take place in the preparation work for a new budget year or, if of sufficient urgency, it can be done during a budget year by reallocating resources in the relevant programme. It is likely that the policy shift can be accommodated by including new elements in the implementation plan. These planning elements should be placed in order of priority when a programme budget is prepared. The inclusion of a new element in line with a policy shift can then be accommodated by deleting low-priority planning elements to release the required resources. The fact that all this information is at hand in a readily usable form results in effective change as far as students are concerned.

Determination of policy in new areas

The call for new policies is frequently reported in the media. The reaction is often a call for schools to develop new activities that, properly instituted, will solve the problem. Increasing educational opportunity for students of post-compulsory school-age is an example. Such proposals are clearly of value but teachers may shudder when thought is not given to the allocation of resources or to choosing which existing programmes must be modified or withdrawn.

It often appears that the approach to accommodating new policies could be termed the 'introduce and hope' technique. The pressure related to the need for the new policy is such that introduction is often a necessity, but little thought is given to how the policy will work, and there is a fond hope that somehow resources and planning will stretch just that bit more and that we will 'get away with it again'. Of course we never really 'get away with it' at all and already stretched resources must be reallocated or be so thin that they are ineffective across a broader and broader field.

Another technique can be called the partial introduction approach, in which those aspects of a new policy that 'don't cost anything' are introduced with the rest to follow some time later. Of course, apart from the name, there is always some cost and the same problems as those found in 'introduce and hope' eventually surface. It is little wonder that new policies so often fail. Inappropriate approaches to change may lead to frustration and disenchantment on the part of those directly involved and eventually to the failure of the policy. This is most unfortunate, especially if the new policy is an outcome of a real need that will obviously remain.

The Collaborative School Management Cycle suggests that the determination of a policy in a new area should result, first of all, in the inclusion of a new programme. Implementation planning would then proceed for the new programme in line with the purposes and broad guidelines of the new policy. In this planning, elements would be devised through which the purposes could be achieved and listed in priority order. The planning elements would be likely to include personnel required, materials, travel and new equipment and can be relatively easily translated into financial terms in the programme budget. In this way a total amount can be calculated for the likely cost of successfully introducing the new programme. Some people might want to argue about the correctness and appropriateness of the planning and costing, and the ensuing discussion might produce more efficient and effective planning.

When the plan is prepared and the cost is calculated, it is then possible to proceed to introduce the new policy by finding new or additional sources of income. If these are not available then introduction can still proceed. It becomes a matter of determining the priority rating of the new policy and dispensing with programmes relating to lower-order policies until the required resources are available. It might even be possible to proceed by dropping out a number of low-priority planning elements in several programmes to achieve the desired end. In either case, the information on which to base a decision is readily available. This is the real value of programme budgeting and planning: it ensures that detailed information is available on which to base judgements affecting the activities we provide for students.

It is not easy to introduce new policies when existing policies or parts of policies have to be dropped because of the changed priorities. No one likes removing or reducing existing programmes especially in education, but new needs emerge and have to be accommodated somehow. The technique of 'watering down' programmes so that new programmes can be accommodated does not work. It can kill off the new policy and also do immeasurable harm to existing policies.

Reordering of policy priorities

Reordering priorities in order to implement policies assumes that an order of priority already exists. This is not the case in most schools. However, in many schools there may be classifications of policies into at least 'high priority' and 'others'. In some schools this classification may be further extended and policies may be listed in a number of broad groups. Change occurs when the priority for a policy changes from one category to another.

The reordering of priorities is a continual process in the school but changes do not always occur, as a result, in all cases. It seems that often we cannot translate the new order into practice. Reordering priorities should result in changes to the amount of resources allocated to activities but, if the actual resources allocated to programmes are not known in detail, it is difficult to reallocate resources in line with a new order of priorities. A technique in the past has simply been to spend more money on the programmes listed in a higher priority but this technique only worked when additional sources of funds were available. When additional funds were available, they were sometimes used for 'add-on' elements for relevant programmes, when in fact the additional funds should have been allocated as part of a more comprehensive planning effort.

A reordering of policy and programme priorities should result in a reordering of all of the resources allocated to those programmes. Of necessity, this reordering of allocated resources needs to be based on detailed information on the current allocation of resources. This information is readily provided by programme planning and budgeting. Collaborative School Management ensures that additional resources allocated to a programme follow a comprehensive and integrated approach to planning, with the result available in documented form so that all concerned can judge whether the proposed plan is likely to succeed in achieving the intended purposes.

Decreasing (or increasing) school funding

Most schools have encountered reduced funding from government sources in recent years. The resulting changes have been harmful not only because there is a decrease in resources but the changes have often been 'across the board'. This has not only happened in schools but also in the administration and support services designed to assist schools in their operation. It results in situations where a support officer, for example, can be available to a school but there are insufficient travel funds to enable that officer to visit and work with the school and hence provide the support required. Other examples include decisions made by some authorities to accommodate a cut in the education budget by decreasing funding for materials and equipment by ten per cent across the board, or by decreasing or even eliminating teacher relief for professional development.

The situation may improve with the adoption by government and other authorities of a form of programme budgeting. it will enable funding cuts to be translated as programme eliminations or modifications and in this way will detrimentally affect only a small number of programmes in schools rather than affecting all with 'across the board' cuts. It will mean that a high-priority support service will still have sufficient travel funds to function effectively but some programmes may not continue, including the people working within those programmes. It is always a difficult decision to dispense with personnel and far easier to reduce some other resource but if the overall effect is to reduce the effectiveness of many programmes for our clients, the children, then the hard decision must be made.

Even the central authority reducing support to a programme as a means of decreasing expenditure is not without problems. There is often a clear relationship between central authority programmes and school programmes and although the demise of a programme may reflect the government's priority for that policy, it may not reflect local priorities. There may be special circumstances that mean a programme should be retained locally, though it might be dispensed with as too low a priority for the whole system. This is the old problem of how can the central authority accurately provide for the varied needs existing at the local level. The difficulty could be overcome, to some extent, if the central authority would provide resources in the total sense to the school, so that subsequent allocation could reflect local needs. Initiatives along these lines have already been taken in a number of school systems.

Funds for schools are still going to come from a variety of sources and each source is going to have its own restrictions attached. Being prepared to estimate all these amounts and then to develop a budget in programme form does enable a school to make the most of both worlds and to provide best for its students. Dealing with all sources at once enables money to be allocated to various programmes where the restrictions and intentions are complementary. Use of the programme planning and budgeting approach enables programmes to be developed and resources allocated so that local needs are uppermost.

It is evident that Collaborative School Management provides a useful framework for the management of change in general. Its value stems from the fact that planning for programmes and the related resource allocation can be directly linked to policies and that information on which to base sound judgements is readily available in a usable form. A further benefit of having relevant information available is often the elimination of overlap when providing resources for programmes. This efficiency of programme planning and budgeting can release 'additional resources' for allocation to other programmes with lower priority.

Other Issues

Workload and participation in change

The introduction of Collaborative School Management is often regarded, at first, as an 'add-on' to an already overcrowded list of changes occurring in schools. However, a careful consideration of the approach reveals that it is not an 'add-on' in this sense but rather an approach to management that enables those involved with school change to cope with and facilitate the the change in a way that is effective in achieving the objective and makes efficient use of participants' time.

- Those wishing to initiate change have an immediate contact point for the consideration of their ideas — the policy group.
- The necessity and desirability of the proposed change is carefully considered by a group representative of all concerned.
- The proposed change is considered in relation to other needs and goals.
- If considered desirable, the proposed change is the subject of policy-making through selection from alternatives encompassing all aspects of the area of proposed change.
- A priority for the new policy is established indicating the relationship to other policy areas.
- A plan for implementation and a related budget is prepared for a programme through which to implement the new policy.
- The budget is approved and resources allocated in relation to other

priorities to ensure that the policy is effectively implemented.
- A plan for evaluation is prepared for the review of the new policy's effectiveness.
- The roles of the various participants are clearly delineated.

In summary, Collaborative School Management provides a framework within which change can occur, and a framework that also enables the changes to be accommodated in a non-threatening manner. All concerned can anticipate the procedures for managing the proposed change and can be assured that not only will due consideration be given, but also, if it is considered desirable, planning and resource allocation will follow to ensure reflection of the change in the school's work and in students' learning.

Professional development

Collaborative School Management also provides a framework for the professional development of staff and the school community in general. Participation in the process enhances the development of skills in assessing needs, goal-setting, policy-making, setting priorities, negotiating, planning, budgeting, evaluating, decision-making, forming consensus and problem-solving. This development should not take place in isolation, as it quite often does, but in relation to, and integrated with, the reality of providing relevant learning experiences for children. The process not only provides a mechanism for enhancing professional skills through participation, but also provides a means for identifying the general areas of need for professional development. In this way a professional development programme can be drawn up for staff that is based on needs within the school. These needs can be met by sharing existing expertise within the school or by designing specific programmes involving outside experts. Professional development moves from the 'supermarket' approach, where staff 'take what is offered', to addressing real professional development needs within the school. Leadership in this professional development is an important role for the head teacher and senior staff responsible for programmes.

Collaborative School Management can be regarded as the ultimate form of school-based development. The key participants are the parents, students and teachers. They are able to share responsibility for planning for the future and for ensuring that resources are allocated and skills developed so that those plans are fulfilled. In this way the participants are able to chart and take responsibility for their own future and, in so doing, build trust and common values among all concerned.

SUMMARY
LEADERSHIP AND MANAGEMENT OF CHANGE

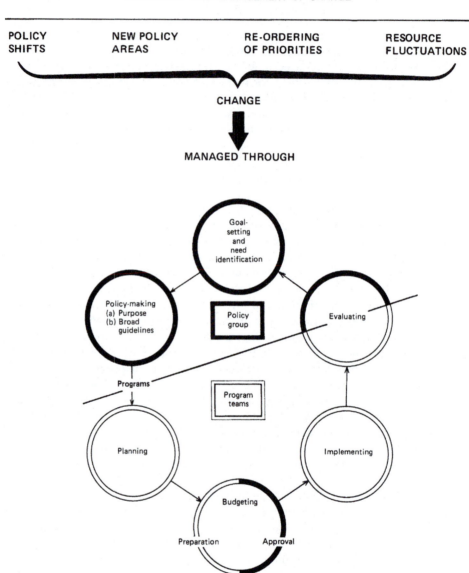

| POLICY SHIFTS | NEW POLICY AREAS | RE-ORDERING OF PRIORITIES | RESOURCE FLUCTUATIONS |

CHANGE

MANAGED THROUGH

Goal-setting and need identification

Policy-making
(a) Purpose
(b) Broad guidelines

Policy group

Evaluating

Programs

Program teams

Planning

Implementing

Budgeting

Preparation

Approval

LEADERSHIP WIDELY DISPERSED
EXERCISED THROUGH

- UNIFIED VISION
- LEADERSHIP FORCES: TECHNICAL, HUMAN, EDUCATIONAL, SYMBOLIC, CULTURAL

12 *Management of Conflict*

There may be concern that Collaborative School Management will create conflict in a school. This fear arises from the view that staff, when organised along programme lines, will be in competition for scarce resources, with hostility resulting and loss of cohesiveness within the school. Better a school-wide perspective, it is argued, than a divided staff. The concern is often expressed for primary schools where organisation along programme lines occurs less frequently than in secondary schools. The opposite view is taken in this chapter: Collaborative School Management is seen as a framework for managing conflict so that its harmful effects are minimised.

This chapter is organised in four parts. First, the nature of conflict is examined, especially in relation to resource allocation. Second, the collaborative approach is offered as an effective framework for minimising the chances of harmful conflict. Third, guidelines are offered for participants in a conflict who wish to obtain a so-called '*win–win*' outcome; that is, who wish to strive actively to satisfy their own interests as well as the interests of others with whom they are in conflict. Illustrations are provided throughout. Finally, guidelines are offered for building consensus through Collaborative School Management.

The Nature of Conflict

Conflict has been defined as 'the active striving for one's own preferred outcome which, if attained, precludes the attainment by others of their preferred outcome, thereby producing hostility.'[1] It is the hostility which is usually seen as the harmful aspect of conflict. The management of conflict thus becomes an effort to eliminate or minimise hostility, acknowledging that it is inevitable, if not healthy, for individuals and groups to strive to attain their own preferred outcomes or to satisfy their own particular interests.

It is useful to start by considering the factors which can give rise to conflict. Three are usually identified.

1 Conflict may occur when the resources of the school are insufficient to meet the requirements of individuals or groups in the school: there is competition for scarce resources.
2 Conflict may occur when an individual or group seeks to control the activities 'belonging' to another group: the issue here is autonomy.
3 Conflict may occur when two or more individuals or groups in the school cannot agree on ends and means in education: the source of the conflict here is divergent goals.[2]

When viewed in this manner there are clearly a host of opportunities for conflict to occur in policy-making and planning. Some decisions which may be the subject of conflict are listed below:

Divergent goals	• What should be the goals of the school? • Which needs (gaps between *'what is'* and *'what should be'*) are high priority at this time? • What should be the school's policy in addressing a particular need? • What should be the goals for a particular programme? • How can the goals for a particular programme be best achieved?
Autonomy	• Which individuals or groups should be responsible for a particular programme? • Who will determine the level of resources to be allocated to a particular programme?
Competition for scarce resources	• What should be the order of priority for activities within a programme when there are insufficient resources to support all activities? • What should be the order of priority for activities among programmes when there are insufficient resources to support all activities?

Conflict associated with these decisions may be minimal in many situations. In some schools there may be little divergence on ends and means; indeed, the staff may have been specially selected for their support of particular goals. Programmes may be stable, with clear areas of responsibility: autonomy is not an issue. Conflict associated with competition for scarce resources may be minimal if a person such as the head teacher allocated those resources and staff have confidence in that person's decisions, or traditionally for one reason or another have never questioned them. It is suggested that such conditions are becoming increasingly rare. It has become almost a cliché that views on means and ends differ in education. The issue of autonomy has become paramount in some systems of education, with teachers' organisations pressing for greater influence in determining conditions within a school, and with community groups seeking similar power as far as programmes are concerned. Both trends have appeared to erode the power and influence of the head teacher. These trends, combined with increasingly scarce resources for schools, have often resulted in a more political climate for resource allocation, and a parallel increase in opportunities for conflict. Indeed, it might be argued that the turbulence of recent times as far as teacher and community influence is concerned has arisen from the three areas which we have defined as factors giving rise to conflict.

Collaborative School Management as a Framework for the Management of Conflict

The issue to be addressed in this section concerns the impact of the collaborative approach. With conflict already evident if not increasing in the manner outlined above, will it ameliorate or exacerbate the situation? It is argued that a well-implemented system of Collaborative School Management provides a framework for the management of this conflict by minimising the hostility and other potentially harmful effects of conflict.

One may turn again to the three factors listed in the previous section as a starting point to identify the way in which the harmful effects of conflict can be minimised. As far as the issue of divergent goals is concerned, opportunities should be created to build agreement on the ends and means of learning and teaching, both in a general school-wide sense and for particular programmes. This suggests some form of collaboration in the goal-setting process. At least there should be a degree of openness so that individual and group preferences can be expressed with the full knowledge of the preferences of others. Unnecessary hostility may often arise because of a lack of knowledge or understanding of other views. A similar advantage may be achieved through collaboration in identifying needs and formulating policies. With Collaborative School Management there is staff and community involvement when needs are identified, goals are established and policies are formulated. Where harmful conflict is evident one should examine the extent to which provision has been made for appropriate involvement.

Problems as far as autonomy are concerned often arise because of a failure to clearly and/or appropriately specify responsibility for particular activities or programmes. The contribution which the collaborative approach can make arises from the opportunity it provides for, and the extent to which it requires, a clear specification of responsibility. Some time must be devoted, for example, to determining the programme structure within the school. Ideally, all activities of staff should be placed in a programme category. Further, the individual who is to have responsibility for a programme must be specified in each case. This responsibility can be dispersed quite widely, since the number of programmes invariably exceeds the number of people formally occupying positions of responsibility. There will, of course, be differences among participants as the structure is determined and responsibility is assigned. The point to be made is that decisions in these areas must be made: they cannot or should not be ignored or remain unclear. As in all facets of Collaborative School Management, the decisions are made with a degree of openness, allowing differences to be expressed with knowledge and understanding of the views and preferences of others. When a decision has been made to adopt Collaborative School Management and the level of conflict seems undesirably high, one should examine the care with which structure and responsibility for programmes have been determined.

Conflict arising from competition for scarce resources is virtually inevitable. The benefits of programme budgeting in minimising hostility and other harmful effects are derived from the rich source of information it provides. Unnecessary conflict can appear where there is inadequate knowledge or understanding of what others wish to do. With a well-implemented system of programme budgeting all relevant information should be available in written form. A list of priorities also assists in this regard: the participants determine priorities within programmes, with the knowledge that not all may receive the resources required for successful implementation. Priorities can also help in the formulation of options for funding based on time. A decision on whether to fund a particular priority need not necessarily be made on a 'yes/no' basis; instead, a decision may be made to support the priority in the next year.

In summary, the benefits of Collaborative School Management for the management of conflict are associated with three characterisitics of a well-implemented approach: the opportunity it provides for appropriate involvement of staff and community, the openness of the process, and the large amount of relevant information which may be generated. Other approaches may give the same benefits but Collaborative School Management provides a systematic and readily understandable framework which warrants special attention if management of conflict is a particular concern.

Guidelines for Managing Conflict

It was suggested in the previous section that the adoption of a system of Collaborative School Management may minimise from the outset the emergence of hostility and other harmful effects of conflict. Attention is given now to guidelines for managing conflict once it has emerged, regardless of whether the collaborative approach has been implemented.

Five patterns of behaviour in conflict

A starting point is the identification of behaviour which participants are likely to reveal during conflict. The classification suggested by Thomas is now used almost universally for this purpose.[3] Thomas suggested that two types of behaviour may be revealed in a conflict; one, which he termed 'co-operativeness', refers to the extent to which one party to the conflict wishes to satisfy the concerns of the other party; the other, which he termed 'assertiveness', refers to the extent to which a party wishes to satisfy his or her own concerns. If one imagines three levels of behaviour for each type — low, moderate and high — it is possible to identify five different styles or orientations which will be evident in a conflict. These are illustrated in Figure 12.1 and explained below.

Competition in conflict is characterised by high assertiveness and low co-operativeness in the search to satisfy one's own concerns — at the expense of others if need be. The effect is domination in what is the classic '*win–lose*' view of conflict. This behaviour is evident when one participant in a discussion on the allocation of resources insists on a high priority for a programme or a programme element regardless of the merits of preferences expressed by others. Actions designed to undermine the case presented by others might also be evident. One instance of competitive behaviour is the use of formal authority to secure a preferred allocation, for example, when a senior teacher allocates funds for his or her own programme element even though discussion with colleagues has revealed a more appropriate decision.

Avoiding is characterised by low assertiveness and low co-operativeness, behaviour manifested by withdrawal, apathy or indifference. Teachers who decline to participate in the instructional planning process, even though priorities for resource allocation related to their programmes are under consideration, would be demonstrating a pattern of avoidance. Hostility may arise when their colleagues or students suffer because of this neglect. Such behaviour is likely to be rare in programme budgeting because of the negative impact on instruction. Avoidance may be evident in the early stages of the implementation of programme budgeting, but it will probably give way to more active involvement once the implications of non-participation are noticed.

Accommodation is characterised by low assertiveness and high co-operativeness, with behaviour typically described as appeasement. This behaviour is demonstrated by teachers who 'go through the motions' of putting a case for their programme or programme element but who give ground immediately a case is put by another, even though there may be strong arguments in favour of their own positions. As with the pattern of avoidance, hostility from colleagues may be the consequence when needed resources are not secured. Effects as far as students are concerned may also be of concern with this pattern of behaviour.

Figure 12.1 Styles of behaviour which may be evident during conflict (from Thomas, 1976)

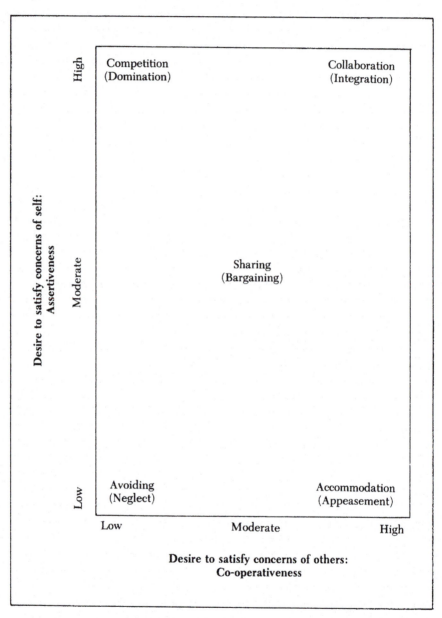

Sharing is characterised by a moderate degree of both assertiveness and co-operativeness. It typically appears as a form of bargaining, with the different parties to the conflict believing that each must give ground if agreement is to be reached. This behaviour often reflects the classic 'zero–sum' view of conflict, the belief that the outcomes are fixed and that gains secured by one party must be at the expense of those secured by the other. The sharing or bargaining pattern is, of course, a common feature of resource allocation. Many would argue that it is the ideal, when participants are encouraged to come to agreements based on each giving up something.

Collaboration is characterised by high degrees of both assertiveness and co-operativeness, with energy devoted to attempts to satisfy the concerns of all parties. In discussion related to the allocation of resources, a collaborative approach is marked by the search for ways to achieve this end. This pattern of behaviour is referred to as '*win–win*' in much of the literature. Guidelines for collaboration are given in another section.

An 'all depends' approach

Each of the patterns described above would appear to be appropriate in some circumstances. A competitive approach, for example, would appear to be acceptable and understandable if there is only a fixed sum of money available and no more than one item can be funded. There are also occasions when a decision must be made quickly or when two parties in conflict cannot agree; the concerns of some parties may often not be considered in determining the outcome. In general, however, the competitive approach would appear to have little in its favour. Avoiding and accommodation also have little to offer except in the short term when time might be gained to permit a more constructive approach. The optimum approach would appear to be collaboration, though it may be a time-consuming endeavour with much energy invested in identifying options which will permit the concerns of all to be satisfied. If collaboration cannot be attained, the sharing or bargaining approach at least ensures that the interests of all parties are addressed to some extent. It has been suggested that bargaining may serve as a useful 'bridge' as a school moves from the traditional competitive, or '*win–lose*' approach, to the more desirable collaborative, or '*win–win*' approach.[4]

Some guidelines for collaboration

Consideration will now be given to guidelines for a collaborative approach in the management of conflict. Some would argue that pure collaboration is impossible if the conflict arises from competition for scarce resources. It may be more appropriate to seek guidelines for behaviour which lies somewhere in the sharing-collaboration continuum. The most promising guidelines are related to the process of negotiation, defined here as a process in which people in disagreement try to reach a settlement, with some measure of satisfaction on the part of each, as far as the achievement of preferred outcomes is concerned.

A straightforward and commonsense approach which has ready application to Collaborative School Management has been proposed by Fisher and Ury, arising from their work in the Harvard Negotiation Project.[5] They argue that traditional approaches to negotiation are really what they term 'positional bargaining' where positions are taken from the outset. In positional bargaining, the behaviour of participants really becomes a contest of wills, with defence and attack based on the basis of established positions. Concessions are made during the course of what can be a long and drawn out affair. The behaviour of participants really falls in the competition-bargaining continuum rather than the bargaining-collaboration continuum. Two variants of the traditional approach are evident, termed by Fisher and Ury 'hard' and soft' . The former is characterised by distrust, with participants viewed as adversaries and victory seen to be the goal, while the latter is an attempt to build trust, with participants viewed as friends and agreement seen to be the goal. But they are both manifestations of bargaining over fixed positions. The solution according to Fisher and Ury[6] is the adoption of what they term 'principled negotiation' or 'negotiation on merit', based on four simple principles:

People: Separate the people from the problem.

Interests: Focus on interests, not positions.

Options: Generate a variety of possibilities before deciding what to do.

Criteria: Insist that the result be based on some objective criteria.

These principles may be applied to Collaborative School Management in a number of ways. The following provide useful guidelines.

1 **Separate the people from the problem.** This guideline does not mean that personal considerations are not taken into account. On the contrary, it is advisable to pay due attention to personal factors but to treat them separately from the problem. Fisher and Ury contend that relationships can be kept on a favourable plane with careful attention to three factors: perception, emotion and communication.[7] One should attempt to see the problem from the other person's point of view. Why do they place a need high in their priorities? Why do they prefer a particular policy alternative? In the face of emotion, one should acknowledge its existence for all participants but not react in the face of an outburst. Communication is critical throughout. The written material in a programme plan and budget must be complemented with effective verbal and non-verbal communication when needs and priorities are considered. All the techniques for effective communication are demanded in and facilitated by a well-implemented system of Collaborative School Management.

2 **Focus on interests and not positions.** This guideline is critically important at every point in the policy-making and planning process. Two apparently conflicting policy alternatives should be analysed in terms of their basic, underlying purposes. What is it that proponents really seek in each instance? A listing of interests may give rise to commonality from

which an acceptable third alternative, substantially meeting both sets of interests, can be formulated. Similarly with decisions related to the allocation of resources among two different programmes. The priorities which have been submitted represent positions. If at first sight both cannot be supported, participants should move away from the list of priorities to a statement of interest. Why is this placed first in the list? What interests do others have which prevent them from supporting this priority? Analysis along these lines may lead to a recasting of priorities or the devising of new priorities which reflect common interests and which can be funded. Fisher and Ury remind us that the most powerful interests are basic human needs which include security, economic well-being, a sense of belonging, recognition and a desire to exercise control over one's life.[8] In general, the key lies in looking behind positions to underlying interests and seeking common ground among these interests. This guideline should be applied at every point in the policy-making and planning process.

3   **Invent options for mutual gain.**   Attention has been given elsewhere to the desirability of preparing options. Guidelines for policy-making, for example, call for the identification of at least three alternatives. The aim is to identify the alternative or combination of alternatives that best satisfies the criteria of desirability, workability and acceptability. Consistent with the second guideline, the identification of three options increases the chances of satisfying common interests. While the guideline applies particularly to the policy-making process, it also has merit when resources must be allocated. Alternatives may be provided within and among priorities in a manner which allows common interests to be readily identified and supported.

4   **Insist on objective criteria.**   This guideline provides a contrast to the traditional approach of positional bargaining which invariably becomes a test of will. The alternative is for participants to try to reach agreement early on the criteria which will shape the decisions to be made. These criteria may include demonstrated impact on students' learning, cost and acceptability to people who must implement the policy or teach the programme or use the resources.

Illustrating the guidelines

Four 'mini-cases' are presented below as illustrations of the manner in which the guidelines may be applied. In each instance the application is being made by the head teacher or another member of staff with responsibility for a programme.

Case 1: 'Who misses out?'
Problem: In contributing to the planning for a particular programme, two teachers present proposals for additional equipment for their classrooms,

each carefully costed and explained. Both teachers feel that their proposal should have first priority. It is known that both plans cannot be funded. There is hostility between the two teachers, who have been arguing about, and lobbying for, their respective proposals for several days.

Solution: principled negotiation. Focus on interests, not positions. Invent options for mutual gain. Set aside the positions for the time being and identify the personal and educational interests underlying the proposals. Develop alternative approaches for satisfying these interests which will bring the costs for the two proposals within feasible limits.

Case 2: 'The empire builder'
Problem: A teacher has sought and obtained substantial financial support in recent years for a number of programmes for which he has responsibility. Colleagues have become sceptical as they see little in the way of results. This year the teacher's request for further substantial funding is meeting with resistance and some measure of resentment. Battle lines are being drawn prior to the meeting.

Solution: principled negotiation. Separate the people from the problem. Focus on interests, not positions. Insist on objective criteria. Redirect the attention of the teacher to objectives related to teaching and learning. Try to see the situation from the teacher's point of view. Does he have personal interests and needs for say, recognition and esteem, which he has been satisfying by securing a large 'slice of the cake'? Can these personal needs be satisfied in other ways? Secure from all teachers an agreement that criteria for programme evaluation will be included in all programme plans with results used as the basis for planning in future years.

Case 3: 'The avoider'
Problem: A member of senior staff is losing the support of his colleagues because he is perceived to be unassertive in meetings where resources are allocated among programmes. The programme and the students are seen to be suffering as a result.

Solution: principled negotiation. Reinforce the principle and the view that people are problem-solvers. This teacher seems uncomfortable with what he sees as a competitive, adversarial system. Reinforce all behaviour which supports the view that participants are problem-solvers seeking the best match of resources to student needs. Focus discussion on issues related to teaching and learning. Direct questions to this teacher to bring out the merits of his programme.

Case 4: 'An interfering council?'
Problem: Some members of the school council (policy group), including some teachers' representatives, have questioned the programme budget prepared by the head teacher and staff, suggesting that proposed expenditure for paintings is wasteful in times of economic restraint. Some were incensed, given that the budget also contained a proposal for an increase in

student levies. Staff who prepared the proposal for this particular programme are equally incensed at what they see as interference and criticism of their professional judgement.

Solution: principled negotiation. Insist on objective criteria. Refer again to the priorities and policies of the school council. Reconsideration of the programme budget is indicated if the allocation is either inconsistent with priorities or policies or if a priority has been omitted in the budget and could now be addressed if the paintings were not acquired.

What if others will not collaborate?

Guidelines for collaboration and '*win–win*' orientations in negotiation are frequently criticised for their impracticality on the grounds that they assume that all participants in the conflict are prepared to follow the guidelines. Fisher and Ury address this concern by suggesting action which should be followed when (a) the other party is more powerful, (b) the other party won't co-operate and (c) the other party plays dirty tricks.

When the other party in a conflict has the power to determine the outcome and is intent on using it — a dominating '*win–lose*' position — the least desirable response is accommodation. Fisher and Ury suggest the development of a BATNA, A Best Alternative to a Negotiated Agreement, by determining the action to be taken if agreement is not reached. Possibilities include improving previously undeveloped but promising ideas and presenting these as options. The essence of the approach is some careful planning when it is clear that you will lose when your preferred options are considered. What the other party might consider to be a win for him and a loss to you may, in fact, turn out to be a partial win if you prepare a BATNA. A BATNA may be prepared at any stage of the policy-making and planning process.

Fisher and Ury propose an interesting strategy of 'negotiation jujitsu' in situations where the other party won't co-operate in an attempt at collaboration. They warn against instinctive reactions; for example, rejecting a firm position announced by the other party, or defending your preference if it comes under attack. Such responses move the conflict back into the traditional positional bargaining arena. The best response is to hold firm to the principled negotiation approach by actions such as the following:

1 When the other party sets out its preferred outcome, neither accept nor reject it: treat it as one possible option. Questions should be posed seeking information as to how the outcome will solve the problem under consideration. In the case of preferred policy, this calls for questions on the effects of the policy. In the case of proposed budget, this calls for questions on the impact of a

particular pattern of resource allocation.

2   Avoid getting into a position of defending your ideas; indeed, take the initiative and invite questions and criticism. In what ways does this option fail to solve the problem we are considering? Modify your options when improvements are suggested.

3   Redirect personal attacks so that they focus on the problem. If the other party accuses you of showing indifference to the learning needs of students, agree that indifference is unacceptable but pose questions asking how you can reach an agreement together about ways of satisfying those learning needs.

4   Use questions and silence to good effect. Fisher and Ury believe that 'statements generate resistance, whereas questions generate answers' and that 'silence often creates the impression of a stalemate which the other side will feel compelled to break....'[9]

The guidelines for principled negotiation and collaboration would appear to be worthless in the face of actions by others which fall into the 'dirty tricks' category: deception, personal attacks, threats, delays and the like. Principled negotiation can be applied, however, by addressing the same four points: separate the people from the problem, focus on interests not positions, invent options for mutual gain and insist on objective criteria — all focused on the process itself. If this effort fails, the BATNA may well be a 'walk out', to be resolved by formal authority.

Building Consensus

Aspects of the collaborative approach would appear to be facilitated in part by the achievement of a consensus, for example, as far as agreement on policies and priorities for the school as a whole is concerned. Going further, however, the approach may in fact do much to contribute to the achievement of consensus. The purpose of this section is to explore these possibilities and to propose guidelines for the building of a consensus when it is appropriate to do so.

Consensus is sought or discussed in two contexts. First, we often talk of building a consensus among groups which, for one reason or another, may normally be considered in conflict or at least differing on significant issues. As far as a school is concerned, the different groups may include the head teacher and other senior staff, teachers, support staff, students, parents and others in the school community. In the approach to policy-making and planning under consideration, it is desirable to build a consensus among these groups for the goals, policies and priorities of the school. There is usually the hope that this consensus can be maintained.

Another context in which the term is used is in decision-making, when reaching a consensus on a course of action to be followed is seen as an alternative to an autocratic decision or some form of consultation or taking a vote. In the approach to policy-making and planning under consideration, consensus is thus the style of decision-making at one or more points in the process. Consensus might be sought, for example, in determining policy when, say, three options have been generated by a working party: the policy which is adopted might incorporate facets of each option. Consensus might also be sought when priorities within and among programme plans must be considered in the light of limited resources. In both of these situations, consensus is an alternative to the frequent use of decision by majority vote, the merits of which will be considered in another section.

Consensus and theories of decision-making

These perspective on consensus were described without a definition of the term. It is helpful at this point to clarify the concept and briefly review theory in decision-making related to consensus. Guidelines will then be offered for building consensus.

For decision-making in groups, consensus is reached when there is substantial agreement among members, a state which should not be confused with unanimity. Hall described it in these terms:

> Complete unanimity is not the goal — it is rarely achieved. But each individual should be able to accept [the decision] on the basis of logic and rationality. When all group members feel this way, you have reached consensus as defined here. . . .[10]

Developing this view further, one may envisage members of a group approaching a decision with different preferences. When they share opinions on these differences it may be apparent that no one approach is the preference of a majority or even a significant minority of the group. But as a result of discussion and debate, a course of action may emerge that can be supported by all or most members, each of whom is saying, in effect, 'this may not be my first preference as far as the outcome is concerned, but I am prepared to accept it because it will achieve our purposes and it will be accepted by all or most members of the group'. This view may be extended to include the first of the two contexts described above where broad agreement is sought among groups to produce a relatively enduring relationship.

Implied in the foregoing is the belief that two criteria must be satisfied in achieving consensus: (a) the decision or outcome must be high in quality, that is, it must be effective in terms of solving the problem or achieving the goal, and (b) the decision or outcome must be acceptable to those who must implement it or who will be affected by it. This contrasts with an occasionally expressed view that a consensus decision is a mediocre decision, that it is a compromise which necessarily affects the quality of the decision or outcome. Quality and acceptance should be the goals of a consensus as they are in all approaches to decision-making.[11]

Guidelines for building consensus

Seven guidelines for building consensus are offered. Some are implications of theories about decision-making, while others are derived from guidelines for managing conflict through negotiation. The guidelines apply to both contexts or perspectives described earlier, namely, the building of a relatively enduring relationship among groups with different interests, and the use of a particular leadership style within decision-making. Illustrations for policy and planning are provided.

1   Highly participative approaches —consulting relevant groups or reaching a consensus —are indicated when acceptance of the outcome is critically important, especially if it is not certain that (a) a decision of the head teacher or other leader, depending on the context, will be accepted, (b) acceptance is important for effective implementation, and (c) there is conflict among members of the school community as far as preferred outcomes are concerned. These conditions seem to apply in particular to those aspects of policy and planning which involve the setting of goals, the identification of needs, the ordering of priorities and the formulation of policies.

Contrary to an often-held view, an implication of the foregoing is that the likelihood of conflict is a reason to bring people together rather than to revert to a relatively autocratic decision. Hostility is minimised if people have the opportunity to explain their preferences: discussion and debate can proceed with full knowledge of other points of view.

2   The guidelines for management of conflict through negotiation are especially applicable to building consensus. Those offered by Fisher and Ury as described and illustrated earlier are especially recommended: separate the people from the problem, focus on interests and not positions, generate a variety of possibilities before deciding what to do and insist that decisions are based on some objective criteria. In practice, this approach calls for participants to state their preferences, with encouragement to describe these in terms of interests rather than fixed positions. A series of options are then identified, with a consensus likely to emerge when common interests can be satisfied from the creation of a new option or combination of existing options. Other guidelines offered by Fisher and Ury should be followed when some participants decline to co-

operate in the collaborative or consensus approach. The twin goals of decision-making should be paramount throughout: a high-quality decision and an acceptable decision.

3   Decision by majority vote should be kept to a minimum. It is of interest that the range of decision-making or leadership styles in the various decision-making models rarely contain provision for taking a vote. Consistent with the first two guidelines, the view is offered here that voting may inhibit the process of identifying interests and formulating options in an attempt to build consensus. Head teachers in staff meetings and chairpersons of policy groups may need to depart from traditional practice in this regard. Similarly, consideration of a single discussion paper may be inappropriate. Expressed another way, voting can be divisive, with hostility often arising and continuing after a polarisation of views.

4   Flexibility in leadership style is important. An autocratic decision is appropriate in some situations, especially when the leader has the information to make a high-quality decision and members of the school community are prepared to accept and implement that decision. The leader, when selecting a leadership style, must also be sensitive to the distinction between a decision which will make efficient use of time, and a decision which will require an investment of time. The former refers to decisions which can and should be made quickly, and the latter refers to situations where other benefits can be achieved by spending time on the decision. Benefits of an investment in time include cohesiveness and team spirit, as well as the acquisition of technical skills in collaborative decision-making.

5   Individual behaviour is important for the process. Some useful tips follow. Avoid arguing in order to win as an individual. Present your views as lucidly and logically as possible, but listen to the reactions of others: consider them before pressing your point. Do not change your mind simply to avoid conflict. When a dissenting member finally agrees on one issue, do not feel that the person must be rewarded by having his or her own way on another. Do not assume that someone must win and someone must lose when discussion reaches a stalemate: look for the next most acceptable option. Finally, each member has the responsibility to monitor the processes through which work gets done and to initiate discussions of process when it becomes ineffective.[12]

6   The first five guidelines are concerned with decision-making. They should be followed regularly and consistently if enduring relationships are to be built among different groups. An expectation must be raised for continuing participation along the lines illustrated. One assumes that this is the intention in building and maintaining a consensus among government, business and labour in the current

economic context. Similarly, the expectation and intention should be clear for participation of the various groups in the school community in the policy and planning process.

7 Consensus should only be sought in groups of up to sixteen or twenty in number. Research has shown that it is difficult to reach consensus in a larger group because a fragmentation of interests may result in self-sustaining groups based on fixed positions.[13]

Summary

The theme of this chapter is that Collaborative School Management provides a framework for coping with the conflict which is inevitable when there are different views of the ends and means of education, and when people with different, often ambiguous areas of responsibility seek to achieve their purposes with limited resources. The collaborative approach is helpful in that it brings people together to determine goals and formulate policies. With the substantial but concise information base, whatever differences exist will occur in the light of knowledge of what others are seeking to do. The focus is shifted from competitive, avoiding or accommodating behaviour in the management of conflict, to the collaborative. Approaches identified in recent studies of effectiveness in negotiation have resulted in straightforward guidelines which are especially suited to Collaborative School Management, especially those put forward by Fisher and Ury: separate the people from the problem, focus on interests not positions, generate a variety of possibilities before deciding what to do, and insist that results be based on objective criteria. When these guidelines are combined with well-known approaches to building consensus, all schools will have at their disposal a workable and acceptable means for managing conflict.

SUMMARY
MANAGEMENT OF CONFLICT

CONFLICT ARISES WHEN:

Individuals and groups with
different views on

ENDS AND MEANS ← ⎰ BRINGING PEOPLE
⎱ TOGETHER
⎰ OPENNESS
⎱ INFORMATION

and with different and often
ambiguous

AREAS OF RESPONSIBILITY ← ⎰ PROVIDING A PROGRAMME
⎱ STRUCTURE SPECIFYING
RESPONSIBILITY

seek to achieve their purposes
with

LIMITED RESOURCES ← ⎰ POLICY FRAMEWORK
⎱ PRIORITIES
⎰ OPENNESS
⎱ INFORMATION

COLLABORATIVE SCHOOL
MANAGEMENT ASSISTS BY:

GUIDELINES FOR MANAGEMENT OF CONFLICT BY COLLABORATION
Fisher and Ury suggest:
- Separate the people from the problem.
- Focus on interests not positions.
- Generate a variety of possibilities before deciding what to do.
- Insist the result be based on objective criteria.

GUIDELINES FOR BUILDING CONSENSUS
- Consensus is especially appropriate when acceptance is important for effective implementation and when conflict is evident about ends and means.
- Flexibility is still important: there are times and places for decisions to be made by one person alone.
- Decision by majority vote should be kept to a minimum.
- Build the right group atmosphere and develop appropriate individual skills.
- Keep group numbers below 20, or your task will be very difficult.
- Follow Fisher and Ury's guidelines.

---

13 *Management of the Staff Resource*

Planning for the allocation of human resources is the subject of this chapter. This is a necessary and important aspect of management in every school but there are special considerations in the self-managing school as far as budgeting is concerned. Should specification in financial terms (pounds or dollars) be included in programme plans and budgets for staff in the school? In the case of the school which is entirely self-managed or which pays the staff from funds which are received at the school, the answer is, of course, in the affirmative. For schools in systems where the hiring, deployment and payment of staff generally remains a central responsibility, the issue is problematic. We see benefits in the inclusion of the staff resource in the preparation of programme budgets, regardless of the location in the centralisation-decentralisation continuum of responsibility for hiring, deployment and payment. The first section of the chapter presents the case for inclusion. Then follows a relatively detailed explanation and illustration of how this can be accomplished in an open fashion which has been found to be generally acceptable.

The Case for Inclusion

If programmes are natural and logical divisions of the curriculum then these programmes concern students and their learning. It follows that programme plans should contain details of what people, including the staff, do to support learning. In fact it can be seen that as the teaching staff is by far the most important resource for students' learning, its inclusion is an absolute necessity in this sense. This view emphasises the importance of the 'planning process' in programme budgeting with its associated allocation of all resources in addition to the allocation of money.

With the inclusion of the staff resource in programme budgeting, the focus becomes people — teachers and students — and what they do. The need to include the staff resource in order to obtain this focus is demonstrated by a comparison of existing school-based programme budgeting with and without the staff resource. Those not including this resource tend to see programmes as a way of providing materials and equipment to learning areas. The emphasis is on the provision of these items rather than on students' learning.

Comparisons of different approaches to programme budgeting demonstrate that inclusion of the staff resource is more likely to result in the development of programmes as natural and logical divisions of the curriculum. When staff are not considered, programmes tend to be defined across related learning areas. For instance, in early attempts to budget for K–10 schools, it often occurred that many programmes were defined on a K–10 basis. That is, programmes such as K–10 Science, K–10 Language and K–10 Physical Education were detailed separately. However, when staff resources were included it became obvious that these programmes were not necessarily 'natural divisions' of the curriculum. In K–2 and 3–6, language and science were really incorporated in K–2 and 3–6 General Studies Programmes, because the same teacher taught all of these 'subjects' as an interrelated group to a particular class. It differed in 7–10 where specialist groups of teachers were responsible for the particular programmes. The importance of the staff resource in determining natural curriculum divisions was highlighted by the ready acceptance and workability of K–10 Physical Education Programmes and 3–10 Music Programmes where most of the actual teaching was conducted by the specialist staff concerned. Experience has shown that an important aspect in gaining the full benefits of programme budgeting is this ready relation between the programmes and how staff work in groups. It suggested that the number of programmes in which any individual teacher 'works' should be kept to a minimum. None of the foregoing benefits should be attained at the expense of curriculum development on a K–6 or K–10 or K–12 basis.

Another important aspect of programme budgeting is that it involves planning at one point in time the allocation of *all* available resources. This planning ensures that best use is made of these resources because their use is integrated. Is it possible, therefore, to integrate the use of all the resources to be available without including the key resource, and in fact the most costly resource, the teacher? Experience has shown that the best time to negotiate teaching conditions for staff is during this planning stage. At this time staff are very much aware of the ramifications involved and are able to balance teaching conditions against developing more desirable programmes for students. An outcome can be staff agreement to increase teachers' loadings so that class sizes are decreased, or to introduce a new programme for students, or to expand the provision of an existing programme for students with special needs. On the other hand, if staff wish to decrease teachers' loadings, it is immediately apparent that programme changes will result for students unless additional staff are provided.

Some would argue against the inclusion of the staff resource where the school does not have 'control' of this resource. Perhaps the school does not have control in that individual staff cannot be hired or fired, but control can be exercised. Usually this occurs in the composition of the teaching staff, that is, in deciding which specialist areas are to be included, in what proportions, and how they are to be used. This type of control enables full consideration of the staff resource in programme budgeting and again emphasises that programme budgeting really concerns planning related to student learning and the related use of all resources. Of course this planned use of staff is not new to schools, although it may be a different approach to consider it at the same time as the budgeting of other resources. After all, the biggest decision about resource allocation made each year is in the construction of the school timetable. Why not integrate this aspect of planning with those aspects related to non-human resources?

The possibility of including the staff resource also gives rise to the question of what to do if planning on a needs basis indicates that staff in a particular area are no longer required, or are no longer required to the same extent. It is as well to realise that this situation is not created by programme budgeting, but programme budgeting does provide a framework for action based on students' needs. Obviously, deployment of personnel within a school system has to be a system-wide matter, but programme budgeting as an approach to planning draws attention to the issue of whether students' needs are more important to school planning than providing work for the existing staff.

It is considered that these points establish the relevance of including the staff resource in programme budgeting. It now remains to develop methods for this inclusion.

Including the Staff Resource in Programme Planning

The timetable already details how the staff resource is used in terms of units of time, proportions with respect to areas of the curriulum, and other related aspects. This planning is usually undertaken separately from the consideration of the other resources available, but there are advantages to be gained in planning the use of all available resources at the one time. The existing timetables point the way in plans to include the staff resource. It is a matter of considering what students need to do or experience in programmes in order to achieve the programmes' purposes. This leads to considering how much of the staff resource is required to ensure that the learning activities for students proceed as planned. It is then possible to determine the staff required by considering desirable group sizes in relation to the total number of students in the programme, the physical environment in which the programme is to operate, safety factors, and so on. This information is detailed for each programme. In the reconciliation of 'resources required' with 'resources available' it is likely that compromises will be necessary and decisions must be made in line with established needs and policy priorities.

In order to take account of the differing needs and priorities between programmes it is necessary that there be a common approach within a school to detailing the staff needed for programmes. Usually this takes the form of detailing the amount of 'teacher time' required per week for the programme to operate as designed to meet students' needs. This 'teacher time' can be expressed in hours or units of time specifically selected to meet an individual school's circumstances. Often this unit of time is referred to in schools as a 'period' and may vary in length from half an hour to one hour.

Usually, the existing timetables are too simplistic to be used solely as the basis for considering the staff resource in programme budgeting. Services provided by staff are complex and diverse. Normally, timetables only record 'teacher time' spent with classes in subject learning. Sometimes 'free lessons' or planning times are also recorded but there is a need to detail the nature of all the services provided by staff, and to allocate these as required by programmes and as the total resource allows. This aspect can be illustrated by describing the approach developed at Rosebery District High School where it is considered that teachers provide services in the categories of:

Class/subject teaching
Preparation/Marking/Organisation (PMO)
Programme supervision
School administration and pastoral care

The first category is self-explanatory. The second, commonly referred to as PMO, is required to facilitate learning and teaching. Programme supervision is necessary for the overall development of programmes, and is usually provided by senior members of staff. School administration and pastoral care involve those services related to the care and welfare of students, reporting to parents, counselling of students about courses and development, yard duty, school organisation, and so on.

Programmes require different quantities of these categories of services, depending on the nature and purpose of the programmes. For each programme, each category of service required is detailed as a specific number of units per week, and these unit requirements are justified in each instance. Particular attention is directed to the Administration and K–2 General Studies Programmes in the Appendix which demonstrate different requirements for teachers' service-units.

The quantities of services provided need to be taken into account so that later, the availability of staff can be matched with the staff required for programmes. Senior staff, for example, provide units of service in all four categories while other staff may only provide units of service in two categories.

In order to quantify the available staff resource it is necessary to make

Figure 13.1 A sample provision of teacher service-units

Classification	Class/subject teaching	Lesson PMO	Programme supervision	School administration	Total
Teachers	28	7.	–	5	40
Senior staff	20	5	9	6	40
Vice principals	10	2	8	20	40
Principal (head)	4	1	10	25	40

certain assumptions that give some rationality to the complex way that teachers work in their schools. It is assumed that all teachers provide a certain minimum number of units of service each week. It is recognised that all staff in any school will probably provide more in the way of additional preparation, extra-curricular activities and pastoral care, and that this additional service will vary from teacher to teacher and from time to time.

At Rosebery, it is considered that teaching staff each provide forty units of service per week, a unit of service being three-quarters of an hour. The numbers of service units provided by the respective groups of staff are shown in Figure 13.1.

When looking at Figure 13.1, the following points should be noted.

1 The total number of staff and the number of staff within each classification are determined by formulae based mainly on enrolments.

2 Senior masters/mistresses (SM), the infant mistress (IM) and senior teacher (ST) constitute the senior staff along with the principal (head teacher) and vice principals.

3 The agreed ratio of PMO units to class/subject teaching units is approximately 1:4 for all groups of staff. This is based on an amendment, determined by staff, to the State Staffing Agreement. It was also recently agreed to attempt to decrease the teaching units to 26 or 27 for teachers and to increase the number of PMO units accordingly.

4 Rosebery is a K-10 school. The school week consists of 30 units for classes K to 6, and 35 units for years 7 to 10.

Using Figure 13.1 and the staff quotas, it is possible to calculate the total quantities of units available as the staff resource. This information is shown in Figure 13.2.

When information is available about the quantities and nature of the services provided by the staff resource, it is possible to balance it with the staff services which programmes require. This balancing and reconciliation could result in the identification of a mismatch between the services in a particular subject that a teacher can provide and the services that are required. The problems resulting have been mentioned previously, as well as the possible solutions. If the mismatch is in the nature of too many staff,

Figure 13.2 A sample list of available teacher service-units

Classification		Class/subject teaching		Lesson PMO		Programme supervision		School administration	
	Quota	Units	Total	Units	Total	Units	Total	Units	Total
Teachers	34	28	952	7	238	–	–	5	170
Senior staff	6	20	120	5	30	9	54	6	36
Vice principals	2	10	20	2	4	8	16	20	40
Principal (head)	1	4	4	1	1	10	10	25	25
TOTALS			1096		273		80		271

it is usually impossible to convert the excess staff to another kind of resource. However, if the imbalance is the other way, it is possible in Tasmania to increase this resource by using Commonwealth Schools Commission Recurrent Grants.

The example illustrates how the inclusion of the staff resource can be realistically accomplished in programme planning. Other approaches can easily be developed to suit the particular circumstances of different schools. The next question to face is whether it is now necessary to convert the staff allocation in programmes from time to money. Quite obviously it is not necessary and the staff resource can be handled in terms of units of time. However, the possibility of translating these time units into financial units raises certain issues we consider worth exploring.

In the budgeting process, resources are allocated to programmes from different sources. These resources could be viewed as supplying different aspects of programmes and these aspects could be recorded in more descriptive ways, for instance the teacher resource could be expressed as 'teacher time' or the excursion resource for isolated schools could be expressed as kilometres of bus travel. It becomes apparent that such an approach does not allow for easy comparison between the different types of resources available and it is argued that there are benefits in being able to make such comparisons. To make comparisons, there needs to be a common method for expressing quantities of different resources. Obviously the simplest common approach is the translation of all resources to monetary terms.

When all resources allocated to programmes are translated into financial terms, the first thing that is immediately apparent is the cost of staff in comparison with other resources. Of course this information has always been known and often quoted but the real significance and importance of the staff resource is clearly brought to the attention of all concerned. Consideration of some of the sample programmes in the Appendix illustrates this point. The cost of staff in comparison with the total cost of some sample programmes is shown in Figure 13.3.

Making It Work

Figure 13.3 A sample comparison of staff resource and total programme cost

Programme	Staff resources	Other resources	Total resources
Special education	$ 28 846	$ 1 777	$ 30 623
7–10 Technical subjects	79 707	9 152	88 859
K–2 General studies	110 933	16 060	126 993

In the face of such evidence, teachers clearly see the importance of their contribution to the success of programmes and it is noticeable that there is less blame given to a lack of some item of equipment or materials, when a programme fails. In a sense, translation of all resources to financial terms assists teachers to recognise and accept their accountability for the development of programmes.

In schools there has always been the argument that programmes which rely on material and equipment attract all the money, while book-intensive programmes are given little money by comparison. If the teaching resource is expressed in financial terms and added to the other resources in such programmes, then the real situation becomes evident. The inclusion of the staff resource in financial terms demonstrates a more equitable allocation of resources.

Another consideration assisted by the inclusion of the staff resource in financial terms is the relationship between priorities and programme expenditure. It is apparent that some kind of relationship exists between the priority assigned to, and money allocated for, any programme. If a programme is given a higher priority then it can be expected that it will be allocated increased resources. Often the increased priority is reflected in the staff resource. Such increases are clearly seen in comparison with other programmes by the inclusion of the additional staff resource in the total funding of the programme.

At some point in the evaluation of programmes, efficiency as well as effectiveness must be considered. Effectiveness is concerned with whether the purposes are being achieved and to what degree. Efficiency is concerned with whether effectiveness is being achieved at an acceptable cost. With this kind of information available, taking into account priorities, the policy group is in a better position to make decisions about programme expansion, continuity or curtailment when faced with changes to the total resources available. In coming to terms with measures of efficiency, finance has to be considered in the context of the total programme, not just the material input.

Reaction to this inclusion of the staff resource in financial terms generally varies, depending on the degree to which the staff concerned are involved with programme budgeting. Naturally there is hesitation at first, but when people accept the inclusion of the staff resource in the budget allocation, and experience the benefits that can be derived, it seems to be a

Management of the Staff Resource

Figure 13.4 A sample determination of average costs of class/subject teaching units

1. The average cost per annum for a member of staff in each staff category is
   established from information supplied by the employing authority

Staff category	Average annual cost*	Number	Total cost
Teachers	$22 846*	34	$776 764
Senior staff	29 525	6	177 150
Vice principals	32 368	2	64 736
Principal**(Head)	40 114	1	40 114
TOTALS		43	$1 058 764

* includes isolation area allowances
** confidentiality of the principal's salary is not maintained as the exception

2. The cost of any unit of service provided by any category of the staff is calculated by
   dividing the average annual cost by 40 to give the cost of a unit per week for a year.

Staff category	Average annual cost	Cost per unit
Teachers	$22 846	$571
Senior staff	29 525	738
Vice principals	32 368	809
Principal (Head)	40 114	1 003

3. It is then possible to calculate the average cost of a class/subject teaching unit
   irrespective of the category of staff providing the unit, as illustrated below.

Staff category	Quota number	Units provided per staff member	Total units provided	Cost per service-unit	Total
Teachers	34	28	952	$571	$543 592
Senior staff	6	20	120	738	88 560
Vice principals	2	10	20	809	16 180
Principal (Head)	1	4	4	1 003	4 012
TOTALS	43		1 096		$652 344

Average cost of a class subject teaching unit for a year = $ 652 344 ÷ 1 096 = $ 595

4. On a similar basis it is possible to calculate the average cost of a PMO unit as the
   same amount ($595) as they are provided on a constant ratio of 1 : 4 for all
   categories of staff.

Figure 13.4 cont.

5. Programme supervision unit costs can be determined using the average unit cost for each category of staff as calculated in step 3.

Supervision units:	Senior staff	$ 738
	Vice principals	809
	Principal (Head)	1 003

6. School administration and pastoral care unit cost can also be determined using the average unit cost for each category of staff as calculated in step 3.

Administration and pastoral care units:	Teachers	$ 571
	Senior staff	738
	Vice principals	809
	Principal (Head)	1 003

further development and refinement to translate the staff allocations into financial terms. After all, this development is only a monetary expression of the existing timetable.

If translation of the staff resource into financial terms is accepted as a desirable development, then it becomes necessary to develop a system to do this which reflects the costs involved as realistically as possible. It is important to take into account the fact that different staff are paid different salaries, yet there is obviously a need to protect the confidentiality of each teacher's salary. As well, costs need to be expressed realistically in the sense that the level of experience of the staff members concerned should not be a factor if there are staff changes.

At Rosebery, each member of staff provides 40 units of service, divided, as described earlier in the chapter, among the categories of:

- Class/subject teaching
- Preparation/Marking/Organisation (PMO)
- Programme supervision
- School administration and pastoral care

Different types of staff provide these services in different proportions as shown in Figure 13.1.

In allocating class/subject teaching units to programmes in the budgeting process, it is not desirable to list who is actually to provide these units at the time of planning and yet 'the who' determines the cost. This problem is overcome by averaging the cost of class/subject teaching units of the category of staff or the experience levels of the staff providing the units. A desirable side benefit of this approach is that the confidentiality of individual teachers' salaries is maintained. The actual determination of these costs for 1985 is summarised in Figure 13.4 as a series of steps. A summary of these service-unit costs is contained in Figure 13.5.

With this information available, it becomes possible, when preparing programme budgets, to detail the number of different staff service-units required and to calculate the associated cost. Examples can be seen in the sample programme budgets included in the Appendix. Following the

Figure 13.5 A sample of staff service-unit costs

Classification	Class/subject teaching	PMO	Programme supervision	School admin. & pastoral care
Teachers	$595	$595	—	$571
Senior staff	595	595	738	738
Vice principal	595	595	809	809
Principal (Head)	595	595	1 003	1 003

eventual reconciliation of the suggested budgets and resources available, the actual staff needed to provide particular services to the various programmes can be determined.

From this consideration of the staff resource in relation to programme budgeting it is apparent that it is desirable to include the staff resource along with all other resources because of its significance to the planning and operation of programmes. From experience we know that it is normal development in programme budgeting to progress from programmes detailing only material resources to programmes detailing organisation for student learning, including the staff resource. It may be desirable to start including calculations of the staff resource in financial terms at a later stage, as staff acceptance of this approach to planning grows and benefits to the school of translating the staff resource are recognised. Different schools will develop particular approaches to the inclusion of the staff resource to suit their own circumstances.

SUMMARY
MANAGEMENT OF THE STAFF RESOURCE

WHY INCLUDE THE STAFF AS A RESOURCE IN PROGRAMME PLANNING AND BUDGETING?

- Teachers are the key resource in educational programmes for students.
- Inclusion of the staff resource ensures that teaching and learning are the focus in programme planning.
- Teachers are central to the organisation of the school. Programmes need to closely relate to the way in which teachers work.
- Effectiveness is increased when planning involves the consideration of all resources at the one point in time.
- The composition of the staff resource needs to match the purposes of programmes for students.

HOW TO INCLUDE THE STAFF AS A RESOURCE IN PROGRAMME PLANNING AND BUDGETING

1. Determine categories of staff based on terms of appointment.
2. Determine types and quantities of services provided by teachers in and out of the classroom.
3. Determine proportions between types of services provided by each category of staff.
4. Introduce a measure of time (period or unit) to describe quantities of services provided.
5. Calculate the quantities of different services provided by the total number of staff on the school quota.
6. Determine the service needs of all programmes through planning.
7. Balance teachers' service-units required with those available.
8. Determine the priorities considering flexible resource. More teachers' units *or* materials *or* ????

EXPRESSION OF THE STAFF RESOURCE IN FINANCIAL TERMS

- Is it *necessary* to express the staff resource in financial terms in programme planning and budgeting? *No!* Expression as units of time suffices.
- Expression of all resources in common form allows realistic comparisons to be made.
- The cost of the staff resource reflects the importance of the staff resource to learning programmes.
- Attention directed to the cost and importance of the staff resource in programmes increases recognition of teachers and acceptance of accountability for the development of programmes.

14 *Questions That People Often Ask*

The approach outlined in this book has been used extensively as the basis for more than 100 seminars, involving some 5000 people in several Australian states from 1984 to 1986, as well as in seminars in Britain, Canada and the United States in 1987. Questions raised by participants have been carefully analysed and those most frequently raised have been identified and are addressed in this chapter. The questions fall into four categories:

- Introducing the approach
- Policy-making and planning
- Identification of resources and budgeting
- Evaluating programmes.

Introducing the Approach

Question: Where in the Collaborative School Management Cycle does a school start the process?

In a literal interpretation of the Collaborative School Management Cycle a school should start with goal-setting and need identification, and then follow the sequence of policy-making, planning, budgeting and evaluating. In reality, however, schools will rarely follow this pattern; indeed, in some instances, it may be undesirable to do so. Some schools have started at the point where a budget in traditional line-item form has been adopted and the schools have literally 'worked backwards', rearranging the approved resource allocation into programme categories. Staff are then invited to write statements of purpose and broad guidelines and provide a plan for implementation and evaluation. In the following year, statements of purpose and broad guidelines are expanded to produce a one-page policy. This approach is appropriate for a school which is working well but lacks statements of policy and a framework for planning. It obtains these by working from 'what is'. Other schools have begun the process with a school-wide, comprehensive evaluation or review as part of a school improvement project. In these instances, the Collaborative School Management Cycle provides a framework for dealing with the outcomes of their evaluation, so that identified needs lead to policies, plans and the allocation of resources in programme budgets. The formulation of policy has been the starting point for some schools, with planning the budget along programme lines following in the second year. There may, in fact, be significant disadvantages if an attempt is made to begin the process with an extended period of goal-setting. Substantial amounts of time may be devoted to the task, often causing impatience because immediate results are not obtained. It is important, then, for the 'starting point' to be determined on the basis of the school's current approach to management and to needs which are evident at the time.

Question: How does this recommended approach to school management differ from PPBS which failed?

PPBS stands for Planning Programming Budgeting System, a concept which was introduced in North America in the 1960s and which was largely a failure. It failed for several basic reasons. There was an emphasis on tedious and lengthy documentation for each programme, detailing very specifically the material requirements and other aspects of the plan. There was a concentration on identifying specific targets to be achieved and emphasis given to measuring that achievement. There were inadequate links with curriculum statements and curriculum policy. Without adequate staff development, the time allowed for introduction was too short. Overall, the emphasis was on detailing targets and measurements rather than on planning and implementing. The distinction is drawn between that approach and the approach recommended in this book, which emphasises brevity in documentation: *one-page* policies, *two-page* plans, *one-* or *two-page* evaluation reports. Our approach provides sufficient information, allows for flexibility to meet emerging needs, and recognises that in education some purposes can only be evaluated by subjective methods provided that those methods involve professional, informed opinion.

Question: How should this approach to school management be introduced to a sceptical staff who believe that they are already overworked?

We recommend that no attempt be made to introduce the whole approach within a school in a short period of time. Rather, once staff have been introduced to the ideas, a small number of programmes should be trialled using volunteers. This trial group of programmes can then be expanded in later years as the benefits of the approach become obvious to all concerned. It is also important to emphasise to staff that this approach to school management is not an 'add-on'. Teachers already make policies, prepare plans, identify resources required and evaluate. The approach enables teachers to link these activities together in a meaningful and systematic way. Another aspect that can be emphasised to staff is that eventually the approach saves time, because planning ahead for the next year is completed at one point in time and staff in the programme teams control the selection and ordering of materials as they are required and within the budget guidelines. In this way, providing resources is not likely to cause frustration to staff who are implementing learning programmes for students.

Question: Does the introduction of this approach to school management require additional support?

In answering this question, we would emphasise that the approach to school management does not entail any new tasks for school personnel. School staffs are already involved in policy-making, planning, budgeting and evaluating. This approach to school management brings these activities together in an integrated and systematic way. From this point of view, additional support to introduce the approach is not required. It is recognised, however, that especially in the earlier years of introduction, there is an additional requirement in preparing and documenting policies and programme plans. For this reason, among others, it is recommended that the approach be phased in over some three to five years to minimise this task. Not all policies and programmes change dramatically from year to year and in most cases developments from one year to another are a matter of fine tuning. Experience also indicates that, in fact, time is saved once the approach is completely in place. This frees staff even more to undertake the associated preparation of learning programmes and evaluation work. The removal of frustrations caused by supplying materials is also a bonus for staff.

Question: Can this recommended approach to school management work in small schools and is it needed in small schools?

Collaborative School Management is an integrated approach to policy-making, planning, budgeting and evaluating which may involve the community as well as the head teacher and staff. One outcome is a very clear linking of policies to learning programmes for students. The desirability of this approach is the same for all schools irrespective of size. Of course, in a small school the programme structure and the actual number of programmes will match the way in which the school is organised. It should be noted that the programme structure of a school is an outcome of how teachers work and children learn in that school. It follows, therefore, that it is unlikely that any two schools will have the same programme structure. A very small primary school might only have four programmes, namely, Administration, P–2 Studies, 3–6 Studies, and P–6 Special Programmes.

However, it would still be possible to plan and budget appropriately for these programmes and to demonstrate which policies are addressed in each programme.

Question: Is there a danger that programme budgeting will become a means of greater control by a central authority?

Two important aspects of programme budgeting are relating programmes to locally determined policies, and evolving a programme structure that best suits the way a school is organised. In both aspects, schools will differ from one another. In fact, Collaborative School Management, involving programme planning and budgeting, encourages the development of this diversity among schools. An outcome of this diversity of policies and programmes is the difficulty of making comparisons between schools. Without the capacity to compare programmes from school to school, it is impractical to view programme budgeting as a control measure by a central office. The very volume of information provided by all schools would also prohibit its use as a control measure especially as the information provided concerns educational planning in schools rather than merely expenditure of funds. Programme budgeting does provide key information for *all* concerned with a school and demonstrates the relationship between the policies of the school and its programmes. With decentralisation of authority to schools, an approach with these characteristics is required to keep teachers, parents and other interested parties informed and to facilitate the participation of all concerned in the exercise of their responsibility.

It is possible and desirable, of course, for senior officers of an educational system to monitor the implementation of programmes which reflect government or system policy for all schools. Programme plans and budgets enable schools to provide such information without special effort. A system of programme accounting in schools will also facilitate the auditing process which is a continuing requirement for all schools.

Question: Can Collaborative School Management succeed in an era of detailed industrial agreements between teachers and employing authorities?

Collaborative School Management is essentially policy-making and planning at the local school level involving teachers, parents, students and the local community in general. It is an expression of the decentralisation of decision-making and responsibility from the central authority to the local level. This desire for decentralisation of responsibility and the sharing of responsibility is in keeping with ideas central to present-day industrial agreements between teachers and employing authorities. Policy-making and planning at the local level must always take place in the larger context of government or system policies and regulations. That is to say, a policy established in a school must not be contrary to government or system policy on the issue in question. Usually, such policy allows some variation from school to school on any particular policy issue. In a sense industrial agreements between teachers and employing authorities are policy guidelines within which schools must work when establishing their own policies relating to how teachers work. The amount of flexibility within these industrial guidelines that can be exercised at the local level varies from authority to authority. Viewed in this context, experience has shown that teachers are more than willing to vary conditions to the benefit of students when they can share in the decision-making process.

Question: How can this approach to school management accommodate government initiatives where submissions are required?

The accommodation of these programmes within the approach can obviously present problems due to the fact that information concerning submission success, funding and programme continuity from year to year is not known at an early date. Obviously one way to deal with the situation is the approach adopted within most schools at present, that is, to consider these schemes as additional to the normal programming and operation of the school and hence deal with them separately. This is less than satisfactory as it means that these programmes become 'add-on' rather than integral to the total education process within the school. The alternative is to consider them as other sources of funding and include them in the total planning and budgeting process for the school. This does require prediction of submission success and funding levels, which may not always be entirely accurate. Mechanisms for dealing with funding adjustments have been detailed elsewhere.

Question: Does Collaborative School Management or programme budgeting become just another 'add-on' for staff along with special initiatives of government which add to the workload of teachers?

No! The Collaborative School Management Cycle becomes the framework for *all* processes that involve goal-setting, policy-making, planning, budgeting and evaluating. Many schools in Victoria, Australia, for example, have introduced programme budgeting at the same time that a school 'improvement' plan has been implemented. A school which already has Collaborative School Management has a framework for curriculum and policy review of a kind which might be undertaken in such initiatives. Governments and other authorities might bring submission-writing into line with recommendations for programme plans and budgets set out in this book. The time-consuming process of writing substantial submissions which are rarely given more than a superficial reading is replaced by the more convenient set of two-page plans and budgets we have recommended.

Question: What happens during the introduction of this approach when there are teachers who do not want to be involved?

We recommend that no attempt be made to introduce the approach across the whole school at once. Instead, we recommend that once an appropriate programme structure has been identified, then volunteers be sought to trial the introduction with a small selection of programmes. These will be programmes within which the volunteer teachers normally work. In each case a programme plan and budget should be prepared with reference to appropriate policies and implemented following the necessary approval process. The remainder of the school programmes can be managed by the methods already in place within the school. This trial enables all staff to assess the situation over a period of time and further programmes can be added to the 'trial group' as appropriate. Experience has shown that this approach demonstrates the benefits of programme planning and budgeting to all staff; it reassures and convinces those who may, at first, be sceptical. All staff come to realise that they can contribute to policy-making and planning and gain a greater control over the day-to-day operation of programmes, with a resulting reduction in frustration, especially concerning material requirements.

Question: How long does it take to fully implement Collaborative School Management within a school?

The actual time will vary from school to school depending on local circumstances but it will probably take between three and five years. Such a time-scale allows for gradual implementation so that everyone concerned is able to observe and recognise benefits before proceeding with further implementation. It is suggested that in the first year only a small number of programmes be developed using volunteer staff. The number of programmes can be increased year by year as circumstances allow. In the early years the non-contentious policies can also be documented for information and the contentious policy areas addressed a few at a time. This gradual approach enables the programme structure to be changed and developed as policy and programme areas are clarified. Another important aspect of this gradual implementation process is that staff and the policy group are not overloaded, and skills developed in policy-making, planning and budgeting in the early stages can be used to good effect with later policies and programmes. We further recommend that major evaluation of programmes should not be attempted until the later years of the introduction period. This allows time for programmes to be developed and the relationship between the purposes of policies and programmes to be clearly established.

Policy-Making and Planning

Question: Conditions invariably change within a school year. Do programme planning and budgeting enable emerging needs to be met?

We recommend that planning within programmes provide a built-in capacity for flexibility. This needs to be reflected in the budget allocation especially for such things as expendable materials for students to use. Sufficient quantities can be ordered for the commencement of the year but some funds retained to allow response to emerging needs throughout the year. With these funds under the control of the programme teams, the response can be as fast as required without unnecessary reference to other bodies for approval, as long as the expenditure involved is within the guidelines of the approved plans and budgets. It is also recommended that each programme budget include a sum for 'contingency purposes' in the manner illustrated in sample programmes set out in the Appendix.

Question: Can programme planning and budgeting accommodate a major policy change in the middle of a budget year?

A major policy change will require extensive modification to an existing programme or perhaps even the development of a new programme. Either way, the preparation of a plan for implementation and the identification of the appropriate resources will need to be undertaken. This will require time. Therefore, it may be appropriate to include the major modification or new programme in the work for the next budget year. In this way due care and consideration are given to planning to ensure the success of the policy initiative. On the other hand, it may be that the policy initiative is so important that immediate implementation is required. In this case resources can be allocated from within the programme to be modified or from programmes which have lower priority. This latter possibility is not recommended and it can be argued that a few months' delay in implementing a policy initiative is not that serious when considered in the long term.

Question: What action can be taken if a programme is phased out or reduced in priority and specialist staff within that programme exceed requirements?

This situation can occur when programmes are designed to meet the emerging needs of students. It is already occurring through falling enrolments in schools, which emphasises that it is not a problem particularly related to this approach to school management. This approach does enable the early identification of staff required for the next year, and thus provides a longer period in which the school system, as a whole, can endeavour to match the needs of students and the needs of teachers. Changing circumstances also emphasise the need to consider the possibility of retraining which is already a reality in other professions. This particular problem cannot be solved at the school level alone; it usually requires a system-wide approach.

Question: Who can initiate changes to policy?

Provision should be made for any person or group in the school community to initiate a review of policy. It is important that such endeavour be initiated through the policy group and that an accepted procedure be developed to deal with these initiatives. It is equally important that the accepted procedures be widely known. Conflict more often results from the fact people do not know how to bring about change than from the nature of the change in question. It is recommended that a policy be developed to facilitate suggestions for change. Such a policy should preclude the possibility of agreement to the proposed change at the time the issue is raised. Rather, it should ensure that, if the issue is deemed worthy of consideration, then a working party is appointed to explore the issue and prepare options (at least three) relating to the issue for later consideration by the policy group. This working party should include those with relevant expertise and stake in the outcome. A date should be set for the completion of the task. The development of options rather than a single position ensures that all aspects of the issue are considered and makes public the fact that this wide consideration occurred. Both facets are important in arriving at the best decision and in gaining commitment by all concerned to the decision that is eventually made.

Question: Do you really need to consider options in policy-making?

The traditional approach to policy-making has been the preparation of a single position paper possibly at the end of an investigation by a committee or working party. When the position paper is presented for approval, there is an expectation that it will be adopted because it represents the 'best thoughts' of the working party. It often happens that members either accept or reject the position stated, leading to a 'defend–attack spiral'. This approach is not necessarily the most desirable in bringing a policy group together and yet consensus is desirable because it helps the group to gain the necessary commitment to ensure successful implementation. However, if the working party presents a number of options, then it makes clear that it has considered many aspects of the particular issue in the investigation. The working party may state a preferred option but no one is pushed into accepting or rejecting the options offered. It emphasises that there is more than one possible solution and so invites further suggestions. By considering all of the options available concerning students' needs, the working party can reach agreement on the most appropriate option. It often occurs that a minority supporting an extreme option can see that their particular view will not be accepted by the majority but are satisfied that their view has not been ignored. As well, the option which is finally adopted is often a modification of an earlier option which has had aspects from other options added to it. The result is a policy with which there is overall agreement and which best suits the existing situation.

Question: What happens in this recommended approach to Collaborative School Management if the parents and the community are not interested in policy-making?

This assumption of so-called 'community and parent apathy' often comes from looking at the situation too broadly. If a meeting of parents is called to look at policy-making in general then the response is likely to be poor, but if a meeting is called to consider policy on a well-advertised and specific issue that is contentious in that community, then the response is likely to be very good indeed. This emphasises the need in policy-making to identify those policy areas where there is satisfaction, and, over a period of time, to document these policies for the information of all concerned. As well, there is a need to identify those policy areas where there is dissatisfaction and to involve parents, teachers and the wider community in determining new policies in these areas by considering options and adopting a policy statement that best suits the local situation. Similarly, in drawing up a schedule to review programmes, distinctions can be made between those of obvious concern and others. Parents willingly respond to being involved in reviews where there is concern and an opportunity to suggest a different approach which will be more in keeping with students' needs.

Question: Does this approach to school management stereotype the curriculum or is it possible for new ideas to be introduced?

New ideas can be brought forward for possible introduction not only by teachers but by others as well. The point of contact in this respect is always the policy group. If the group is convinced that the idea has merit then a policy statement is developed and adopted. The adoption ensures that the idea must be encompassed in the next planning year either by its own programme or as an element in one or more existing programmes. In this way, planning is undertaken to implement the new policy and the necessary resources are identified and provided through the budgeting process, according to priorities established. We acknowledge that this means the new idea cannot be introduced immediately but must wait for the next planning year. Of course, if the idea is only minor in nature, then it may be addressed immediately as an emerging need in an appropriate programme. But if the new idea is important, then the short delay is desirable because it enables time for thorough investigation and policy determination, followed by appropriate planning and resource allocation. Experience has shown that this approach ensures the successful introduction of a new idea and provides a documented basis for its continuation when the person who initiated it leaves.

Question: When a school council or board of governors is the policy group and the head teacher is responsible for ensuring that policies are implemented within the school, what happens when a head is required to implement a policy with which he or she disagrees?

This question can be 'answered' by asking the reverse question—what happens when a head teacher endeavours to implement a policy with which no one else agrees? Both questions are irrelevant in Collaborative School Management. Policies are determined only after thorough investigation of the issues involved and exploration of possible alternatives. In this work the basic criterion is relevance to the needs of the students involved. The head teacher has a key role in this investigative and policy selection work. The approach gives rise to policies that are relevant to students' needs and for which consensus has been gained. A head teacher, therefore, should not be required to implement a policy with which he or she disagrees. Rather, the head teacher is required to implement policies to which all have had opportunity to contribute and to which there is commitment. In this way there is a high probability of successful implementation.

Identification of Resources and Budgeting

Question: Schools do not receive funds from the various sources at the one point in time. How does this affect programme planning and budgeting?

Planning and budgeting of programmes are facilitated if the total funds involved are known at the one point in time and prior to commencement of the year in question. There are moves in some places towards this situation. It is possible to predict the resources that will be made available from various sources with sufficient accuracy to allow realistic planning and budgeting to take place. This prediction can be based on anticipated enrolments and patterns of resource provision in the preceding two or three years. It is also necessary to consider the implications of possible changes in government policy to anticipate changes to resource provision. Experience has shown that resource provision predicted with at least 90–95% accuracy is sufficient for planning purposes. A minor budget review can be carried out at the commencement of the following year when the actual resources are known. Minor changes can be made to programmes by adding previously omitted, lower-priority planning elements within programmes, or by subtracting further elements to accommodate the difference between predicted and actual resources. We emphasise that it is possible to predict with sufficient accuracy for such changes to be very minor, and there is little detraction from the value of the preplanning.

Question: Sources of funds provided for a school often have particular 'restrictions'. How is this aspect accommodated in the recommended approach to programme planning and budgeting?

It is difficult to take all these restrictions into account during the planning and budgeting processes. Obviously the processes would be facilitated if all funds came from the one source without any restrictions other than that they must be used to improve children's education. Experience has shown that in fact this approach can be adopted and that it is possible to proceed with planning and budgeting as if all resources (except staff) are 'restriction-free'. It does mean that planning and budgeting for the total situation must be completed at the one time. When planning and budgeting have been completed, then it is possible to match the school's preferred use of funds with the restrictions placed by the various sources of funds. Examples have been given in chapter 7 of the mechanics of such a system, using colour coding. Staff are greatly assisted in their task when the necessity to consider these restrictions in planning and budgeting is removed.

Question: The main function of staff is teaching and preparing for teaching. Should they waste their time by being involved in budgeting?

Preparing for teaching involves planning for the future and the effectiveness of the programmes provided for students is dependent on the quality of this planning. An important aspect of planning is identifying the resources that are required to enable the planning to be properly implemented. This identification of the required resources forms the basis of budgeting. Staff may require assistance in costing the required resources and this is a role for support staff. Appropriate identification of the required resources during planning, and the assurance of their provision prior to the commencement of the year in question, allows teachers to prepare and provide lessons for students without the frustrations of not having the exact resources, or not knowing whether in fact these resources can be made available. In this way budgeting as well as educational planning may enhance the quality of teaching and learning.

Question: Do programme planning and budgeting require teachers to have training in economics and/or accounting?

Teachers are trained to plan educational programmes within schools. An aspect of this planning is the identification of the resources required to implement the planning through learning programmes for students. Teachers already carry out this task, although in this approach to programme planning and budgeting it is advisable for resources to be identified well ahead of time so that appropriate provision is made for them in the budget. The actual selection and ordering of the material resources is seen as a role for the staff in programme teams. Accounting for expenditure through bookkeeping is seen to be the role of administrative staff such as the bursar or registrar. Coding systems were illustrated in chapter 8 showing how the ordering and, later, accounting can be readily co-ordinated.

Question: What happens if a programme budget is exceeded?

It is necessary that support staff provide programme teams and the policy group with monthly statements giving up-to-date details of programme receipts and expenditure. It is also advisable that this information be available to programme teams at other times on request. Programme teams are accountable, so they must contain expenditure within the approved budget and take that into consideration when they place orders. Nevertheless, unexpected rises in costs can occur and unforeseen circumstances may arise requiring additional expenditure. These situations can be accommodated by including a contingency reserve in the budget. Experience has shown that if such a reserve is provided in a general way for *all* programmes then there is competition for the reserve *among* programmes, which may result in undesirable or hasty expenditure. It is better to include a small reserve in each programme to be used only in emergencies. It can still happen that for some reason a programme will exceed this reserve, in which case a further amount can be 'borrowed' from the reserve of a more fortunate programme with the proviso that this amount may have to be 'paid back' in the future. When these principles are followed programme budgets are unlikely to be exceeded.

Question: Can funds within the budget of a particular programme be carried forward to the next budget year?

Funds provided within the budget of each programme are related to the plans approved for that budget year. It follows, therefore, that funds should be expended for each programme within the year concerned. However, sometimes there will be delays in the supply of items and some orders may not be filled in time for all accounts to be paid within the budget year. In these cases it is obviously desirable to carry forward the relevant amounts to the following year. The emphasis needs to be on the commitment of all funds within the budget year rather than on the actual expenditure. As well, it is possible for programmes to gain major items of a very expensive nature by the allocation of funds over two or more budget years. This provision will, of necessity, involve carrying forward the appropriate amounts. Auditing regulations usually enable this to occur if prior approval is given.

Question: To allow planning and budgeting for the following year, must schools receive financial information at an earlier date than is now the case?

We recognise that this information is required for the recommended approach to work at its optimum. There are signs in several places that this information could be made available earlier. In the interim, experience has shown that it is possible to predict the resources that will be available with sufficient accuracy to make the approach work. The various aspects of this prediction of resources are dealt with in chapter 7. It should be noted that absolute accuracy in this prediction is not required. For planning purposes, accuracy of 90–95% is sufficient, and small adjustments can be made early in the year in question to accommodate minor variations. The listing of planning elements within programmes in order of priority facilitates this accommodation of variations by enabling the subtraction of low-priority elements or the addition of elements that may have been omitted earlier. An important point to note is that a well-considered plan exists which can be implemented, with some variations if necessary. This is preferable to attempting to plan at the various times at which resources become known as definite amounts.

Question: Does the introduction of programme planning and budgeting require the keeping of two sets of accounts—new accounts for programmes and traditional accounts for lines of expenditure or sources of finance?

It could be necessary to keep two sets of accounts, depending on audit requirements. There is a need for authorities encouraging the introduction of this management approach to review audit requirements and to institute changes so that programme accounting parallels programme budgeting. In the interim it is possible to design accounting systems that serve both needs, by accounting according to programmes and using an associated coding system to identify finance from different sources and/or specific lines of expenditure.

Question: Is it necessary to introduce computerised accounting systems in association with programme planning and budgeting?

Programme budgeting needs to be supported by a system whereby accounts are kept according to programmes rather than the traditional lines of expenditure or sources of finance. This enables monitoring of expenditure according to how it has been allocated in the various programmes. Programme accounting as such does not involve any more work than traditional line accounting. It is the same procedure but with a change of focus. From this point of view, it is not necessary to introduce computerised accounting systems for programme accounting, but the introduction of any system that will make the accounting process easier and/or improve the accessibility of information to those concerned is always desirable.

Question: What happens in this approach to school management if there is a turnover of staff?

Irrespective of the approach to school management adopted, there are problems with continuity of programmes when staff changes, but our experience with this approach in schools with considerable staff turnovers has indicated that there is improved continuity. New staff have immediate access to documented policies and plans that are in an easily read format. Resources required have been identified and a budget prepared and approved. The new teacher therefore has the information and resources to carry forward the programme as planned. After some months in the school, new staff become involved in the planning for the next year and are able to contribute to that planning on the basis of knowledge gained of the local situation and their particular background of experience and training. In this way relevant information is guaranteed to assist new staff in their first year and during that year use is made of their expertise to plan the following year.

Question: Who should select and order materials and equipment for programmes once plans and budgets have been approved?

We recommend that this task be the responsibility of the teachers who form the programme teams. For each programme, these staff are familiar with the actual requirements and the times that different materials must be selected and ordered to ensure supply. Staff can be assisted in the task by bursars to ensure co-ordination and economy in ordering. With responsibility for ordering resting with staff within the guidelines established by the programme plans and budgets, many frustrations relating to the supply of equipment and materials are eliminated. There can be a ready response to emerging needs, and it is possible to ensure that items are to hand when required. The staff's time saved is paralleled by a saving of the policy group's time, because the group does not have to continually authorise purchase. The time saved allows time for further policy review and development.

Evaluating Programmes

Question: What action needs to be taken if an evaluation shows that a programme is not working? What action needs to be taken if this programme failure is related to staff incompetence?

If an evaluation indicates that the purposes of a programme are not being achieved, then at the same time evidence needs to be sought as to why the purposes are not being achieved. This will indicate whether the purposes are, in fact, realistic, or whether appropriate changes should be made to the plan for implementation or the method of implementation. On the basis of this information changes can be initiated and further reviews conducted. If the information gathered points to the problem being in the delivery of the programme to students, then those in positions of responsibility in the school need to ensure that appropriate professional development and advice are provided for the staff concerned. Of course this situation is always with schools and is not a product of this approach to school management.

Question: Can minor evaluations of programmes be regarded as valid if they are carried out by the staff that work within the programme?

The test of an evaluation is whether it enhances the relevance of the programme to the students concerned as judged by parents, teachers, students and the community in general. We agree that it would be preferable if all programme evaluations each year were major, and involved others as well as the teachers implementing the programme, but this is just not possible because of time constraints, so a cycle of major and minor evaluations has been recommended. Although the minor evaluations are carried out by the teachers concerned, the evaluations are realistic because they are directed towards establishing indicators of success as well as areas of concern. Teachers are asked to provide this balance of information in their professional capacity based on their training, expertise and experience. The information provided is published openly throughout the school and general community so its validity must stand up to questioning. Although a schedule of major evaluations is drawn up for a period of several years, it is possible to bring forward the major evaluation of a particular programme if there is due cause for concern.

Summary

Rather than providing a summary of the questions that are often asked about Collaborative School Management, we pose here a series of questions that readers might answer in order to assess policy-making and planning processes in their own situation. To some extent this will provide an opportunity to identify starting points for this approach to self-management. These questions are based on criteria for effectiveness in resource allocation which were identified in the Effective Resource Allocation in Schools Project described in chapter 2.

1 Are there written statements of policies for all programme areas in your situation? Policy is meant here to be more than a statement of goals, purpose or philosophy. In addition, a policy contains guidelines which shape the manner in which programmes are implemented. Policy is not so specific that it contains rules and procedures. A policy is not a curriculum or a course of study but would be a basis for developing these.

2 Do policies for your programme areas shape the setting of priorities and the allocation of resources?

3 Are learning and teaching needs for the next year identified and placed in an order of priority?

4 Does the order of priority among learning and teaching needs take full account of local as well as system needs?

5 Are resources, both human and material, allocated according to priorities among learning and teaching needs?

6 Is there opportunity for appropriate involvement of staff, students and the community in policy-making and planning?

7 Is consideration given in your planning to evaluating the effectiveness of programmes?

8 Is a budget prepared for each of your programme areas which outlines for staff and others the financial plan in an understandable fashion?

9 Are there appropriate accounting procedures to monitor and control expenditure according to programme areas?

10 Can money be transferred from one category of the budget to another as needs within programmes change or emerge?

11 Are high-priority needs in your programme areas consistently satisfied through the planned allocation of resources?

12 Does actual expenditure match intended expenditure in your programme areas, allowing for flexibility to meet emerging and/or changing needs?

13 Do participants in policy-making and planning generally understand and broadly accept the processes and outcomes?

Notes and References

Chapter 1

1. Conservative Party (Britain), *The Next Moves Forward*, Manifesto for 1987 election, May, pp. 18–20.
2. National Governors' Association, *Time for Results*, Washington, D.C., 1986.
3. Walter I. Garms, James W. Guthrie and Lawrence C. Pierce, *School Finance: The Economics and Finance of Public Education*, Prentice-Hall, Englewood Cliffs, N.J., 1978.
4. Charles Perrow, *Organisational Analysis: A Sociological View*, Wadsworth, Belmont, Ca., 1970.
5. Thomas J. Peters and Robert H. Waterman Jr, *In Search of Excellence: Lessons from America's Best-Run Companies*, Harper and Row, New York, 1982.
6. *ibid.*, p. 14.
7. Stewart C. Purkey and Marshall S. Smith, 'School reform: The district policy implications of the effective schools literature', *The Elementary School Journal*, Volume 85, 1985, pp. 353–389.
8. *ibid.*, p. 355.
9. *ibid.*, p. 358.
10. *ibid.*, p. 362.
11. *ibid.*, p. 363.
12. *ibid.*, p. 364.
13. Chester E. Finn, 'Toward strategic independence: Nine commandments for enhancing school effectiveness', *Phi Delta Kappan*, February, 1984, pp. 518–524.
14. *ibid.*, p. 518.
15. *ibid.*, p. 320.
16. *ibid.*, p. 521.
17. *ibid.*
18. *ibid.*, p. 523.
19. Carnegie Forum on Education and the Economy, *A Nation Prepared: Teachers for the 21st Century*, Carnegie Forum, New York, 1986.
20. Holmes Group, *Tomorrow's Teachers: A Report of the Holmes Group*, The Holmes Group, East Lansing, 1986.
21. *ibid.*, p. iv.
22. Conservative Party (Britain), *op. cit.*, pp. 18–20.
23. See, for example, Philip Merridale, 'The power and the accountability', *The Times Educational Supplement*, February 20, 1987, p. 4. [Philip Merridale is Chairman of the Association of County Councils]

229

24. The critical views of several head teachers are reported in *The Times Educational Supplement*, May 1, 1987, p. 12.
25. Geoffrey Morris, 'The County LEA', in S. Ranson and J. Tomlinson (Eds.), *The Changing Government of Education*, Allen and Unwin, London, 1986.
26. *ibid.*, p. 48.
27. See Colin Humphrey and Hywel Thomas, 'Making efficient use of scarce resources', *Education*, August 12, 1983, pp. 125–126; Colin Humphrey and Hywel Thomas, 'Counting the cost of an experimental scheme', *Education*, August 19, 1983, pp. 145–146; Colin Humphrey and Hywel Thomas, 'Giving schools the money', *Education*, May 10, 1985, pp. 419–420; Colin Humphrey and Hywel Thomas, 'Delegating to schools', *Education*, December 12, 1986, pp. 513–415.
28. Humphrey and Thomas, 'Making efficient use of scarce resources', p. 125.
29. Humphrey and Thomas, 'Delegating to schools'.
30. Morris, *op. cit.*, p. 43.
31. See Murray Frazer, Jeffrey Dunstan and Philip Creed, *Perspectives on Organisational Change*, Longman, Melbourne, 1985, for a detailed account of developments in Victoria.
32. Ministry of Education (Western Australia), *Better Schools in Western Australia: A Programme for Improvement*, 1986.
33. Robert Fordham, *Decision Making Processes in Victorian Education*, Ministerial Paper No. 1, Victorian Government Printer, Melbourne, 1983, p. 4.
34. Robert Fordham, *The School Improvement Plan*, Ministerial Paper No. 2, Victorian Government Printer, Melbourne, 1983. p. 6.
35. Ian Cathie, *The Government Decision on the Report of the Ministry Structures Project Team*, Ministry of Education, Victoria, 1986.
36. James W. Guthrie and Rodney J. Reed, *Educational Administration and Policy: Effective Leadership for American Education*, Prentice-Hall, Englewood Cliffs, N. J., 1986.
37. *ibid.*, p. 18.
38. John Lindelow, 'School-based management', in S.C. Smith, J.O. Mazzarella, P.K. Piele (Eds), *School Leadership: Handbook for Survival*, ERIC, Eugene, Oregon, 1981.
39. *ibid.*, p. 95.
40. National Governors' Association, *op. cit.*, p. 59.
41. National Education Association — National Association of Secondary School Principals, *Ventures in Good Schooling*, A joint report, NEA — NASSP, Washington, D.C. and Reston, Virginia, 1986, p. 13.
42. Theodore R. Sizer, *Horace's Compromise*, Houghton Mifflin, Boston, 1984, p. 214.
43. John I. Goodlad, *A Place Called School*, McGraw-Hill, New York, 1984, p. 275.
44. *ibid.*, p. 276.
45. National Commission on Excellence in Education, *A Nation at Risk*, Government Printing Office, Washington, D.C., 1983.

Chapter 2

1. Tasmanian Parliament. *White Paper on Tasmanian Schools and Colleges in the 1980s*. Education Department, Tasmania. 1981.
2. The Report of the Effective Resource Allocation in Schools Project, published by the Centre for Education, University of Tasmania (Hobart, 1986), is in five parts as follows: Brian J. Caldwell, *Effective Resource Allocation in Schools: A Summary of Studies in Tasmania and South Australia*. Part 1: Josie Misko, *Effective Resource Allocation in Government Schools in Tasmania and South Australia*. Part 2: Josie

Misko, *Case Studies of Effective Resource Allocation in Government Schools in Tasmania and South Australia*. Part 3: Kingsley Curtis, *The Development of Funding and Resource Management in South Australian Government Schools*. Part 4: Chris Smith, *Effective Resource Allocation in Non-Government Schools in Tasmania and South Australia*, Part 5.

3. Thomas J. Peters and Robert H. Waterman Jr, *In Search of Excellence: Lessons from America's Best-Run Companies*, Harper and Row, New York, 1982.
4. Josie Misko, *Effective Resource Allocation in Government Schools in Tasmania and South Australia, op. cit.*, chapter 2.

Chapter 3

1. Based on a definition offered in the Program Accounting and Budgeting Manual (interim edition) prepared by the Alberta Department of Education, Canada, 1972, p. 216.
2. Roger A. Kaufman, *Educational System Planning*, Prentice-Hall, Englewood Cliffs, New Jersey, 1972, p. 8.
3. This view of policy is based on a definition proposed by Bryant L. Stringham in 'The School Act, 1970: A Case Study of Public Policy Making in Education', Ph.D. dissertation, University of Alberta, Edmonton, 1974.
4. Adapted from Stephen P. Robbins, *The Administrative Process*, 2nd edn, Prentice-Hall, Englewood Cliffs, New Jersey, 1976, p. 128.
5. Based on the view of budgeting offered by Leon Ovsiew, William B. Castetter and Adolph J. Koenig, in their article 'Budgeting' in Warren E. Gauerke and Jack R. Childress (Eds), *Theory and Practice of School Finance*, Rand McNally and Co., Chicago, 1967.
6. Based on the definition of Stufflebeam *et al.* cited in William A. Mehrens and Irvin J. Lehmann, *Measurement and Evaluation in Education and Psychology*, 3rd edn, Holt, Rinehart and Winston, New York, 1984, p. 5.

Chapter 4

1. Russell L. Ackoff, *Creating the Corporate Future: Plan Or Be Planned For*, John Wiley and Sons, New York, 1981. p. 53.
2. *ibid.*, pp. 65–66.
3. *ibid.*, p. 65.
4. *ibid.*, p. 66.
5. *ibid.*
6. *ibid.*
7. *ibid.*, p. 71.
8. *ibid.*, p. 73.
9. *ibid.*, p. 74.
10. Thomas J. Peters and Robert H. Waterman Jr, *In Search of Excellence: Lessons from America's Best-Run Companies*, Harper and Row, New York, 1982.
11. *ibid.*, p. 14.
12. *ibid.*, pp. 13–14.
13. *ibid.*, pp. 9–11.
14. See, for example, Don Hellriegel and John W. Slocum Jr, *Management: Contingency Approaches*, 2nd edn, Addison-Wesley, Reading, Massachusetts, 1978, p. 487.

Chapter 6

1. This view of policy is based on a definition proposed by Bryant L. Stringham in 'The School Act, 1970: A Case Study of Public Policy Making in Education', Ph.D. dissertation, University of Alberta, Edmonton, 1974.
2. A summary of a variety of views on policy-making is provided by Grant Harman's 'Policy making and the policy process in education', in Robin Farquhar and Ian Housego (Eds), *Canadian and Comparative Educational Administration*, University of British Columbia, Vancouver, pp. 54–75.
3. This view of the policy process is described and illustrated in more detail by Brian J. Caldwell in 'Policy making at the school level', paper presented at the Eighth National Conference of the Australian Council for Educational Administration, Melbourne, 1 September 1981, reprinted in *ACEA Bulletin*, 24, August 1982, p. 2. The view was adapted by Brian J. Caldwell and J. Lawrence Tymko in *Policy Making for Education: A Guide Book for Boards of Education*, Alberta School Trustees Association, 1980, from J.K. Friend, J.M. Proer and C.J.L. Yewlett, *Public Planning: The Inter-corporate Dimension*, Tavistock, London, 1974.
4. J. Lawrence Tymko, 'Accreditation of Alberta Senior High Schools: A Case Study of Public Policy Implementation', Ph.D. dissertation, University of Alberta, Edmonton, 1979, p. 4.
5. Adapted from Wayne K. Hoy and Cecil G. Miskel, *Education Administration: Theory, Research and Practice*, 2nd edn, Random House, New York, 1982, p. 282.

Chapter 9

1. Gary D. Borich and Ron P. Jemelka, *Programs and Systems: An Evaluation Perspective*, Academic Press, New York, 1982, p. 1.
2. Norman E. Gronlund, *Measurement and Evaluation in Teaching*, 4th edn, Macmillan, New York, 1981, p. 6.
3. A description of the way in which evaluation plays a continuous and important role in the school programme is contained in Gronlund, *op. cit.*, pp. 6–13.
4. *ibid.*, p. 12.
5. Useful guides to school-based evaluation are provided by Phillip W. Hughes *et al.*, *A Guide to Evaluation*, Curriculum Development Centre, Canberra, 1979 and by Marie Brennan and Ruth Hoadley, *School Self Evaluation*, Education Department, Victoria, 1984.

Chapter 10

1. Everett M. Rogers, *Diffusion of Innovations*, The Free Press of Glencoe, New York, 1962.
2. Everett M. Rogers, 'What are innovators like?' in Richard O. Carlson et al., *Change Processes in the Public Schools*, The Centre for the Advanced Study of Educational Administration, Eugene, Oregon, 1965.
3. Kurt Lewin, 'Frontiers in group dynamics', *Human Relations*, 1, 1947, pp. 5–41. A useful summary is contained in Robert G. Owens and Carl R. Steinhoff, *Administering Change in Schools*, Prentice-Hall, Englewood Cliffs, New Jersey, 1976, pp. 142–148.
4. Ronald G. Havelock, *The Change Agent's Guide to Innovation in Education*,

Educational Technology Publications, Englewood Cliffs, New Jersey, 1973, pp. 122–124.

Chapter 11

1. See, for example, R.M. Stogdill, *Handbook of Leadership: A Survey of Theory and Research*, Free Press, New York, 1974.
2. See, for example, Paul Hersey and Kenneth Blanchard, *Management of Organisational Behavior: Utilising Human Resources*, 4th edn, Prentice-Hall, Englewood Cliffs, N.J., 1982; Fred E. Fiedler, Martin M. Chemers and Linda Mahar, *Improving Leadership Effectiveness: The Leader Match Concept*, John Wiley and Sons, New York, 1977.
3. Warren Bennis and Bert Nanus, *Leaders: The Strategies for Taking Charge*, Harper and Row, New York, 1985.
4. Robert J. Starratt, *Excellence in Education and Quality of Leadership*, Occasional Paper No. 1 of the Southern Tasmania Council for Educational Administration.
5. Thomas J. Sergiovanni, 'Leadership and excellence in schooling', *Educational Leadership*, February, 1984, p. 6.
6. The descriptions are adapted from those offered by Sergiovanni, *op. cit.*
7. Thomas J. Sergiovanni, 'The theoretical basis for cultural leadership' in L.T. Sheive and M.B. Schoenheit (Eds), *Leadership: Examining the Elusive*, 1987 Yearbook of the Association for Supervision and Curriculum Development, ASCA, Alexandria, Va., 1987, p. 122.
8. See, for example, findings in relation to principals in J.E. Rouche and G.A. Baker, *Profiling Excellence in America's Schools*, American Association of School Administrators, Arlington, Va., 1986.

Chapter 12

1. Rensis Likert and Jane Gibson Likert, *New Ways of Managing Conflict*, McGraw-Hill, New York, 1976, p. 7.
2. Based on a classification by Louis R. Pondy, 'Organizational conflict: concepts and models', *Administrative Science Quarterly*, 12, September 1967, pp. 296–320.
3. Kenneth Thomas, 'Conflict and conflict managment', in Marvin D. Dunnette (Ed.) *Handbook of Industrial and Organizational Psychology*, Rand McNally, Chicago, 1976, pp. 889–935.
4. Robert G. Owens, *Organizational Behavior in Education*, 2nd edn, Prentice-Hall, Englewood Cliffs, New Jersey, 1981, p. 296.
5. Roger Fisher and William Ury, *Getting to Yes: Negotiating Agreement without Giving In*, Hutchinson, London, 1983.
6. *ibid.*, p. 11.
7. *ibid.*, chapter 2.
8. *ibid.*, p. 50.
9. *ibid.*, p. 117.
10. Jay Hall, 'Decisions, decisions, decisions', in James B. Lau (Ed.), *Behaviour in Organizations: An Experiential Approach*, Richard D. Irwin Inc., Homewood, Illinois, 1975, p. 77 (reprinted from *Psychology Today*, November 1971, pp. 51–54, 86–88).
11. The twin goals in decision-making of quality and acceptance are suggested by Victor Vroom and Phillip Yetton, *Leadership and Decision-making*, University of

Pittsburgh Press, Pittsburgh, 1973. Several of the guidelines which follow are based on the model for decision-making described in this book.

12. The suggestions in paragraph 5 combine those offered by Hall, *op. cit.*, and John E. Jones, 'A gestalt approach to collaboration in organizations' in J. William Pfeiffer and John E. Jones (Eds) *The 1976 Handbook for Group Facilitators*, University Associates, Iowa City, Iowa, pp. 203–210.

13. Lau, *op. cit.*, p. 81.

Appendix

ROSEBERY DISTRICT HIGH SCHOOL

EXCERPTS FROM
1985 POLICY HANDBOOK
1985 PROGRAMME BUDGET DOCUMENT
AND OTHER PAPERS

Explanatory Notes

The Appendix contains examples of various products of Collaborative School Management drawn from the *1985 Policy Handbook* and the *1985 Programme Budget of* Rosebery District High School in Tasmania. Information from other documents published at the school is also included.

A starting point for Collaborative School Management can be the setting of goals. It will be quickly realised that this task also entails consideration of beliefs or philosophy. These beliefs serve as the background for the development of goals and the associated identification of needs. The statement of school philosophy for Rosebery is given together with the statement of goals. These statements illustrate the relationship between school philosophy and goals.

A sample of school policies has been included together with the priority order of policies of 1985. It should be noted that policies are listed in three categories of priority, designated simply as 1, 2 and 3. Although these indicate relativities between policies, Priority 3 policies are not considered unimportant. Attention is drawn to the policies on Excursions and Decison-making in the School, which are examples of 'policies without programmes' in that they are reflected across a number of programmes rather than one specific programme.

Sample documents reflecting all aspects of the process for the Special Education Programme are included in the Appendix. Further explanatory notes are given preceding that section.

A selection of three programmes has been included. Each programme is preceded by the relevant key policy statement, to illustrate the relationship between policy-making and programme planning and budgeting. These examples are followed by the summary chart of programme budgets for 1985, containing the planned expenditure by categories for all programmes.

Statement of School Philosophy

The school philosophy consists of a series of statements that are held to be fundamental in curriculum design and in the overall operation of the school. Our philosophy is an outcome of a curriculum review undertaken in 1980. This review clearly identified the basic premises that all concerned agreed should determine and guide developments. These basic premises are given in twelve statements. Initially they were adopted for a period of three years, beginning in 1981, but our work since then has confirmed that our philosophy is useful and its continued implementation has never been challenged.

Statements

1. The basis of all our dealings with each child is that the child will receive respect, care and love. The central concern of the school is the child. This orientation for education at our school is in line with a humanistic model which has the child as the focus. This model stresses the complete development of the individual as a unique personality. The school curriculum should be appropriate to the stage of development of the child.

2. We recognise and take account of the differences between individual children in our planning and in all our dealings with them. Children are not stereotypes: they develop along recognisable, sequential steps but the rate depends on the individual. This approach embraces the physical, emotional, intellectual, social and moral aspects of development. Progress through each successive stage is dependent on a high level of competence at a preceding stage, and proceeds at a completely individualistic rate. It is possible to recognise a child's level of progress at any stage. Learning regression can occur due to a lack of experience, lack of motivation and/or emotional blockage.

3. We base our curriculum on the continuous development of children from kindergarten to year 10.

4. We take account of the fact that the community as a whole expects students to have achieved certain educational goals by the time that they leave school. External statements about goals and expectations for our students exist and require responses. Guidelines for courses have been established by the Schools Board of Tasmania. Fixed entry-requirements are stated by the Apprenticeship Commission, the Tasmanian State Institute of Technology, TAFE, and the University. Employers are accustomed to using the School Certificate for evidence of general education and proficiency in basic skills in possible future employees.

5. We recognise that the achievement of specific goals becomes more important as the child proceeds through the school but also that personal needs remain the first priority.

```
┌─────────────────────────────────────────┐
│   The Child as the centre                 │
│                          Specific goals    │
└─────────────────────────────────────────┘
    K  ─────────────────────────────→  10
```

This model shows the change in emphasis as the child proceeds through the school.

6. The school's curriculum must provide a general education for each child, be useful and highlight common purposes to which all can subscribe. The curriculum should provide children with skills to enable them to approach, use and deal with the ever-increasing body of knowledge. The curriculum should allow for, and make the most of, the individual differences of teachers and children. The school should prepare a child so that he or she can become a self-sufficient member of society and cope with the changing nature of society. The curriculum should develop in students self-awareness and an awareness of others, as well as tolerance and acceptance of individual and cultural differences. The curriculum should display a wide range of learning approaches. The curriculum must be useful. The three common purposes in a curriculum should be to develop the skills of 'communicating', 'thinking' and 'valuing'.

7. We must set goals which identify the experiences, the knowledge and the skills which all children need before they leave school, and we must ensure that these goals are met. This care for the basic and essential learnings and experiences for all students should be sustained. A list of subject matter is insufficient. Subject matter, teaching–learning processes and learning situations should be organised around this statement. When they leave school, all children should possess certain intellectual and social competences and the acquisition of these should be monitored.

8. We make the school environment safe, warm, secure and stimulating for the child. It must be tidy, friendly, businesslike, comfortable and aesthetically appealing.

9. We give high priority to the activities which foster the physical development of children. The school should give priority to developing children's physical health and skills. There is a well-known correlation between physical health and academic performance.

10. In planning our curriculum we take account of the nature, interests, values, expectations and ambitions of our community. Our community views the school in a favourable light and feels that its openness is important. Our community members want to be included in the process even though they do not wish to be involved in day-to-day matters.

11. We take account of the interests, values, expectations and ambitions of our students. Our children have demonstrated that they are aware of their needs. They develop a mature approach in their view of what their years at school should mean to them. Statistical data available show that our children are typical and conform to state standards of expectation.

12. We practise shared decision-making. An effective curriculum will result from all of us helping to make a decision when we are directly affected by that decision. Our involvement in relevant decisions — those which call on our expertise or fall within our area of jurisdiction — will improve us as people, increase our enthusiasm and lead to improved relationships.

Statement of School Goals

A set of goals has been developed which lists the expectations and aspirations for students with respect to their school education and also identifies expectations of the systems required to support students' achievements. The statements about goals result from expressions of opinion within both the school and the community. Before a goal is accepted, it must be in keeping with our stated philosophy.

Goals are included in our statement irrespective of whether they are short-term or long-term. As well, there has been an attempt to write goals as specific statements rather than as generalised expressions of ideas. It is considered that writing specific statements about goals aids those using the statements for planning purposes to interpret them uniformly. A result of these approaches has been the large number of actual statements written.

The large number of statements has led to the development of a categorisation of goals to assist staff and council members to relate the goals to planning and policy-making. Most goals naturally relate directly to students and have been divided into those that indicate outcomes considered as being desirable and necessary for students, and those that indicate learning experiences considered to be worthwhile in the school education of the student. Other goal statements relate to the provision of resources for students to facilitate the achievement of outcomes and experiences. Further goals statements relate to the management of the school with management goals being designed to enhance students' achievements.

Categorisation of goals

1   Outcomes for students
2   Learning experiences for students
3   Provision of resources
4   Management

In the following pages the goal statements in each category have been listed. Within each category a numbering system has been used to identify individual goals although this system is not necessarily designed to indicate an order of importance. There has been an attempt to assemble the goal statements in groups within each category, with each group having a common aspect and with a natural 'flow' from one group to the next. To some extent, the groups of goal statements have also been arranged in order of importance with the most important groups preceding those of lesser importance.

It is not envisaged that our statements of goals are a never-changing set but rather a target for a specific period of time, usually a year. Some goals will always be included but others will be discarded when they are achieved or when circumstances change. Our policies and their resulting programmes are designed to enable our goals to be achieved. The evaluations of programmes and policies will make a major contribution to the review of goals from year to year.

1. *Goals related to outcomes for students*
1.1   Develop each student's ability to use language as a successful tool of thought and communication.
1.2   Develop each student's knowledge of, and skill in using, mathematics.
1.3   Give students knowledge and understanding of the world in which they live and the relationship between people and their environment.
1.4   Enable students to attain the skills, including respect for oneself and respect for others, which are necessary for successful and comfortable participation in society.
1.5   Help students to an understanding of those factors that have contributed to our Tasmanian and Australian way of life.
1.6   Develop in students a sense of pride in being an Australian.
1.7   Give students the skills, knowledge and attitudes necessary to participate in the political process of Australian life.
1.8   Train students in the skills needed to make a successful transition from school to life after school.
1.9   Develop in students a love of learning and a realisation that learning is a life-long activity.
1.10 Develop in students the necessary skills for successful participation in a technologically oriented society.
1.11 Develop each student's creative talents in the various artistic fields.
1.12 Develop in students an appreciation of the arts and crafts and the part these activities can play in our lives.
1.13 Develop students' skills in finding, understanding and using information.
1.14 Develop students' skills of analysis on which to base decision-making.
1.15 Develop students' skills in problem-solving.
1.16 Develop each student's physical capacity and general sporting skills.
1.17 Develop in students an appreciation of sportsmanship.
1.18 Develop in students skills and attitudes necessary for a meaningful use of leisure time.
1.19 Develop students' skills in living in the outdoor environment.
1.20 Develop students' skills for coping with life in a city.
1.21 Help students to understand and practise the ideas of health and safety.
1.22 Enable students to attain a certificate based on achievement levels for subjects as moderated by the Schools Board of Tasmania or by the school.

2. *Goals related to learning experiences for students*

2.1   Ensure that all students experience the use, meaning and development of language through stories, poetry, drama and related activities.

2.2   Provide learning experiences for students in all the major academic areas.

2.3   Ensure that students' learning is through direct experience when possible.

2.4   Develop students' self-respect and self-discipline by giving them experience at school which is designed to foster harmonious working relationships.

2.5   Provide learning opportunities for students so that they gain an awareness of the individuality and abilities of their peers.

2.6   Provide opportunities for students to participate in self-motivated learning.

2.7   Provide opportunities for students to participate in activities in large groups designed to promote a sense of belonging.

2.8   Facilitate later formal learning by providing opportunities, especially in the early years of school, for children to develop sociability.

2.9   Provide opportunities for talented children to pursue and develop their talents.

2.10 Provide experiences for special students specifically related to overcoming their disabilities.

2.11 Provide experience for students in a wide variety of arts and crafts to enable them to select those most suited to their interests and needs.

2.12 Provide students with direct experience in the use of computers and related technology.

2.13 Provide opportunities for students to develop skills in scientific method as an approach to problem-solving.

2.14 Provide a physical education programme that offers a balanced range of activities conducive to healthy development.

2.15 Provide direct experience for students in a wide variety of sports to enhance students' ability to identify those sports appropriate to their interests.

2.16 Provide opportunities for students to compete in various fields of endeavour and to learn to cope with this aspect of living.

2.17 Provide experience for students in specific technical and related fields because of the nature of local employment and leisure activities.

2.18 Provide a wide variety of option subjects in senior years to cater for students' differences and to enable students to explore possibilities for later learning.

2.19 Enable students to experience first-hand the variety of living environments in Tasmania.

2.20 Provide support programmes to assist parents in preparing children for school. In some circumstances this could involve limited early entry.

2.21 Provide an opportunity for students to learn a second language.

2.22 Provide opportunities for extra-curricular activities in line with the school's philosophy and in keeping with the expressed interests of students.

2.23 Provide students who are likely to proceed to further education with experience of prolonged examinations.

3.   Goals related to provision of resources

3.1 Provide resources in the general sense to facilitate all school programmes at a level at least commensurate with Tasmania-wide standards.

3.2 Continue the development of the school as an aesthetically pleasing environment designed to best meet the needs of our students.

3.3 Continue the development of the school building to include change-rooms, showers, and toilets for use by students undertaking physical education and sport.

3.4 Continue the development of the recently provided playground area to facilitate school sport, accommodate spectators and enhance the aesthetic appeal of the area.

3.5 Provide an adequate administration area to facilitate the operation of the school, including improved provision for accommodating visitors to the school.

3.6 Continually update resources so that students are able to have 'hands-on' experience of appropriate new technology.

3.7 Promote the appropriate use of the community and its members as a school resource.

3.8 Provide a wide range of support personnel to help identify students' learning difficulties and to propose and activate remedial pro-grammes.

3.9 Provide teacher and programme support for children with special needs.

3.10 Provide support programmes to assist the professional development of teachers and, particularly, beginning teachers.

3.11 Acquire a collection of art that may serve as a teaching collection and demonstrate the value of such work.

3.12 Provide a canteen for students so that they do not have to leave the campus if parents and/or the school so desire.

3.13 Provide opportunities for fund-raising within the school to finance specific projects.

3.14 Provide transport for excursions, sport and general school activities, at relatively small cost to students.

4. *Goals related to management*

4.1 Ensure that children are supported and cared for and are assisted in making the most of the opportunities that the school provides for them.

4.2 Develop an organisational structure and pattern that is reflective of the continuity of the curriculum from K to 10.

4.3 Develop a School Council as the major policy-formulating body of the school, with the community and the school staff jointly sharing this responsibility in equal partnership.

4.4 Develop an approach to school management which reflects the constitution of the School Council. The key points of this management approach are the role of the Council in setting goals, identifying needs and determining policy, the role of the staff in preparing plans for programme implementation and budget preparation, the role of the Council in approving the budget, the role of the staff in the operation of programmes and the joint school and Council role of evaluation.

4.5 Develop ways in which students can actively participate in school decision-making.

4.6 Provide means for regularly informing parents about school matters and the progress of their children. Such means should include the opportunity for face-to-face communication.

4.7 Organise staff meetings in a way that expedites staff participation in decision-making.

4.8 Develop staff skills in programme planning and budgeting because this approach to planning and resource allocation enhances the operation of the School Council in its budgetary control.

4.9 Develop skills in programme evaluation as the next specific step in the evolution of our management approach.

4.10 Develop staff skills in management practices appropriate to their level of involvement and/or interest.

4.11 Provide a wide variety of opportunities for parental involvement in the activities of the school.

4.12 Foster the operation of the Parents and Citizens Association as an advisory body in the implementation of school policies.

4.13 Develop a reward system appropriate to the age of students which recognises and applauds excellence in achievement.

4.14 Pursue a vigorous public relations programme to project the image and achievements of the school to the community at large.

ROSEBERY DISTRICT HIGH SCHOOL
POLICY PRIORITIES 1985

PRIORITY 1

04 Computer education
05 Commerical education
09 Excursions
10 Early intervention
13 K–2 General studies
14 3–6 General studies
22 Language development
23 Learning to read
24 Motor mechanics
26 Mathematics
28 Physical education
30 Pastoral care
32 3–6 Regrouped language
34 Special education
38 Sport
41 Technical subjects
64 Support services
81 Budget & planning
82 Beginning teacher development
83 Communications — Parents & Citizens
84 Council communications
86 Decision-making
91 Student council
65 Staffing
66 Book sales
80 Administration
85 Formation of classes
88 School organisation
89 Professional development
90 Public relations

PRIORITY 2

01 Arts & crafts
03 Student assessment
06 School Certificate
07 Discipline
08 Drama Festival
15 Homework
16 Handwriting
20 Journalism
21 Kindergarten and Preparatory education
25 Music
27 Option subjects 9–10
29 Preparing for school
31 Presentation Day
33 Your Child's Report
35 Social studies
36 Science
39 Talented children
40 Transition education
42 Visual arts
44 School magazine
60 Buildings & grounds
62 Community bus
63 Curriculum resource

PRIORITY 3

02 Art acquisition
11 Extra-curricular activities
12 Foreign languages
17 History
18 Home economics
19 House system
37 Speech & drama
43 School assemblies
61 Canteen
87 Fund-raising

Appendix

ROSEBERY DISTRICT HIGH SCHOOL
09: POLICY STATEMENT: THE PURPOSES AND NATURE OF SCHOOL EXCURSIONS

22 November 1983

Excursions are regarded as an essential part of the learning programme for all children. Basically the purposes of excursions are:

1 to enhance children's learning through the provision of real or first-hand experiences;
2 to increase knowledge, understanding and appreciation of the local area and other areas that are different from our own;
3 to develop skills in observation, recording and reporting;
4 to assist in the development of children's confidence, independence, sense of adventure and sense of responsibility, particularly towards their own safety and the safety of others;
5 to help children learn to live and work with others.

To achieve these purposes throughout the school life of the student, excursions increase in difficulty, nature and length from kindergarten to year 10. It is intended that skills developed on an excursion in a particular year can be built on in the following year. As well, it is intended that over the school life of a student, a wide variety of experience and areas will be covered without involving repetition.

For kindergarten-to-year-2 classes, excursions are held in the local area. Any excursion only occupies a maximum of one day and total travel is a maximum of $2\frac{1}{2}$ hours. In this way children visit local points of interest and deal with the immediate environment of our town. Parents' involvement is considered vital to the success of some of these excursions.

In years 3 to 6, some excursions are longer than one day and include staying away from home overnight. Year 3 children visit and study a farming environment while year 4 children study a city environment, usually Hobart. Year 5 children visit a country area and usually have some first-hand experience with farm animals. Year 6 children visit an outdoor recreational environment which is also closely related to their study of Australian history. Parental involvement is considered essential to the success of some of these excursions.

In years 7 to 10 excursions are of at least five days' duration and will usually take the form of outdoor education and camping experience to develop students' independence and self-reliance and the ability to fend for themselves in a bush environment. It is necessary, though, that in one of the years, students have an excursion to a city, so that they can experience city life, finding their way and generally coping with city living.

R.J. CHAPMAN
Chairman

ROSEBERY DISTRICT HIGH SCHOOL
30: POLICY STATEMENT: PASTORAL CARE

6 December 1983

The development of the child can be viewed as encompassing intellectual, physical, social and emotional aspects. It is generally accepted that the school is very involved in the intellectual and physical development of the child. If school education concerns the education of the whole child then the school is also involved with the child's social and emotional development. The acceptability of school involvement with a child's social and emotional development is not only based on the idea of the education of the whole child, but also on the idea that without satisfactory development of an emotional and social kind, then satisfactory intellectual and physical development is unlikely to occur.

The idea of school involvement in the education of the whole child emphasises the sharing of the educational development of the child between the home and the school, with the home taking the leading role in emotional and social development, and the school taking the leading role in intellectual development.

The school policy on pastoral care is based on these ideas. The purpose of pastoral care in the school sense is to assist each child in reaching his potential in intellectual, physical, social and emotional development and to gain the maximum value possible from all school programmes.

The nature of pastoral care is based on the idea that the purposes described are best achieved by each child being able to develop secure, warm and trusting relationships with the adults in the school and with other children. Specifically there are always two members of staff who have the responsibility for the overall well-being and development of each child. A senior member of staff has responsibility for all children in a grade area and works with each child's class teacher in caring for the child's best interest. Of course other staff to some extent share in this responsibility, especially in the more senior years. To assist the process, changes in staff responsible for any child are kept to a minimum.

In providing pastoral care for a particular child, staff endeavour to:

- ensure that the child is familiar with the necessary school organisation;
- mantain communication with the parents on the child's development;
- counsel the child on his or her school courses;
- ensure that the child's social and emotional development is assisted and that any problems are resolved if at all possible.
- be available to the child to give assistance and advice as the child may require.

Senior staff in charge of grade areas and class teaching staff are assisted by the principal and vice principals in their pastoral care in particular when children experience extreme emotional or social difficulties. Support staff, such as guidance and welfare officers, are also able to assist in such circumstances.

Our pastoral care policy tries to ensure that every child is cared for in a total sense and assisted to the maximum extent possible in benefiting from school programmes.

CHRIS WILLOUGHBY
Senior Master

ROSBERY DISTRICT HIGH SCHOOL
86: POLICY STATEMENT: DECISION-MAKING WITHIN THE SCHOOL

12 May 1983

Our school philosophy states that we practise shared decision-making. The School Council, as our major policy-formulation body, reflects this statement in that it is an equal partnership between the staff and the parents. Once policy is formulated, it is the role of the staff to implement that policy by appropriate planning, programming, budgeting and organisation. The subsequent review process is a joint function of the staff and the Council.

The planning, programming, budgeting and organisation processes performed by the staff are again carried out on the basis of shared decision-making. It is not practical that all staff will share in all decisions, rather, it is appropriate that those staff with a direct interest and/or relevant expertise will share in any particular decision.

Decisions about general matters of significant importance to the whole staff will be made by all staff at general staff meetings which will be run democratically. Significant decisions relating to curriculum development will be made at curriculum staff meetings, we hope as the result of consensus of the whole staff.

Due to constraints of time, many decisions relating to the whole school in all respects will be made by senior staff, but minutes detailing their decisions will be made available to all staff on the staffroom noticeboard. Any staff member can call into question a decision by senior staff by placing the item on the agenda of the next general staff meeting.

Decisions will also be made by other staff groups with related interests and/or expertise. These include year areas (K–2, 3–6, 7–10), subject areas (7–10 or K–10) and special purpose groups. Again, decisions of any of these groups can be questioned at a general staff meeting.

It is the prerogative of senior staff members to make decisions concerning their areas of responsibility on a day-to-day basis. These decisions will be organisational in nature rather than on issues of larger significance.

The policies of the School Council, our statement of school philosophy and the policies of the Education Department form the basis for all our decision-making. The educational process for our students should therefore proceed on a predetermined, reasoned and planned basis. Changes will occur, with justification, to the ultimate benefit of students.

Obviously, in the decision-making process care should be taken not to confuse areas where it is our prerogative to decide and areas where we are legally bound by the Education Act and Regulations. This can often occur where the principal or a member of senior staff implements a regulation which at the time may be unpopular in some quarters. Again, there is a mechanism for seeking redress if it is thought to be necessary; such a request is made to the Department through the principal or through the Tasmanian Teachers Federation.

JIM M. SPINKS
Principal

DOCUMENTS RELATING TO SPECIAL EDUCATION

Explanatory notes

1 These documents relating to special education in the school illustrate all stages of collaborative decision-making: policy options, policy adopted, programme budget and plan, minor evaluation report and major evaluation report.

2 The three policy options are clearly labelled 'OPTION ONLY'. These options were prepared by a working party of the Council. It should be noted that although some material is common to all three, they differ in important areas.

3 The policy statement adopted by the Council is a modification of Policy Option Two. The modification concerns placing the emphasis of special education in the early years, including pre-school years as explained in paragraphs 6 and 7 of Option Two. This emphasis was suggested in Option One.

4 The programme plan and budget are printed opposite the policy statement adopted, to enable consideration of the relationship of the plan and budget to the policy.

5 The minor and major evaluations of the programme are examples only and are included to illustrate the possible nature of such evaluations. It should be noted that the minor evaluation mainly concerns implementation while the major evaluation is more concerned with the achievement of programme purposes. These reflect, to some extent, the distinction between formative and summative evaluation respectively, a distinction often found in the literature on evaluation. It should also be noted that the information-gathering is more extensive for the major evaluation.

POLICY OPTION 1: SPECIAL EDUCATION

Special education is the education of children with specific learning difficulties or other special needs. The school recognises the fact that all children are different and that some have problems in one or more of the following areas of development: intellectual, physical, sensory, social, emotional, behavioural, speech and language. These problems mean that such children do not function well in a normal, mixed classroom. They require special help which is better given outside the normal classroom and by specialist teachers. Accordingly the special education policy ensures that:

1 Individual differences in children are recognised and problems identified.
2 Children with particular problems receive different treatment from the majority, according to their special needs.
3 The education of 'normal' children is the main concern of the school and it is considered detrimental to their development to be placed in the same classes as those with difficulties.

In order to achieve these purposes the school will:

1 Employ a teacher to undertake special education within the school. Such a teacher will preferably be provided from outside the normal staff quota but if this is not possible will be provided from within the normal staff quota.
2 Identify children in need of special education and develop plans to deal with their problems.
3 Involve school support staff where appropriate.
4 Concentrate special education resources, *in the main*, in the early childhood area, on the basis that prevention is better than cure.
5 Create a special class of the children identified as in need of special education. They will be withdrawn from normal classrooms and all, or almost all, responsibility for their education will be taken by the special education teacher.

In the event of no suitable special education teacher being available, the special education needs of particular children will be met by the normal classroom teachers with assistance, where appropriate, from support staff and senior staff. However, as this would jeopardise the chances of the best possible education for the majority of children, it is recommended that the policy as outlined above be given Priority 1 status.

POLICY OPTION 2: SPECIAL EDUCATION

Special education is the education of children with specific learning difficulties or other speical needs. The school's policy on catering for such children is guided by the philosophy expressed in The COPE Report (*Primary Education in Tasmania*, Education Department, Tasmania, 1980). That is, wherever possible it is considered desirable to have mixed groups of children so that they are able to have contact with as wide a range of people as they will meet in society as adults. The only exception to this would be children who are severely intellectually handicapped, because such children require resources which we are unable to provide. However, for the other categories of 'difference' —

- specific learning difficulty
- speech impairment
- language disability
- mild to moderate intellectual handicap
- behavioural disturbance
- physical disability
- sensory disability

— it is considered that there are benefits in catering for children with special needs in the normal classroom (The COPE Report p. 65). These benefits apply equally to all children, whether or not they have problems.

However, children with special needs, such as those listed above, may at times require a more specialised programme than the normal classroom is able to provide. We place a very high priority on the need to provide the best possible education for such children, no less than for children who display no learning difficulties or other problems.

Accordingly, the school will:

1. Ensure that staff are employed to undertake special education within the school. Such staff will preferably be provided from outside the normal staff quota, but if this is not possible will be provided from within the normal staff quota.
2. Develop plans to deal with children who have specific intellectual, physical, social, emotional, behavioural or speech and language-related problems.
3. Consider, in drawing up plans for special education provisions, all variables such as the age of the child, the nature of the problems and the type of programme operating in the child's own classroom.
4. Cater for the mobility of children with physical handicaps.
5. Involve school support staff where appropriate.
6. Ensure that special education resources are evenly distributed to meet the needs of students from kindergarten to year 10.
7. Recognise that the classroom teacher is the person most responsible for children with special needs, and ensure that the special education staff are used as a resource, providing all possible support to that teacher in dealing with children who have difficulties in surviving in the normal class group.

The special education policy thus outlined is considered to be category 1 priority in our school, and every effort will be made to secure the appointment of highly suitable and well-trained special education staff. If no such staff are available then the special education needs of children will be met by the normal classroom teachers, with support staff and senior staff assistance.

POLICY OPTION 3: SPECIAL EDUCATION

Special education is the education of children with specific learning difficulties or other special needs. The school recognises that there are a certain number of children who fall into this category because of problems in one or more of the following areas of development: intellectual, physical, sensory, social, emotional, behavioural, speech and language.

At issue is the attempt to meet the needs of such children, balanced against the needs of the majority. It is considered that the likelihood of gaining a special education teacher from outside the normal staff quota is virtually non-existent. The provision of such a teacher from within the minimal staffing quota would disadvantage the greatest number of children as it would have the effect of increasing class sizes and/or decreasing the range of options available to students.

The purpose of this policy is thus to ensure that children with learning difficulties and other special needs receive no special considerations above other students.

It is seen as the task of the classroom teacher to cater for the full range of children. In so doing, the resources available to the classroom teacher will be in the form of support service staff and senior staff assistance.

Many other policy statements already in existence deal with the 'how' and the 'what' of children's learning. There would appear to be no great advantage in singling out children with difficulties for special attention and accordingly special education is considered to be of category 3 priority in our school.

THE ADOPTED POLICY FOR SPECIAL EDUCATION

Special education is the education of children with specific learning difficulties or other special needs. The school's policy on catering for such children is guided by the philosophy expressed in The COPE Report (*Primary Education in Tasmania*, Education Department, Tasmania, 1980). That is, it is considered desirable to have mixed groups of children wherever possible so that they are able to have contact with as wide a range of people as they will meet in society as adults. The only exception to this would be children who are severely intellectually handicapped, because such children require resources which we are unable to provide. However, for the other categories of 'difference' —

- specific learning difficulty
- speech impairment
- language disability
- mild to moderate intellectual handicap
- behaviour disturbance
- physical disability
- sensory disability

— it is considered that there are benefits in catering for children with special needs in the normal classroom (The COPE Report, p. 65). These benefits apply to all children, whether or not they have problems.

Children with special needs, such as those listed above, may at times require a more specialised programme than the normal classroom is able to provide. We place a very high priority on the need to provide the best possible education for such children, no less than for children who display no learning difficulties or other problems.

Accordingly, the school will:

1 Ensure that staff are employed to undertake special education within the school. Such staff will preferably be provided from outside the normal staff quota, but if this is not possible will be provided from within the normal staff quota.
2 Develop plans to deal with children who have specific intellectual, physical, social, emotional, behavioural or speech and language-related problems.
3 Consider, in drawing up plans for special education provisions, all variables such as the age of the child, the nature of the problem and the type of programme operating in the child's own classroom.
4 Cater for the mobility of children with physical handicaps.
5 Involve school support staff where appropriate.
6 Concentrate special education resources, **in the main**, in the early childhood area on the basis that prevention is better than cure.
7 Identify and cater for children under normal school age who are at risk in any of the categories of 'difference' defined earlier.
8 Recognise that the classroom teacher is the person most responsible for children with special needs, and ensure that the special education staff are used as a resource, providing all possible support to that teacher in dealing with children who have difficulties in surviving in the normal class group.

This special education policy is considered to be a category 1 priority in our school, and every effort will be made to secure the appointment of highly suitable and well-trained special education staff. If no such staff are available then the special education needs of children will be met by the normal classroom teachers, with support staff and senior staff assistance.

Signed: _____ Chairman

1985 BUDGET FOR SPECIAL EDUCATION

ROSEBERY DISTRICT HIGH SCHOOL	1985 BUDGET

PROGRAMME: Special Education   RESPONSIBILITY: M.S.   CODE: 173

1. **Purpose:** We aim to have all children achieve their full potential in all areas of development during their school years. It is recognised, however, that some children fail to achieve their potential due to some specific disability which affects their capacity to learn. A purpose of the Special Education Programme is to identify these children, determine the nature of their disability and to devise and implement plans to overcome the disability where possible.

    A further purpose of the programme is to identify children who have overall a very low potential, and have great difficulty in learning, and to assist these children achieve their potential by designing individual programmes for them and providing the necessary intensive help.

2. **Broad guidelines:** Children with specific disabilities or general low learning potential will be identified through consultation amongst the relevant people.

    Fundamental to the programme is the philosophy that children should remain part of their peer group in as many respects as possible, and that by its very nature, special education requires a highly individualised approach to achieve maximum benefits. Those who design the teaching programme must, therefore, ensure that the programme is appropriate for each individual. A programme could involve extraction as part of a group, or a totally individualised programme to operate within the normal classroom.

    The main thrust of the programme will be towards the younger children in need of special help so that problems can be overcome or reduced as early as possible. It is recognised, however, that older children can need special education, and that this need should be met if possible.

    It is vital that opportunities are provided for close liaison between the special education teachers and the classroom teacher of each child involved.

3. **Plan for implementation:**

    3.1   The equivalent of one full-time and one half-time special education teachers will be employed.

    Three rooms will be provided as teaching areas for extraction purposes, at least two of which will also be set up as resource centres for special education materials.

    3.2   Senior staff will supervise the programme.

    3.3   A part-time aide will be provided for the programme to assist in the preparation of learning materials.

    3.4   Sufficient materials and equipment will be provided for the effective operation of the programme, including structured language and maths materials, manipulative equipment, art and craft supplies, and part-purchase of an additional large-print typewriter.

    3.5   Additional stocks of appropriate reading materials will be provided to enhance the effective operation of the programme, particularly in the areas of high interest/low ability reading material of upper primary and lower secondary students, and teachers' resource material.

4. Resources required:

Planning elements	*Teaching staff*	*Non-teaching staff*	*Materials & equipment*	*Books*	*Services*
4.1 Teaching units provided by special education staff 37° units × $595/unit	22 015				
Related units of Planning, Marking and Organisation (PMO) 9 units × $595/unit	5 355				
4.2 Senior supervision of the programme by infant mistress 2 units × $738/unit	1 476				
4.3 Provision of teacher aide services to develop support materals 2 hrs × $7.22 × 40 weeks		577			
4.4 Support items for students' use			750		150
4.5 Books for students and staff to use, including a special focus for 1985				300	
	$28 846	577	750	300	150

Programme total = $30 623

(*Units for 3–6 Regrouped Language Programme included in Programme 114)

5. **Evaluation (minor):** Keeping individual records for each child will provide the basis for evaluation reports. These reports will be given to teachers and parents although their form will vary according to the situation.

The criteria used to determine children in need of the programme may also be used to measure the progress of the total group and thus the effectiveness of the programme.

Programme team:
Liz Brient   Michele Davison   Trudy Drukin   Marilyn Spinks   Carol Titley

REPORT OF MINOR EVALUATION FOR SPECIAL EDUCATION

PROGRAMME: Special Education   **RESPONSIBILITY:** M.S.   **CODE:** 173

EVALUATION REPORT FOR 1984

This report should be red in conjunction with the policy and programme plan for special education. Resources were allocated to implement fully the programme plan.

SUCCESS INDICATORS

1. Many teachers have indicated that the Special Education Programme is assisting them to deal more effectively with children who have special needs in the classroom. This has been particularly evident since the increase in provisions for special education at the beginning of this year.

2. Parent-teacher interviews conducted under the regular schedule have indicated strong support for the programme.

3. A number of children on the programme show evidence of increased self-esteem and ability to cope with learning tasks.

4. A small number of children in the early childhood area are likely to be coping well enough in the near future to come off the programme.

AREAS OF CONCERN

1. There has been insufficient time for classroom teachers to consult with special education teachers on the progress of children.

2. Some classroom teachers are unaware of the need to consult, so that work can be followed up in the classroom.

3. Some children with problems 'slip through' and are put on the programme too late, due to lack of continuity in monitoring their progress as they cross from one grade to another.

4. There are problems with the supply of books needed for teachers' resources due to:
   (a) lack of opportunity to select appropriate materials;
   (b) delays by suppliers in meeting orders.

COMMENTS AND RECOMMENDATIONS

- Senior staff need to create opportunities where possible for classroom teachers to consult with special education staff.

- Special education staff need to make themselves available at department meetings so that they can make teachers aware of the resurces available. This includes resources in the form of support materials, and information about learning-teaching processes which take place through the individualised programmes.

- Better liaison is needed between senior staff of the different grade areas to ensure that provisions for special education give continuity for particular children when they cross grade levels.

- The school should budget for professional development time so that special education staff can visit language and special education resource centres where they can select suitable materials and either purchase them or borrow them.

Prepared by members of the programme team.

REPORT OF MAJOR EVALUATION FOR SPECIAL EDUCATION

PROGRAMME: Special Education   **RESPONSIBILITY:** M.S.   **CODE:** 173

INTRODUCTION
For this year the Special Education Programme was upgraded to provide an increased teacher component (1.5 teachers as compared to one teacher in the previous year). In evaluating the results of this programme the evaluating group held a series of informal meetings with all teachers concerned, interviewed the guidance officer and speech pathologist connected with the school to ascertain objective indications of progress or otherwise of the children concerned, and interviewed a representative sample of parents who have children involved with the programme. Child studies, with names removed to ensure anonymity, were also made available to the group. The findings of this evaluation are summarised below.

INADEQUACIES AND PROBLEM AREAS IDENTIFIED
1. The lack of ready access to some support staff (particularly guidance officer and speech pathologist) means that there are sometimes lengthy delays in obtaining information on which to base individual programmes.

2. One parent interviewed was confused about the provision of 10 hours of teacher aide time (provided from an external source) to cater for mobility of the physically handicapped, and thought that this provision was teacher time to assist in overcoming intellectual handicap.

3. A very small minority of children show evidence of 'opting out' of the normal classroom, preferring the special education situation all the time, probably due to the greater feeling of security.

4. Children are sometimes not identified as being in need of special education until they are too old for their problems to be overcome.

5. There is insufficient time for classroom teachers to consult with special education teachers on the progress of children, and in some cases teachers are unaware of the special education resources available.

SUCCESSFUL OUTCOMES OF THE PROGRAMME
1. Many teachers have indicated that the Special Education Programme is assisting them to deal more effectively with children who have special needs in the classroom as they are given help with implementing individualised programmes developed out of the work. The special education teachers do this with the children concerned. This feeling of receiving increased support is directly attributed to the increased provision.

2. A number of children on the programme are showing evidence of increased self-esteem and ability to cope with learning tasks. Tests administered (refer guidance officer) give objective evidence of this.

3. A small number of children in the early childhood area are likely to be coping well enough in the near future to come off the programme. This reinforces the benefits of early identification of children with problems and of early intensive help.

SUMMARY AND RECOMMENDATIONS
1. There is little if anything that can be done about the amount of the guidance officer's and speech pathologist's time provided to the school as this is an

Education Department matter. The group feels that it is worth noting, however, that as yet the Special Education Programme is in its infancy and that as the special education staff become more confident in their task of dealing with a wide range of disabilities and learning problems, the lack of ready access to support staff should be less of a problem.

2. The confusion that became evident about the nature of the provisions for special education for particular children points out the need for improved liaison between staff and parents. Consideration should be given to increasing the frequency of parent-teacher interviews with respect to children in the Special Education Programme.

3. Particular staff members should be nominated to undertake special pastoral care of the small minority of children having unusual difficulty in coping with the normal classroom situation, particularly in the secondary years.

4. The need to identify children early and the benefits of early intensive help as previously outlined, underline the need to continue the main thrust of the programme towards the early years. It is essential that continuity in monitoring children 'at risk' throughout the school is further developed and maintained.

5. Senior staff should create opportunities where possible for classroom teachers to consult with special education staff. The special education staff should make themselves available to department meetings so that they can make teachers aware of the resources available. This includes resources in the form of support materials, and information about learning-teaching processes which take place through individualised learning programmes.

Prepared by the Evaluation Group including members of the Council and Programme team.

ROSEBERY DISTRICT HIGH SCHOOL
80: POLICY STATEMENT: SCHOOL ADMINISTRATION

The purpose of school administration is to ensure that all concerned with the school are part of a harmonious whole and that their involvement in the relevant activities of the school is facilitated. This means that there must be two-way communication with parents, the Education Department and organisations external to the school as well as communication within the school. School administration also ensures that people in the school are physically provided for and that rights and privileges are respected. These activities take place in the context of policies of the School Council and the Education Department.

Further purposes are to provide organisation and co-ordination of school routines, secretarial and similar services, financial accounting, maintenance of school records, copier services, security of property, maintenance and development of school properties, and suitable housing for staff.

An additional purpose of this policy is to provide staff development and support for curriculum development and planning in school programmes. Also included is the assessment of teachers for promotion and other purposes. It is emphasised that decision-making is a shared process in the school, and the functions of senior staff are seen to be co-ordinating, influencing and encouraging to effect planning and decision-making rather than directing the work of others.

The school has staff in the categories of senior staff, teachers and clerical staff. From the senior staff, major administrative tasks are performed by the principal and vice principals. The principal provides supervision and leadership and deals with matters particularly related to staff assessment and development, communication and liaison. One vice principal is responsible for organisation, while the other is predominantly concerned with curriculum support. Other senior staff are responsible for organisation, in conjunction with teaching staff, providing the organisation within age-grade groups as well as throughout the school. Clerical staff, namely the bursar and office assistants, provide secretarial support, financial accounting, school records and maintenance.

Staff meetings are operated to facilitate the various activities covered within this policy and to enable decision-making on substantive matters to be shared.

JIM M. SPINKS
Principal

Appendix

1985 BUDGET FOR ADMINISTRATION

ROSEBERY DISTRICT HIGH SCHOOL	BUDGET 1985

PROGRAMME: Administration　　　**RESPONSIBILITY:** J.M.S.　　**CODE:** 103

1. **Purpose:** The Administration Programme sets out to ensure that all concerned with the school are part of a harmonious whole and that their involvement in the relevant activities of the school is facilitated. This means that there must be two-way communication with parents, the Education Department and organisations external to the school, as well as communication within the school. School administration also ensures that people in the school are physically provided for and that rights and privileges are respected. These activities take place in the context of policies of the School Council and the Education Department. Further purposes are to provide organisation and co-ordination of school routines, information for long-term planning, secretarial and similar services, financial accounting, maintenance of school records, copier services, security of property, maintenance and development of school properties, and suitable housing for staff.

    An additional purpose of the programme is to provide for staff development and support for curriculum development and planning in school programmes. Staff development includes the assessment of teachers for promotion and other purposes.

2. **Broad guidelines:** The school has staff in the categories of senior staff, teachers and clerical staff. From the senior staff, major administrative tasks are performed by the principal and vice principals. The principal provides supervision and leadership and deals with matters particularly related to staff assessment and development, communication and liaison. One vice principal (VPO) is responsible for organisation, while the other (VPC) is predominantly concerned with curriculum support. Other senior staff are responsible for organisation in conjunction with teaching staff within age-year groups as well as throughout the the school. Clerical staff, namely the bursar and office assistants, provide secretarial support, financial accounting, school records, and maintenance, etc. Staff meetings are conducted to facilitate the various activities within this programme and to enable decision-making on substantive matters to be shared.

3. **Plan for implementation:**
    3.1 Allocation of principal's service units to supervise the programme and to work within the programme, particularly on communication, liaison, long-term planning, senior staff and teacher development, planning for implementation of policies, participation in policy formulation and staff assessment.

    3.2 Allocation of VPO's service units to facilitate communication with the home, organisation of school routines and dissemination of information, student attendance, school security, and maintenance of school photographic records.

    3.3 Allocation of VPC's service units to provide curriculum development support to other programmes throughout the school.

    3.4 Allocation of senior staff and teachers' service-units to facilitate students' routines as well as ensuring the security of buildings and equipment.

3.5 Clerical staff, namely the bursar and office assistants, to provide liaison with the Education Department and external organisations on routine matters, financial accounting, secretarial support to senior staff, maintenance of school records, maintenance organisation and security of buildings, organisation of maintenance of staff housing, and printing services to other programs.

3.6 Allocation of 10 teacher-relief days to be used at the discretion of the school to facilitate school organisation when the Department's policy does not enable relief staff to be employed.

4. Resources required:

Planning elements	Teaching staff	Non-teaching staff	Relief days	Materials & equipment	Services	Minor materials	Reserve
4.1 Principal's function							
Supervision: 7 × $1,003	7,021						
Administration: 20 × $1,003	20,060						
4.2 VPO's function							
Administration: 10 × $809	8,090						
Materials for PB, DM, staff HB, att, photos, meetings				2,000			
4.3 VPC's function							
13 units × $809	10,517						
4.4 SS & Tr. function							
SS = 6 × 3 × $738	13,284						
Tr. = 27 × 2 × $571	30,834						
7 × 5 × $571	19,985						
4.5 Clerical function							
Bursar (75% of time)		17,717			1,400 (postage)		
Full-time office assistant		15,106		5,000	4,000 (telephone)		
Part-time office assistant (17.5 hours)		3,633				250	533
4.6 Discretionary relief staff			760				
	109,791	36,456	760	7,000	5,400	250	533

Total = $160,190

5. Evaluation (minor)

1985 represents the first year that the Administration Programme has not encompassed pastoral care. The evaluation will endeavour to review whether, after this separation of administration and pastoral care, the purpose of administration continues to be caring for people.

ROSEBERY DISTRICT HIGH SCHOOL
41: POLICY STATEMENT: TECHNICAL SUBJECTS

8 November 1983

Technical Subjects is the programme in the school which incorporates the subjects wood work, metal work, technical drawing and technology for years 7–10. The programme allows students the opportunity to develop a knowledge and understanding of a wide range of materials, tools and equipment. The courses are concerned with identifying and developing those areas of technical knowledge and skill that will be of assistance to the individual student in both a vocational and recreational sense. Students are given the opportunity to think creatively by participating in the design of projects. Constant explanation of safe working practices features in all aspects of the programme.

The sequence and detail of tasks undertaken by students is organised according to the child's level of co-ordination and expertise. The result of this practice is reflected in the levels of study offered in years 9 and 10 where specialisation is allowed.

Students in years 7 and 8 have two 45-minute periods each week of workshop experience in a subject we call manual arts. Students are given the opportunity to work with a wide range of hand tools and a limited number of machine tools. They work with materials such as metals, timbers and plastics. All students in years 7 and 8 study two periods of technical drawing. This subject allows students to develop drawing skills and gain an understanding of simple working drawings.

Year 9 and 10 students are able to specialise in the areas of study they prefer, as shown below.

Wood work in these years gives students the opportunity to work on larger and more complex projects. Students are able to use a wider range of power tools.

Metal work gives students the opportunity to perform more involved machining processes as well as a wide range of welding skills.

Technical drawing develops students' ability to communicate knowledge, ideas, and solutions to problems in a graphic form.

Technology in year 9 is designed to equip the student with a basic understanding of the internal combustion engine and its associated systems so that students will develop the confidence needed to undertake and successfully complete minor repair tasks. In year 10 students study basic electronics. This enables students to learn about electronic components and circuitry.

The Technical Subjects Programme provides students with the opportunity to develop skills that will be of great assistance in post-school life and to gain experience in possible vocations.

PETER BRADLEY
Senior Master

1985 BUDGET FOR TECHNICAL SUBJECTS

ROSEBERY DISTRICT HIGH SCHOOL	1985 BUDGET
PROGRAMME: 7–10 Technical Subjects RESPONSIBILITY	CODE: 161

1. **Purpose:** Technical Subjects can be defined as a programme incorporating wood work, metal work, technical drawing and technology for years 7–10. The programme will allow students the opportunity to develop knowledge and understanding of a wide range of materials, tools, equipment and processes unique to the area. Courses will be concerned with identifying and developing those areas of technical knowledge and skill that will be of assistance to the individual in both a vocational and recreational sense.

2. **Broad guidelines:** The programme will be activity-based. Children will be given the opportunity to think creatively through participation in the design of projects. Children will be encouraged to look at and analyse their work critically, and this will lead to further development of communication skills. Constant reference to and explanation of safe working practices will be a feature in all aspects of the programme. The sequence and detail of the tasks undertaken will be organised according to the level of co-ordination and expertise displayed by the individual. The logical result of this practice will be reflected in the levels offered in years 9 and 10 where the options offered allow specialisation to occur.

3. **Plan for implementation:**
   3.1 Students in years 7 and 8 will be divided into four groups and each group will study two units each of manual arts and technical drawing. Students in years 9 and 10 will be offered metal work, technology, wood work, and technical drawing as options. Year 10 classes will be allocated four units. Year 9 classes will be allocated three units and four units if on the same line as advanced mathematics.
   3.2 Provide supervision for four units per week.
   3.3 Provide materials and equipment for classes.
   3.4 Duplicate notes and testing materials and print relevant texts for students' use.
   3.5 Provide minor materials required to operate the programme.
   3.6 Through a major equipment replacement programme over two years, purchase a metal lathe of suitable size and quality to enable all the operations required of it to be performed.
   3.7 Provide two relief days to enable staff to participate in seminars or inter-school visits.
   3.8 Telephone charges in relation to ordering of materials and equipment.

4. Resources required:

Planning elements	Teaching staff	Relief days	Materials & equipment	Minor materials	Services
4.1 Teaching groups 7–8 manual arts					
8 × 2 units = 16 units					
7–8 technical drawing 8 × 2 units = 16 units					
9–10 metal work 5 groups = 18 units					
9–10 wood work 5 groups = 18 units					
9–10 technology 5 groups = 17 units					
9–10 technical drawing 4 groups = 15 units					
total = 100 units 100 units × $595/unit	59,500				
Preparation, Marking and Organisation (PMO) 25 + 4* units × $595/unit	$17,255				
4.2 S.M. supervision 4 units × $738/unit	2,952				
4.3 Materials and equipment			5,200		
4.4 Duplication service					1,200
4.5 Minor materials				500	
4.6 'Hercus' 2600 metal lathe			2,000		
4.7 Teacher development		152			
4.8 Telephone					100
	$79,707	152	7,200	500	1,300

Total = $88,859

(*Additional PMO units to reduce teachers' loadings.)

5. Evaluation (major)

1. Identify inadequacies and problem areas as an outcome of discussion on the purpose and nature of the programme.

2. Identify those areas of the programme that have been very successful in meeting the needs of individual students.

3. Consider the results of year 10 students on self-moderation tests in wood work and metal work.

Programme team:
Craig Allen   Peter Bradley   Ron Kamphius
Phil Parish   Allan Snare   Steve Tammens

ROSEBERY DISTRICT HIGH SCHOOL
13: POLICY STATEMENT: K–2 GENERAL STUDIES

29 November 1983

General Studies K–2 is composed of the following curriculum areas: language, maths, science, social studies, art, music, speech & drama, and physical education. All of these subjects are taught by each classroom teacher, with some specialist assistance in the last three mentioned.

Our main purpose in the early childhood area is to use those curriculum areas listed as the basis for developing each child as a whole person. It is essential that children be considered as individuals in this process, for the stages of development they have reached on entering school will differ from child to child, as will their potential for growth in the physical, intellectual, social and emotional sense. Our programme aims to take each child from 'where he or she is' and to build on that at the pace best suited to the individual.

Young children learn best in an atmosphere which takes into account their interests, and provides related real experiences. Therefore the teaching programme is activity-centred, and aims to link together as far as possible the different subject areas, so that skills gained in one area are used to enhance learning in another area.

The development of competence in all areas of language use is central to the K–2 Programme, as without such competence other learning cannot readily take place. In providing for such language learning as reading and writing, teachers work from the children's own interests first, with the main aim being the development of enthusiasm and confidence. Refining of such skill as correct spelling, punctuation, and letter formation takes place as children demonstrate readiness for them.

Maths in the K–2 area involves the development of children's skills in recognising and recording numerals, counting, measuring in all its forms, and introduction to the basic processes of addition, subtraction, multiplication and division — all through activities which are real to the children, rather than abstract.

Science and social studies are essentially related to the children's own environment and involve practical activities such as investigating, observing, recording in various ways, classifying, and problem-solving. Most teachers work on a theme basis, through which many aspects of a topic can be explored at different levels.

Art, music and speech & drama are seen at this stage as opportunities for children to express their ideas using a variety of media. These areas offer scope to extend and express the knowledge gained in other curriculum studies in an enjoyable and self-fulfilling manner.

Physical education is considered to be a vitally important area, because it is generally recognised that problems in the development of physical co-ordination can lead to problems in other areas of learning. Each teacher integrates some form of daily physical activity into her programme in addition to any specialist physical education time provided.

In total, the K–2 General Studies Programme aims to provide:

1 the most appropriate activities to encourage development of each child's individual potential;
2 a balance amongst all curriculum areas, with language growth as the core;
3 opportunities to acquire skills and attitudes which are required for success in future years.

(Mrs) MARILYN SPINKS
Infant Mistress

1985 BUDGET FOR K–2 GENERAL STUDIES

ROSEBERY DISTRICT HIGH SCHOOL   **1985 BUDGET**

PROGRAMME: K–2 General Studies   **RESPONSIBILITY: M.S.**   **CODE: 172**

1. **Purpose:** K–2 General Studies embraces the following curriculum areas — language, maths, science, social studies, art, music*, speech and drama*, and physical education*. (*Complementary to the specialist services provided.)

   The purpose of the programme is to use, and integrate where possible, the above curriculum areas, with a particularly strong emphasis on language, as a basis for the development of each child as a whole person — taking into consideration his or her potential for physical, intellectual, social and emotional growth.

   A further purpose of the programme is to cater for the individuality of children. Thus it will take into account, and build on, the learning that has already taken place prior to the child entering school, and will continue to allow learning to proceed at the pace best suited to the individual child.

2. **Broad guidelines:** Fundamental to the nature of the K–2 General Studies Programme is the concept of children as learners through direct experience: hence the teaching programme will reflect an activity-centred approach which takes into account the interests and capabilities of the children and provides related 'real' experiences. These experiences, to be most beneficial, must take place in an environment which provides a sense of security for the children and at the same time is stimulating and dynamic.

   The children's day will be designed to provide a balance appropriate to the level of development between (a) all curriculum areas; (b) individual and shared experiences. The emphasis will move gradually within K–2 from mostly individual activities to an equal balance of individual and shared activities.

   Parents will be encouraged to be closely involved in their children's education through the most appropriate means. This will vary according to different family circumstances.

3. **Plan for implementation:**
   3.1 Children will be divided into five teaching groups on the basis of chronological age, as follows:

   kindergarten — 1 × 45 children (approximately)
          prep — 1 × 23 children (approximately)
   year 1 & 2 — 3 × 23 children (approximately)

   Each group will be allocated a teacher and provided with a classroom adequately furnished for the numbers.

   Each teacher will take responsibility for teaching all curriculum subjects. As an adjunct to the daily classroom programme, P–2 will have specialist teaching time allocated in the areas of physical education and music/drama for three units per class per week.

   3.2 Senior supervision of the programme will be provided.

   3.3 Each teacher will be provided with a wide range of materials and equipment (classroom-based) so that the K–2 programme can fulfil its purpose of catering for individual differences, and integration of curriculum areas.

   3.4 A part-time aide will be employed specifically for kindergarten to assist the teacher and to take a major responsibility for organising the weekly parent-child sessions.

3.5 A part-time aide will be provided in the P–2 area and will be used by teachers either to assist in the classroom or to prepare learning materals.

3.6 An allocation of money for minor materials will be provided to allow special class projects such as cooking or photography to proceed.

3.7 Special provision will be made for 1985 with respect to materals and equipment to continue to bring maths resources up to a level which will enable programmes to proceed as planned.

3.8 A professional development programme will be devised which will focus on developing teacher skills in the area of reading.

3.9 An extraction system will be devised to assist teachers with students.

4 Resources required:

Planning elements	Teaching staff	Non-teaching staff	Relief days	Materials & equipment	Minor materials	Services	Reserve
4.1 Teaching groups K: 1 × 28 = 28 units P–2: 4 × 27 = 108 units total = 136 units							
136 × $595/unit	80 920						
Related units of Preparation, Marking and Organisation (PMO) 34 + 4* units × $595/unit	22 610						
4.2 Infant Mistress supervision 6 units × $738/unit	4 428						
4.3 Materials and equipment				4 350		150	300
4.4 Kindergarten aide 23 hours/week		6 642					
4.5 P–2 Teacher aide 10 hours × $7.22 × 40 weeks		2 888					
4.6 Minor materials for class/teacher use 5 × $30 × 3 terms					450		
4.7 Maths equipment				900			
4.8 Professional development 5 days relief			380				
4.9 Extraction system teaching: 4 units	2 380						
PMO: 1 unit	595						
Total = $126,993	$110 933	9 530	380	5 250	450	150	300

(* Additional PMO units to reduce teachers' loadings.)

5 Evaluation: (minor)

Evaluation of the programme will be largely subjective in nature and will monitor the development of concepts, skills and attitudes in the curriculum areas listed earlier, through a system of weekly reviews, child studies, checklists and reporting to parents in both the verbal and written form.

Programme team: Sharon Ansell Kim Jansson Cheryl Murray
Trudy Durkin Margaret Johnson Marcell Norton Marilyn Spinks

ROSEBERY DISTRICT HIGH SCHOOL
PROGRAMME BUDGET SUMMARY SHEET
RESOURCES REQUIRED

	Teaching staff	Non-teaching staff	Relief days	Materials & equipment	Book Services & hire	Minor materials	Travel	Services	Contingency reserve	Other	Programme total
101 Extra-curricular activities							380		200		580
102 Art acquisition				410		60					470
103 Administration	109 791	36 456	760	7 000		250		5 400	523		160 180
104 Community bus							500				NRA*
105 Pastoral care	79 694			600							80 794
111 Curriculum resource	23 252	3 910		7 073					100		34 335
112 School council	1 618			10	100	100		200	100		2 128
113 K–10 Music	27 798		152	2 040	30	100		200		290	30 610
114 3–6 Regrouped language	41 102		228		500	50		250	100		42 230
121 Presentation Day				200		110		185	50		545
122 K–10 Physical education	44 077		152	2 530	300	100	600	300	200		48 259
122 K–10 Sport											
124 Support services	2 427			900			2 260	600	100	480	6 767
131 7–10 Social studies	1 618	9 136						200			10 954
132 9–10 History	56 193			1 350	1 800		500	30	168		60 041
133 7–10 Transition education	6 688			500	150	260	50				7 648
134 7–10 Teacher support service	9 806					450	2 650	520			13 426
141 7–10 English		7 859		600							8 459
142 3–10 Foreign languages	61 405			600	2 200			425	200		64 830
143 K–10 Speech & drama	19 778			120	240						20 138
144 Drama Festival											
151 7–10 Mathematics	26 466			596	200	180					27 442
152 7–10 Science	738										738
153 K–10 Computer education	67 069			470	1 474	91		505	254		69 863

	Teaching staff	Non-teaching staff	Relief days	Materials & equipment	Book Services & hire	Minor materials	Travel	Services	Contingency reserve	Other	Programme total
161 7–10 Technical subjects	55 764	1 444	152	3 300	1 775	405	400		300		63 540
162 7–10 Visual arts	12 924		304	3 324	509			110	425		17 596
163 7–10 Home economics	79 707		152	7 200		500		1 300			88 859
164 9–10 Commercial subjects	19 326			860	100	270			200		20 756
171 Early intervention	21 706			1 890	200	470			50		24 316
172 K–2 General studies	17 993		76	690	250	420			100		19 529
173 K–10 Special education	3 713			200							3 913
181 3–6 General studies	110 933	9 530	380	5 250		450		150	300		126 993
182 Public relations	28 846	577		750	300			150			30 623
191 Cleaning	111 814	2 888		5 400		800			100	100	121 102
192 Grounds	738					40			10		788
193 Canteen		65 651		4 467		223			50		70 391
194 Book sales		16 285		350		150			50		16 835
201 9–10 Journalism		591									591
202 School magazine		1 700									1 700
203 Student council	11 900			830	200	150			100	300	13 480
211 K–10 Talented students				1 000							1 000
											NRA*
	3 570		152	300		110		100			4 232
	+ 310 (R.E.)										310
TOTALS	1 058 764	156 027	2 508	60 810	10 328	5 739	7 340	10 625	3 680	1 170	1 316 991

*NRA (no resources allocated)

Index

CPSIA information can be obtained
at www.ICGtesting.com
Printed in the USA
LVOW13s2038140517

534491LV00012B/101/P

9 781850 003311